Stoic Six Pack 9: The PreSocratics

Stoic Six Pack 9: The PreSocratics

By

Benjamin Cocker

George Grote

William Arthur Heidel

John Marshall

Enhanced Media
2016

Stoic Six Pack 9 – The PreSocratics

Anaximander's Book, the Earliest Known Geographical Treatise by William Arthur Heidel. First published in 1921.

The School of Miletus: Thales, Anaximander, Anaximenes and Heraclitus by John Marshall. First published in *A Short History of Greek Philosophy* by John Marshall in 1891.

The Pre-Socratics by George Grote. First published in *Plato and the Other Companions of Sokrates*, Volume 4 in 1888.

The Logic of the Pre-Socratic Philosophy by William Arthur Heidel. First published in *Studies in Logical Theory* 1903.

The Eleatics: Xenophanes, Parmenides, Zeno and Melissus by John Marshall. First published in *A Short History of Greek Philosophy* by John Marshall in 1891.

The Pre-Socratics by Benjamin Cocker. First published in *Christianity and Greek Philosophy* by Cocker in 1870.

Stoic Six Pack 9 – The PreSocratics. Published 2016 by Enhanced Media.

Enhanced Media Publishing
Los Angeles, CA.

First Printing: 2016.

ISBN-13: 978-1537591247

ISBN-10: 153759124X

Contents

Anaximander's Book
The Earliest Known Geographical Treatise
By William Arthur Heidel 7
Introductory Remarks 8
I 9
II 30
III 40

The School of Miletus
By John Marshall 49
Thales 50
Anaximander 53
Anaximenes 57
Heraclitus 58

The Eleatics:
Xenophanes, Parmenides, Zeno and Melissus
By John Marshall 61
Xenophanes 62
Parmenides 64
Zeno 68
Melissus 70

The Pre-Socratics
By George Grote 73

The Logic of the Pre-Socratic Philosophy
By William Arthur Heidel 145

The Pre-Socratics
By Benjamin Cocker 161

Anaximander's Book

The Earliest Known Geographical Treatise

By William Arthur Heidel

Introductory Remarks

Anaximander of Miletus is admittedly one of the foremost figures in the history of thought, and much has been written about him. He remains, however, somewhat enigmatical, and the obscurity which invests his character involves in some measure the entire line of early Milesian thinkers. When one considers the commonly accepted view regarding Anaximander one can hardly escape the impression that it is somewhat incongruous if not wholly inconsistent.

That he wrote a book is not called in question, though one is not sure whether he or Pherecydes is to be credited with writing the earliest prose treatise in Greek. Anaximander is generally called a 'philosopher' and his book is supposed to be properly described by its traditional title *On Nature*. No disposition has been shown to doubt that he was sufficiently interested in geography to prepare a map of the earth, which made a deep and lasting impression, insomuch that it may be said to have fixed the type, preserved with successive enlargements, refinements, and modifications, to be sure, but essentially the same, until in the Alexandrian Age various attempts were made to adjust its outlines in conformity with the newer conception of the earth as a spheroid. Duly considered this admitted fact would of itself suggest the questions whether Anaximander was not a geographer rather than a philosopher, and whether he must not be presumed to have written a geography in addition to drawing a map.

When one finds that he is expressly credited with a geographical treatise in the biographical and bibliographical tradition of the Greeks, one asks why this has been called in question. We have, then, first to canvass the evidence regarding his book and his map.

I

The question regarding Anaximander's book cannot be divorced from that concerning his map. This is not equivalent to saying that the existence of either proves the existence of the other; for maps did exist without accompanying texts, presumably before Anaximander's time; and geographical treatises might, and did in fact, exist without maps. In the case of Anaximander, however, quite apart from general considerations, of which more may be said hereafter, the literary evidence for the geographical treatise is so closely interwoven with that for the chart, that it must all be considered together.

Themistius says that Anaximander was 'the first of the Greeks to our knowledge who ventured to publish a treatise *On Nature*.' This statement, except so far as it bears witness to Anaximander's authorship, deserves no credence; for it belongs to a class of data peculiarly untrustworthy. From early times the Greeks amused themselves by investigating the historical beginnings of various activities and contrivances. These studies gave rise in time to treatises *On Inventions*, and undoubtedly contained much information of value; but pronouncements on matters of this sort are obviously relative to the knowledge of the investigator, and, where the author of a dictum and the sources and limitations of his information are alike unknown, we have no right to accept it as truth. In this instance we may at most conclude that Themistius, or rather his unknown source, did not credit Thales with a treatise *On Nature*.

The entry of Suidas runs thus: "Anaximander of Miletus, son of Praxiades, a philosopher; kinsman, disciple and successor to Thales. He first discovered the equinox, the solstices, and dials to tell the hours, and that the earth lies midmost. He introduced the *gnomon* (sun-dial) and, speaking generally, set forth the essential outlines of geometry. He wrote *On Nature, Tour of the Earth, On the Fixed Stars, Sphere*, and some other treatises." For the moment we may pass over all but the bibliographical data. The title *On Nature* we have already met. *Tour of the Earth* was one of the accepted names for a geographical treatise. *On the Fixed Stars* and *Sphere* would be suitable titles for works dealing with astronomy. What account shall we take of this bibliographical index?

In the times of Anaximander and for long thereafter it was not customary for authors to prefix titles to their writings. Such indication as the writer vouchsafed to give of the contents of his book would ordinarily be contained, along with his name, in the introductory sentence, as was done, for example, by Herodotus, more than a century after Anaximander. Ephorus was, apparently the first geographer and historian who divided his work into 'books.' However reasonable the earlier practice may have been for the writer, it was extremely inconvenient for a librarian. The latter required a con-convenient ticket to attach to the scroll, and hence invented titles where they were not furnished by use and wont. The librarians at Alexandria thus found in current use not only such general titles as *Iliad* and *Odyssey*, but also certain sub-titles referring to episodes or distinct divisions of larger wholes. It is obvious that in the catalogues of the Alexandrian libraries these titles recognized by usage and found in the testimonia, particularly regarding rare books or *desiderata*, were duly listed. Hence it might well happen, and demonstrably did repeatedly happen, that one and the same book was represented in the catalogues by various titles.

Now as regards Anaximander we need not pause at present to inquire whether, assuming the essential truth of the bibliographical data furnished by Suidas, he is to be credited with more than one treatise. The title *On Nature*, though in no sense original or really authentic, is admitted by all to apply to a genuine work of Anaximander from which, it is assumed, derive in the last resort the reports of his 'philosophical' opinions, excerpted by Theophrastus and preserved in the form of tablets triturate in the doxographic tradition. Even the most superficial knowledge of such things must suffice to justify the application of such a title as *On the Fixed Stars* to at least a portion of this treatise. As for *Sphere*, it is true that it is not strictly applicable, because there is no adequate ground for thinking that Anaximander spoke of celestial spheres, the luminaries being according to his teaching annular bodies; but from Aristotle onwards the Pythagorean astronomy and cosmology so established itself that even the best writers spoke of 'spheres' where really 'circles' more accurately described the facts. Hence it would be pressing too far a current expression to object to *Sphere* as a possible sub-title of the treatise *On Nature*. Of the *Tour of the Earth* we need for the movement to remark only that it is included in the list and refers beyond question to a geographical treatise, or in any case to a portion of a work, attributed to Anaximander, supposed to contain matters germane to geography. Whether other evidence of the existence of such a work in antiquity can be discovered elsewhere, we shall have presently to inquire.

Now this bibliographical index has been lightly, perhaps too lightly, set aside as valueless by modern scholars. Generally this is done without even a word of explanation; where anything is said, it is apt to be suggested that there is a mistake or that the titles were read out of references to the map and the celestial globe attributed to Anaximander. As has been already stated, no exception is taken to the datum regarding the title *On Nature*, though it is now agreed to have been of later origin. To Zeller, apparently, it was the multiplicity of titles that occasioned surprise and doubt. Why it should do so, he did not indicate; but one may surmise that he had in mind the probability that Anaximander was the first prose writer and assumed that all beginnings are modest. We may later recur to the question whether Anaximander may with great probability be regarded as the originator of Greek prose; meanwhile it may suffice to say that this is not so certain as to justify *a priori* deductions from the hypothesis. To add to the difficulty, apparently, Suidas, after enumerating the four titles already considered, adds that Anaximander wrote 'some other treatises' not specified by name. Now we shall subsequently find another title, not included in the list of Suidas, which may with probability be referred to our Anaximander.

This circumstance might be considered as aggravating the difficulty to the point of rendering what was before an improbability a sheer impossibility. But this also does not necessarily follow; for it may be that we shall have to revise our notions concerning Anaximander and what is possible or probable in regard to him. It so happens that the title elsewhere cited and not specifically mentioned in the list of Suidas is identical with a title cited in reference to Hecataeus of Miletus. Now Hecataeus, as we shall presently see, was only a trifle over a generation younger than his fellow townsman Anaximander, and pursued studies in good part at least identical with his, taking up and perfecting his map and writing a geographical treatise which enjoyed a great and well-deserved reputation. If it should prove that Anaximander was in intention primarily a geographer, the work of these two eminent Milesians would in fact lie quite in the same plane and run in part parallel, though each extended his line in one direction beyond the other's. Of this we shall have to speak more at length presently: what for the moment concerns us is to point out the fact that there is a striking similarity between these almost contemporary authors in regard to the titles ascribed to them.

Hecataeus seems to have written one work, or at most two, but the recorded titles are quite numerous. That these bibliographical data derived in part from the catalogues of the Alexandrian libraries admits of no doubt, and is in fact not questioned. Why we should not assume the same source for the bibliography of Anaximander does not appear. We have, therefore, thus far found no good reason for rejecting the testimony of Suidas, subject of course to the limitations which apply to all early titles, including that *On Nature*. The only apparently good reason will be presently found on closer examination to confirm the record that Anaximander wrote a geographical treatise.

We have seen that Suidas attributes the introduction of the *gnomon* or sun-dial to Anaximander. Diogenes Laertius reports that "he first invented the *gnomon* and, according to the *Miscellany of Favorinus*, set up at Sparta, in the place called the Dial, one that showed the solstices and equinoxes, and contrived a sun-dial to tell the hours. And he first drew an outline of land and sea, and moreover constructed a (celestial) sphere." Critics have taken exception to certain details of this statement. While Suidas, Diogenes Laertius, and Eusebius agree in attributing the invention of the sun-dial to Anaximander, the Greeks, according to Herodotus, learned the use of the dial and the twelve-fold division of the day from the Babylonians. In view of what we said above regarding the ancient reports of inventions we may well concede that Anaximander did not invent, but merely introduced the instrument. Perhaps even the mere introduction was not due to him; for it is quite possible that dials had been brought to Ionia either from Babylon or from Egypt before his time. We have, however, no reason to doubt that Anaximander was one of the earliest known Greeks to make a scientific use of the instrument. The dial which, according to Favorinus, he set up at Sparta, showed the equinoxes and solstices, and, according to Pliny, Anaximander discovered the obliquity of the zodiac, which, together with the beginnings of the seasons as marked by the rising and setting of certain constellations, could be, and at least in later times were actually, marked on the dial, as connected with seasonal changes in the position of the sun. Such observations are manifestly related to astronomy, with which Anaximander is acknowledged to have greatly concerned himself. The heliacal setting of the Pleiades, long before observed, could with the aid of the dial be definitely dated with reference to the autumnal equinox.

But there is evidence that the risings and settings of the sun at the solstices and equinoxes were in early times used for geographical as well as for astronomical purposes. It is significant that there is no certain reference to the height of the sun at midday until the discovery was made in the time of Eratosthenes that the sun at the summer solstice was vertical over Syene.

By that time the mathematical theory of the globe-earth was fully worked out and the value of the observation could be seen and the necessary conclusions drawn from it, which resulted in the geographical location of the tropics and the equator. But long before that we learn of the use of three equatorials, the central one passing through the straits of Gibraltar and defined with reference to the equinoxial rising and setting of the sun, and two other lines related respectively to the summer and to the winter sunrise and sunset, the former running from the Pyrenees to the Caucasus along the course of the Ister, the latter running parallel along the line supposed to be described by the upper course of the Nile from the Atlas Mountains to the upper Cataracts. This scheme, known from Herodotus, is obviously a geographical projection of the lines of a flat disk sun-dial, which originally concerned itself with the positions of the sun, not at the meridian, but at the rising and setting, where its variations were far more conspicuous. Since this geographical scheme is unquestionably derived from the early Ionians, we naturally think of it as going back either to Hecataeus or to Anaximander; and of the two Anaximander surely has the better claim to it.

But it has been said that the sun-dial at Sparta cannot be attributed to Anaximander, since Pliny says that it was Anaximenes, the disciple of Anaximander, who set it up. It is surprising that this objection should have been seriously considered; for in the same breath Pliny attributes the invention of the science of the *gnomon* to Anaximenes. The latter statement no one accepts, and with good reason; for Anaximenes is in comparison with Anaximander a figure of hardly secondary importance. The natural inference is that in this case Pliny misunderstood a statement in his source, which may well have been superficially ambiguous, since the clause regarding the discovery of the science of the gnomon and the erection of a dial at Sparta, might well have been introduced by a demonstrative susceptible of reference either to Anaximander or to Anaximenes, both of whom were mentioned. In this connection it is well to remark that while there is nothing else in the literary tradition associating Anaximenes with Sparta, it is reported that Anaximander warned the Spartans to abandon their city and houses and live in the open because he anticipated the earthquake which destroyed the entire city. We cannot, unfortunately, rely implicitly on these statements; but if they were true we should have the more reason to suspect that the bronze map of the earth which Aristagoras of Miletus brought to Sparta in his effort to persuade that State to aid the Ionians in over-throwing the Persian power was in fact the map of Anaximander who was commended to the Spartans by personal relations. But whether this map was that made by Anaximander or, as some prefer to think, the revised and perfected map of Hecataeus, who was conspicuously prominent in the Ionian revolt, makes very little difference for our purposes. The presence of a sun-dial at Sparta is as intelligible as that of the map; for both were related to geography, and Anaximander no less than Hecataeus was a geographer. Nor should it cause surprise that Anaximander should thus be supposed to have visited Sparta. It is true that we have no other record of his travels, but in view of the scantiness of the reports regarding him, this is not significant. One can hardly think of a geographer, especially of a pioneer in the field, as confining his studies to his native city and to such information as he could there obtain at second hand. His successor Hecataeus, we are told, had travelled widely.

Of the 'sphere' which Anaximander is said to have constructed we cannot say much. Its relation to his astronomical or cosmological studies is sufficiently obvious. It was as natural that he should attempt a graphic or plastic representation of the heavens as of the earth. Whatever its form, it would serve to visualize the obliquity of the zodiac, which he discovered, and to relate the constellations, in their risings and settings, to the seasons and the changing position of the sun. Anaximander presumably never realized how much this attempt was destined to contribute to the final overthrow of his conception of a disk earth and to the eventual revision of his map; for, once the heavens came to be clearly visualized as a sphere, the advance of geometry, which he is said to have cultivated, and the detailed observation of the stars, to which his sun-dial and 'sphere' must have added impetus, led inevitably to the postulate of a spheroidal earth. This postulate, as is well known, came not from geography, but from the study of the heavens. Indeed, long after the newer conception of the earth had sprung from the speculations of the Pythagoreans, who were geometers and not at all practical geographers, the maps of the geographers, though gradually modified, preserved the impress of their Ionian originators and of their conception of the disk earth.

As to Anaximander's map, we do not know through what intermediaries the notice regarding it came to the handbook of Diogenes Laertius. His testimony does not, however, stand alone, but is supported by the geographical tradition. The filiation in detail of the works on geography in which his map is mentioned need not detain us here. Leaving aside several unimportant notices which add nothing to our enlightenment, we may confine ourselves to the statements of Agathemerus and Strabo. The former says "Anaximander of Miletus, who 'heard' Thales, first had the hardihood to depict the inhabited earth on a tablet. After him Hecataeus of Miletus, a man who had travelled widely, refined his work to the point of admiration. Hellanicus of Lesbos, indeed, a man of wide learning, handed down the fruits of his research unaccompanied with a formal representation. Then Damastes of Sige, borrowing chiefly from the works of Hecataeus, wrote a geographical work; in due order Democritus and Ephorus and certain others composed systematic Tours of the Earth and Geographies." Of this statement it need only be said that it contains a selected fist of geographers, whether they prepared maps or not, extending roughly down to the time of Eratosthenes. The list is carelessly drawn and the phrasing is at more than one point ambiguous; but the difficulties which it presents do not specially concern us here.

To Strabo we are indebted for two passages relating to Anaximander as a geographer. Beginning his geographical treatise he says, "Geography, which I have now chosen to consider, I hold as much the pursuit of the philosopher as any other science. That my opinion is sound is clear from many considerations. For not only were the first who boldly essayed the subject men of this sort, — Homer, and Anaximander, and Hecataeus, (as Eratosthenes also says) his townsman, and Democritus also and Eudoxus and Dicaearchus and Ephorus and others more; and besides, after their time, Eratosthenes and Polybius and Posidonius, philosophers all. But, what is more, wide and varied learning, by which alone it is possible to achieve this task, belongs peculiarly to the man who contemplates all things divine and human, the science of which we call philosophy." Here Anaximander is presented as a geographer who, like numerous other worthies, including Homer, is regarded as a philosopher. The two-fold fact that Eratosthenes is cited as authority for the citizenship of Hecataeus and that the list of worthies falls into two groups of which Eratosthenes heads the second, suggests that that eminent geographer had something to do with drawing up the roll of geographers. His contribution does not, of course, extend beyond the first division; and even there we must except Homer, whom Eratosthenes declined to recognize either as a philosopher or as a geographer, insisting that he was to be regarded solely as a poet bent on entertaining his readers.

Nor can we credit Eratosthenes with rating the others as philosophers; for, aside from the vague conception of what constitutes a philosopher, which is characteristic of Strabo's cast of thought, it is to be noted that Hecataeus, for reasons which will engage our attention later on, was never seriously regarded as a philosopher and hence does not figure in the doxographic tradition. The same is true of Ephorus.

The reference of Strabo, however, to the 'wide and varied learning (polymathy)' required of the geographer recalls that Heraclitus rebuked it, saying "Polymathy does not teach one to have understanding, else would it have taught Hesiod and Pythagoras, and again Xenophanes and Hecataeus." It was apparently the historical and geographical interest of these men that invited the rebuke of the Ephesian recluse. Such breadth of interest was of course characteristic of the whole line of historians and geographers. Pythagoras alone seems strange in such company. Why he should have been decried as a polymath is not clear; but we must recall that he came from Samos, where he may well have imbibed some of the varied knowledge of the Milesian circle, and that we have no authentic account of the range of his interests. What is commonly attributed to him is for the most part true of his school only. He may have been interested in geography, but neither the nature of the reports to that effect nor the record of his school would warrant one in affirming that he was. Heraclitus is said to have referred to Thales' prediction of the eclipse: in what terms he may have done so, we do not know. There is nothing to show what he may have thought of Anaximander.

But to return to Strabo. A few pages after the passage above quoted he resumes: "Let this suffice to justify the statement that Homer was the first geographer; but those also who succeeded him are known as noteworthy men and of the kindred of philosophy; the first of whom after Homer, Eratosthenes says, were two, Anaximander, an acquaintance and fellow citizen of Thales, and Hecataeus the Milesian; the one, he says, first gave out a geographical tablet (map), the other, Hecataeus, left a treatise attested as his by his other writing." The importance of this statement, coming from Eratosthenes the renowned geographer and chronologist, who served as head of the great library at Alexandria, is at once apparent. Just what it signifies is perhaps not quite so clear. Let us consider it somewhat more at length.

This passage bears out the conclusion we reached above in regard to the list of geographers drawn up by Eratosthenes. It was not for their supposed connection with philosophy, but solely as geographers that he mentioned Anaximander and Hecataeus, and Homer was not entered in the roll of honor. As regards the contribution of these pioneers of the science it hardly needs to be said that the testimony of so great an authority as Eratosthenes to the fact of Anaximander drawing a map has been accepted as conclusive evidence by all modern scholars. This conclusion is justified, however, not because Eratosthenes made no mistakes in regard to the authenticity of works, but rather by the circumstances, (1) that we cannot in this instance go farther and check his conclusion by better evidence from other sources, and (2) that in this case his decision is positive and not negative. The first of these principles must always hold in historical inquiries when there is no sufficient reason for impugning the testimony of a generally trustworthy and competent witness. The second is of importance in relation to the judgments of the Alexandrian librarians, because they assumed a critical attitude and erred in general, when they erred, in refusing to admit rather than in affirming the genuineness of works entered in their catalogues. For us, therefore, there remains no alternative but to accept the map as an historical fact.

But what of the geographical treatise attributed to Anaximander? It will perhaps be urged that the statement of Eratosthenes reproduced by Strabo confirms the judgment of those who would reject the report of Suidas, to the effect that Anaximander wrote a *Tour of the Earth*. If this be true, we are on dangerous ground when we refer the list of his works preserved by Suidas to the catalogues of the Alexandrian libraries. But what is affirmed, and what is implied, in the statement of Eratosthenes? The genuineness of Anaximander's map and of Hecataeus' geographical treatise is unquestionably affirmed. One may, if one will, insist that the word 'first' be taken with both statements, so that Eratosthenes shall be made to affirm not only that Anaximander first gave out a map but that Hecataeus first left a geographical treatise. Though possible, the construction is extremely improbable and forced. Yet, even if so much were granted, what is implied in the sentence as a whole? It is not stated that a geographical treatise attributed to Anaximander did not exist or had not existed; rather the affirmation that the claims of such a treatise, attributed to Hecataeus, to be regarded as genuine were confirmed by his other writing, when considered in relation to the sentence as a whole, would seem to imply that Eratosthenes had knowledge of a treatise attributed to Anaximander, which, however, was not so or otherwise sufficiently authenticated. If this exegesis be sound, and I believe it is, we discover in the very text which, "superficially viewed, seems to discredit the bibliography of Suidas, a confirmation of our thesis that the geographical treatise of Anaximander was entered in the Alexandrian catalogues. We may, however, infer from the statement of Eratosthenes that in his time, at least, it was noted as subject to question.

We must now inquire how much weight we should assign to the doubt of Eratosthenes regarding the genuineness of the work attributed to Anaximander. At first sight it would appear that he was as competent a judge in such matters as one could readily find; for one recalls that he was alike eminent as a geographer and as a student of chronology, the former interest seeming to qualify him in a special way to speak with authority on matters connected with the history of geography and in particular with geographical literature, the latter bespeaking for him uncommon credit in regard to the moot questions concerning 'inventions.' But upon closer examination one discovers that these pretensions vanish in thin air. Eratosthenes was, indeed, a geographer and a chronologist of deservedly high repute; but in both fields it was not the antiquarian details, but the scientific principles involved, that chiefly engaged his attention and owed to his efforts a noteworthy contribution. It might well happen, in consequence, that he should err in judgment in regard to matters which lay outside his proper field of study and less invited his interest. We should not be surprised, therefore, if others more directly interested and in such matters more competent should prove to have abandoned his doubts regarding the geographical treatise of Anaximander. That such was in fact the case we shall now try to show with such degree of certainty as is possible in such matters. As is generally the case in historical questions where a conclusive text is not to be produced, the evidence in this instance must be cumulative and must be presented piecemeal with a running commentary. The judicial reader will follow and weigh the arguments in detail, suspending sentence until the whole case has been presented.

We may sum up the conclusions which we have thus far reached in the following propositions, (a) Anaximander wrote a treatise, current in antiquity and accepted as genuine, which was commonly entitled *On Nature*, (b)

There were recorded in the catalogues of the Alexandrian libraries certain other titles purporting to belong to him, such as *Tour of the Earth, On the Fixed Stars, Sphere,* and others not specified, (c) These titles were one and all of later origin, and, being quite possibly at least in part subtitles, indicate at most the scope of his writing without in any way revealing his predominant interest or creating a reasonable presumption in regard to the number of treatises, one or more, which he may be thought to have written, (d) He was credited with the invention or introduction of the sun-dial, which he employed for scientific purposes, certainly as regards cosmology or astronomy, probably in the interest of geography, (e) He drew a map of the earth, which was believed to be the first of its kind and to entitle him to be considered the first scientific geographer, (f) He is credibly reported to have constructed a 'sphere' or representation of the heavens, (g) Eratosthenes had knowledge of a geographical treatise attributed to Anaximander, which he did not consider sufficiently authenticated to justify him in crediting the father of scientific geography with more than the drawing of a map.

So far, then, as the geographical treatise is concerned, down to the time of Eratosthenes the verdict must be *non liquet,* though the admitted interest of Anaximander in the science of geography may be said to favor the presumption that he did not in his book, the existence of which is acknowledged, forego treating a subject so certainly in his thoughts. But Eratosthenes does not mark the close of scientific and antiquarian studies at the Alexandrian libraries in the fields of geography and chronology. The later advances in the science of geography do not concern us here; but it is necessary to direct attention to another scholar whose chosen pursuits especially qualified him to carry forward and revise in detail the historical studies of Eratosthenes. Apollodorus of Athens, the most illustrious disciple of the great Alexandrian critic Aristarchus, devoted himself with zeal and learning especially to the antiquarian aspects of geography and chronology. Attentively reading a vast number of books he published the results of his historical studies chiefly in two works, — his versified *Chronicles,* in which the dates of writers were as precisely as possible fixed, and *The Catalogue of Ships,* in which he gathered about the Homeric *Catalogue* the fruits of his researches in geography. Connected with this learned commentary was his work *On the Earth,* like the *Chronicles,* versified. He wrote, besides, on mythology, prompted by an interest in literary history. Apollodorus is, therefore, of all ancient critics the one whose testimony regarding the book of Anaximander we should most wish to learn.

By a singular good fortune we are in fact in a position to ascertain at least in part what Apollodorus knew of Anaximander's writings. Diogenes Laertius says that Anaximander "gave a summary exposition of his opinions, on which Apollodorus of Athens somewhere chanced, who in his *Chronicles* reports that he was sixty-four years of age in the second year of the fifty-eighth Olympiad and died shortly thereafter." In the light of our foregoing discussion, this most interesting statement deserves somewhat fuller consideration than it has hitherto received.

Whence Diogenes derived this datum is not certain; but one may conjecture from the phraseology that it came mediately or immediately from the late doxographic document which Diels has called the *Posidonian Areskonta*. It is known that Posidonius followed closely in the footsteps of Apollodorus, whose geographical studies he took up and prosecuted to the best of his ability. But in any case Apollodorus made the statement in question in his *Chronicles*. By 'opinions' Diogenes of course means 'philosophical' opinions, and therefore, though Apollodorus does not seem to have cited the title of the 'summary exposition,' it is commonly assumed that it was the treatise appropriately called *On Nature* to which he referred.

Diels has cited as a parallel the chronological datum given by Democritus in his *Brief Cosmology*, and suggests that the year designated was that of the publication of the treatise, which contained autobiographical references capable of astronomical determination.

This is of course conceivable; but, it must be pointed out, this hypothesis, while possibly accounting for the given year, fails to explain the further statement of Apollodorus that Anaximander died shortly afterwards. If, as we are bound to do, we confine ourselves to such information as Apollodorus might derive from the book he had met with, without assuming either data from other sources or unwarranted inferences on the part of the chronologist, we must frame a better theory. Such an hypothesis is in fact not far to seek, and has indeed been already in part suggested by Professor Burnet.

Diogenes dates Anaximander by the second year of the fifty-eighth Olympiad. This statement does not derive directly from Apollodorus, who used the year of the Athenian Archon Eponymus instead of the Olympiad. But the chronological practice of Apollodorus suggests not only that the datum really comes from his work but also that it was based upon information of a peculiarly definite sort.

Ordinarily Apollodorus contented himself (perforce, no doubt) with determining the floruit of a man, taken as forty years of age, with reference to some epoch or the beginning of a king's reign, if a relation could be established. One sees at once the exceptional character of the datum regarding Anaximander; for the age is not forty, but sixty-four, and the year (B.C. 547/6) is not one of his regular epochs. The following year, however (546/5), is one of the important epochs of Apollodorus, being that of the fall of Sardis. The preceding year, moreover, though not marking an epoch for Apollodorus, was one of fateful consequences to the Ionians of Miletus, among whom Anaximander was a man of great prominence; for the march of the Persians under Cyrus against Croesus, whose subject allies the Milesians were, and the defeat of Croesus at the Halys, must have filled Anaximander with dismay. Nothing would be more natural than for him to mention these events, if he dealt at all with geographical or historical matters; for they were obviously of great potential significance from either point of view. If he was personally active in this campaign, as he may well have been, he might properly give his age.

Thus we should have a reasonable hypothesis to account for the report of Apollodorus regarding his age in this precise year. The additional statement that he died not long thereafter would be adequately explained if Anaximander's book made no mention of the fall of Sardis, which soon followed.

It will be seen that this hypothesis carries us beyond the natural scope of a cosmological treatise, such as would necessarily be entitled *On Nature*, into a field more closely connected with history or geography. It may be said, however, that, while this assumption would meet the necessary conditions, others equally as good might be made to fit the requirements. Granted that an hypothesis, however satisfactory, is not to be accepted as proof, we are justified in saying that this particular hypothesis has more probability in its favor than any other that has been proposed, and is at least in a measure supported by the evidence of Anaximander's interest in geography.

But we have not yet exhausted the possible sources of information regarding Anaximander's book. Aside from a fragment preserved by Simplicius, to which we shall later return, there are mentioned certain opinions and passages attributed in our sources to 'Anaximander.' Their status, however, is uncertain, because we hear of another Anaximander of Miletus, to whom they have generally been referred. We are bound, therefore, to consider the new claimant and the validity of his claims.

What we may be said to know about the other Anaximander is little enough, being contained in two brief notices. Diogenes Laertius reports that "there was also another Anaximander, an historian, he too being a Milesian, who wrote in Ionic." The entry of Suidas regarding him runs thus: "Anaximander the Younger, son of Anaximander, of Miletus — historian. He lived in the time of Artaxerxes Mnemon; wrote Interpretation of Pythagorean Symbols, e.g. ' not to step over a cross-bar,' ' not to poke the fire with a poniard,' ' not to eat from a whole loaf,' and the rest." The first gives nothing omitted in the second notice except that be wrote in Ionic, which was natural if he wrote before Attic became the recognized medium for prose, as it did in the fourth century B.C. As Artaxerxes Mnemon reigned 405-359 B.C., and the chronological datum ' he lived in the time of such and such a king' regularly refers to the date of the king's accession (405), this information was not material. Suidas, then, alone gives us significant data.

We gather, then, that Anaximander was a fairly frequent name at Miletus, as this notice acquaints us with two, father and son. If they were not related to the great Anaximander, his fame may account for the perpetuation of the name in his city. Anaximander the Younger is called an historian, which might be significant if we were not immediately informed what sort of history he wrote without getting the least intimation that he produced anything beyond the Interpretation of Pythagorean Symbols.

Though Suidas gives us no specimen of his interpretations and we have no evidence in regard to them from other sources, we fortunately are not without instructive examples of the same literary kind from other hands. At their best they are reports of an antiquarian character regarding curious practices in Greece or foreign lands; at their worst they are stupid attempts at symbolical interpretation. They cannot predispose us to think of Anaximander the Younger as a serious rival of his great eponym; and in any case the fact that he is called an historian, with such a work and such only to his credit, offers no justification for assigning to him every fragment or notice which would be appropriate to an historian.

Having seen what manner of man Anaximander the Younger was according to the only certain information we have regarding him, we must now canvass the data which Greek tradition attributes simply to 'Anaximander' and modern scholars commonly credit to the account of the author of the Interpretation of Pythagorean Symbols. A scholium on Dionysius Thrax reports, "Ephorus among others in his second book says that Cadmus was the inventor of the alphabet; others say that he was not the inventor but the transmitter to us of the invention of the Phoenicians, as Herodotus also in his History and Aristotle report, for they say that Phoenicians invented the alphabet and Cadmus brought it to Greece. Pythodorus, however, in his treatise *On the Alphabet* and Phillis of Delos, in his treatise *On Chronology*, say that before the time of Cadmus Danaus imported it; and they are confirmed by the Milesian writers Anaximander and Dionysius and Hecataeus, who are cited in this connection by Apollodorus also in his treatise *On the Catalogue of Ships*." The word vaguely rendered 'writers' in the foregoing version should probably be translated 'historians,' its usual meaning in later Greek. Possibly it was this consideration that prevailed with modern scholars, leading them to assign this datum to Anaximander the Younger. Diels alone, apparently, has latterly had misgivings; for after ignoring this passage in the first two editions of his invaluable *Vorsokratiker* he included it in the third, but marked it as dubious under the heading of the elder Anaximander.

Intrinsically there can be no valid objection to the assumption that the early Milesians Anaximander, Dionysius and Hecataeus concerned themselves with the question regarding the source of the Greek alphabet. The absurd notions regarding the late beginnings of literature in Greece, based on a few ignorant utterances of late Greeks and fostered by the incomprehensible influence of Wolf's *Prolegomena* might account for the hesitation of some modern scholars to credit such a report, which obviously implies that to the Ionians of the time of Pisistratus writing was so familiar a fact that they must seek its origins in the distant mythical past; but, apart from such preconceptions, there is no ground for calling it in question. It is rather just what the intelligent student should have expected, not only from a reading of the Homeric poems, whose literary perfection and contents are incomprehensible except on the supposition of long literary practice, but also from a critical reading of the extant remains of early Greek historical writings. Herodotus, whose dependence on early Ionian, especially Milesian, writers is unquestionable, has no doubt of the derivation of all higher elements of Greek civilization from Egypt, and constantly presupposes two lines of transmission, one direct, mediated by Danaus, from Egypt to Argos, the other indirect, in which the Phoenicians play the role of intermediaries. In the latter line Cadmus, who is supposed to have come from Tyre to Thebes, is not the only link. It is not necessary here to go into details. Suffice it to say that on the ground of intrinsic probability no objection can be urged against the assumption that Anaximander, the contemporary of Croesus, held the opinion that Danaus brought the alphabet direct from Egypt.

Nor can there be a reasonable doubt that the elder, and not the younger, Anaximander is intended. The datum furnished by the scholiast is referred to Apollodorus of Athens', who had cited 'the Milesian historians Anaximander, Dionysius and Hecataeus' for the opinion in question, in his great historico-geographical treatise *On the Catalogue of Ships*. He it was, we recall, who somewhere met with Anaximander's book, from which he must have derived the information enabling him to date the old Milesian with such singular precision. The character of that information, as we have pointed out, was presumably historical and geographical. The datum regarding the origin of the Greek alphabet, being of the same character, naturally found its way into a work belonging to the same line of tradition.

But the date of Anaximander was, as we have seen, properly given in Apollodorus' *Chronicles*. Since he was especially interested in chronology, we should expect Apollodorus to give the names in chronological order. In the versified Chronicles he might for metrical reasons depart from this natural order, but not in his prose treatise *On the Catalogue of Ships*. He observed, therefore, the order — right or wrong — in which these writers appeared in his *Chronicles*, barring metrical difficulties not likely to occur except in the event that they had to be mentioned in the same clause.

Now it happens that the names Anaximander, Dionysius, Hecataeus actually follow one another in alphabetical order. In the case of Anaximander, acknowledged to be older than the other members of the group, nobody would deny that chronological considerations might nevertheless have determined his position at the head of the list; but in regard to the other two question will at once arise, because Dionysius is commonly considered junior to Hecataeus. We have then to canvass the question of their chronology, especially in so far as Apollodorus may be supposed to have been concerned in fixing it.

The datum unquestionably from his treatise *On the Catalogue of Ships* we have seen, as well as the reasons for regarding his list as arranged in chronological order. Aside from this we have several other statements. Heraclitus, as we have observed, names his polymaths in the following sequence: Hesiod, Pythagoras, Xenophanes, Hecataeus. That this order is roughly chronological will not be denied, though a question might arise regarding the relative ages of Pythagoras and Xenophanes. They were in any case roughly contemporary, and Xenophanes referred to Pythagoras. Hence we may disregard this nice question of chronology, which cannot be settled. Hecataeus, at all events, was younger than both and earlier than Heraclitus. We have, moreover, the evidence of Herodotus, who represents Hecataeus as prominent in the councils of Miletus in the Ionian Revolt (499 and 497/6). The role which he plays in these events proves that he was an 'elder statesman.' In the article of Suidas about Hellanicus there is clearly a confusion, which others have sought to correct. In view of this corruption of the text, one cannot of course adduce it in evidence. Even worse is the entry of Suidas in regard to Dionysius. "Dionysius of Miletus, historian: Events after Darius in five books, Geography, Persian History in the Ionic dialect, Trojan History in three books, Mythical History, Historic Cycle in seven books." Here, as all acknowledge, we have a hopeless jumble arising from the confusion of an indeterminate number of the almost innumerable writers who bore the name of Dionysius. This being so, we must clearly rule out this datum also as incapable of yielding a date; for the only item in this bibliographical farrago possibly serviceable for chronological purposes, the Events after Darius, not only shares the general doubt attaching to the list as a whole, but is in itself ambiguous. That Dionysius of Miletus was an historian we must grant, and that he wrote on Persian history in the time of Cambyses and Darius I is exceedingly probable. Beyond that we have thus far been unable to go.

There is, however, another chronological datum to be found in the entry of Suidas regarding Hecataeus: "Hecataeus, son of Hegesimander, of Miletus; he lived in the time of Darius who was king after Cambyses, when Dionysius of Miletus also lived, in the sixty-fifth Olympiad: a writer of history." This chronological notice, obviously derived from some chronicle, was it would seem, somewhat awkwardly combined with a bibliography, which has in consequence been lost. It admits of no doubt, however, that the chronologist was himself quite clear in regard to the Milesian writers and their date; and I do not entertain the least doubt that the chronological datum comes ultimately from Apollodorus. In form it agrees perfectly with numerous others derived from his Chronicles: it is obviously intended to fix the floruit of Hecataeus and Dionysius at the year 520 B.C., the year in which Darius, the last Persian king with whom the chronologist could establish a connection, became King of Babylon. Apollodorus no doubt dated by the Athenian Archon Eponymus, but some later author converted the date, using the corresponding Olympiad. We thus see that Apollodorus might perfectly well name the two Milesian historians in either order, Dionysius and Hecataeus, or Hecataeus and Dionysius, since he fixed their floruit in the same year. The two statements therefore complement and confirm one another. Regarding Hecataeus, at any rate, the date, which would make him over sixty years of age at the time of the Ionian Revolt, cannot be far wrong: and respecting Dionysius we have no information that in the least justifies us in questioning the correctness of Apollodorus' calculation.

Having disposed of the objections to the acceptance of the statement attributed to Apollodorus and having justified our reference of it to the elder Anaximander, it remains for us to signalize the importance of the fact reported as evidence of the character and contents of his book. So much at least we may confidently affirm: that it did not confine itself to cosmological and other cognate matters which might justify the title *On Nature* to the exclusion of such a title as *Tour of the Earth*; for a glance at the list of authorities whom the scholiast on Dionysius Thrax cites in regard to the origin of the Greek alphabet, as well as a consideration of the logical context of such an inquiry, must suggest that the book of Anaximander, like those of Hecataeus, Dionysius, and Herodotus, belonged at least in part to the historico-geographical line of tradition. Regarding Hecataeus and Dionysius there can be no question; but Anaximander also is classed with these admittedly 'historical' writers.

We may be pardoned for insisting that we are thus abundantly justified in holding fast our faith in the essential correctness of the bibliography of Anaximander preserved by Suidas and in the derivation of the list of titles from the catalogues of the Alexandrian libraries. It was there in all probability that Apollodorus found the book, which, as we have seen, was known by report, if not by sight, to Eratosthenes. It is possible, indeed, that Apollodorus discovered the book of Anaximander at Pergamum, where he was active in later life, and where his interest in antiquities must have made him welcome; but the book must have been rare in his day, and Alexandria is surely the place where we should most expect to find it. If we assume that the book was there in the time of Eratosthenes we shall not violate probabilities; for the case, far from being unexampled, would find a close parallel in the same field.

We know from Athenaeus that Callimachus, presumably in his catalogue, attributed either the *Tour of Asia*, or, more probably, the entire *Tour of the Earth of Hecataeus*, of which the *Tour of Asia* was a part, to one Nesiotes, though we do not know on what grounds. Conjecture is easy but profitless. But Eratosthenes, his successor, as we learn from Strabo, vindicated the authorship of Hecataeus as confirmed by the Genealogies, which he apparently regarded as a separate work and above suspicion. When, therefore, Apollodorus set aside the doubts of his predecessor regarding the book of Anaximander he was merely doing what other scholars, ancient and modern, have done. It was only natural that such indications of doubtful authorship as may have been noted in the Alexandrian catalogues should be expunged, once the doubts of the librarians were resolved.

There still remain to be considered a number of passages before we can be sure that we have garnered in all the notices of Anaximander's treatise. Athenaeus, expatiating on the *skyphos*, a cup or goblet, remarks that the name occurs as both a masculine and a neuter noun and is sometimes written *skyphos*, sometimes *skypphos*. In this connection he says, "Similarly Anaximander in his *Heroology*, in these terms: 'Amphitryon having parcelled out the booty among the allies and keeping the *skypphos* (masculine) which he chose for himself,' and again: 'Poseidon gave the *skypphos* to his son Teleboas, and Teleboas to Pterelaus; this he took and sailed away.' "Athenaeus, you observe, is concerned solely with a grammatical point; it is worthy of remark, however, that he cites as using the form *skypphos*, besides Anaximander, the poets Hesiod and Anacreon, who employ it, as does Anaximander, as a masculine noun of the second declension, and the epic poet Panyassis, a (somewhat older) relative of the historian Herodotus, who treats it as a neuter noun of the third declension. The agreement at this point of the Anaximander in question with Hesiod, who was older, and with Anacreon, who was but slightly younger, than the elder Anaximander, and the disagreement of Panyassis, junior by over two generations, constitute a point, of no great weight perhaps, but taken for what it is worth, in favor of the elder rather than of the younger Anaximander. But this is not the only possible clew; for Athenaeus cites the title of the work from which the quotations derive.

They come, he says, from the *Heroology* of Anaximander. This title occurs neither in the bibliography of Anaximander the Elder nor, of course, in that of the Younger, which contains but the one title, *Interpretation of Pythagorean Symbols*; but, as we have seen, whereas in the case of the latter Suidas does not intimate the existence of other titles, in that of the elder Anaximander he prepares us for more by adding to his list "and certain others." If we attach any weight to the bibliographies of Suidas, the finding of a new title attributed to the elder Anaximander can occasion no surprise; but with his namesake the case is quite different. More important, however, than either of these considerations is the circumstance that the title quoted by Athenaeus is identical with one of the titles of Hecataeus. Respecting the latter we do not know whether the *Heroology* is another name for his *Genealogies* or *Histories*, or a subtitle of that treatise. It can hardly be doubted, however, that it is one or the other. Bearing in mind the close relation which certainly existed between Hecataeus and his predecessor and the established fact that the elder Anaximander included matters of history connected with the mythical past in the book found by Apollodorus, one cannot reasonably question his claim to these passages from Athenaeus. To assign them to Anaximander the Younger, of whom we know nothing except that he lived more than a century after Hecataeus and wrote *An Interpretation of Pythagorean Symbols* is not critical scholarship, but the renunciation of it.

Now if we attribute the words quoted by Athenaeus, as apparently we are bound to attribute them, to the elder Anaximander, we see both by the title and the contents that he dealt with the heroic genealogies which were studied, as we know from Hecataeus, Pherecydes, and Hellanicus, for clues in regard to early history and geography. The scope of his work or works is thus shown, as indeed we were led to infer from his reference to Danaus and the importation of the alphabet from Egypt, to have included not only the beginnings of the cosmos but also the legendary history of Greek lands. In all such cases, whether known from Greek or Hebrew sources, the geographical and ethnographical status at the time of the would-be historian furnished the starting point which was to be explained by reconstructing the past. Whether it be the story of Creation and the genealogical tables of the descendants of Noah, in the Book of Genesis, or the Hesiodic *Theogony* and Catalogues, the purpose and the method are everywhere essentially the same: it is the conception of a universal history. One may call it Genesis, if one will, or Physis, if one prefers; but the central interest of the men who thus set themselves the task of reading the beginnings is always in the earth and its inhabitants as they found them: The description of the earth and its peoples is what constitutes geography, and has always constituted the science. If, as is certain, Anaximander sketched the beginnings of the cosmos and the early history of the Greeks as reflected in the genealogical tables of the heroes, there is no reason why we should doubt that he who constructed a map of the earth actually wrote, as he is reported to have written, a geographical work, which gave the disposition of the peoples and the boundaries of continents and lands in agreement with the pictorial representation of his chart. That was at once the logical thing to do and the thing which by all the tokens we must infer he was most concerned to do.

There is one more reference to an Anaximander which calls for consideration. In Xenophon's *Symposium* the guests are asked to mention the thing on which they severally pride themselves, and Niceratus makes it his boast that his father had compelled him to commit to memory all the verses of Homer and that he could still repeat the entire *Iliad* and *Odyssey*. Antisthenes with the tactless jeer of the Cynic retorts that all the rhapsodes can do as much and that, as everyone will acknowledge, there are no greater simpletons in the world than they. To keep Niceratus in countenance and prevent a possible scene, Socrates with fine urbanity suggests that the stupidity of the rhapsodes is due to their failure to learn the hidden meaning of the poet which is given in allegorical or symbolical interpretation; "But you, Niceratus," he adds, "have paid large tuition fees both to Stesimbrotus and Anaximander and to many others, so that nothing of great value has escaped you." Here then we meet an Anaximander who interprets texts in a manner to bring out their hidden meaning. Nothing more is said about him. Can we with probability identify him with either the elder or the younger Anaximander of our inquiry?

In confronting this question it is necessary to recall the context. As Niceratus does not assert that he has sat at the feet of Stesimbrotus and Anaximander, and does not even assent to the statement of Socrates, which was obviously prompted by a desire to preserve the good feeling of the feast, we are under no obligation to credit Niceratus even with a knowledge of the methods of interpretation practised by Stesimbrotus and Anaximander, much less with having actually studied in the schools of these masters. If Socrates under the circumstances in his ironical manner told a white lie, his well-bred table companions would appreciate and acquiesce in his suggestion. Indeed it is not impossible that with his characteristic plain speaking Antisthenes meant to imply that Niceratus was of a feather with the rhapsodes with whom he flocked. Be that as it may, we are not warranted in pressing the passage to prove either that Stesimbrotus and Anaximander conducted schools in which they gave instruction and received tuition fees, nor that Niceratus attended them. If we assume that Niceratus owed them any instruction, he might equally well have derived it from their books. With regard to the date also we may take a similar view.

As the scene of the Xenophontic Symposium is laid in the year 421 B.C, strict consistency would require that the supposed masters of Niceratus had taught or had at least published their works before that year. This would be true of Stesimbrotus, but would hardly hold of Anaximander the Younger, if his floruit was properly given at 405 B.C.; for in 421 he would have been about 23 years of age. However, an anachronism of this sort on Xenophon's part should not rule the latter out. Again, it is not necessary to assume that all the 'teachers' of Niceratus practised their hyponoetic interpretation on Homer.

Stesimbrotus, who wrote about moot questions in Homer, may be acknowledge to have done so; Anaximander the Younger, who interpreted the Pythagorean symbols, may be said to have fulfilled all that the words of Xenophon require us to suppose if, as is altogether probable, his method of exegesis was essentially the same as that applied to the poets.

Of the elder Anaximander we have not spoken in this connection because very little can be said in favor of him in relation to the hyponoetic interpretation presupposed by the passage from Xenophon's Symposium. It is true that indications are not wanting of somewhat allegorical interpretations of Homer at the close of the sixth century B.C.; but neither is there any evidence that the practice dates back to the middle of that century, nor is there anywhere a hint that the great Milesian would have concerned himself with it, if it did. It was rather in the latter half of the fifth century that the method which was destined in time to enjoy great favor and an extended application won its first laurels. Hence we may with tolerable confidence identify the Anaximander of Xenophon's *Symposium* with Anaximander the Younger, the interpreter of Pythagorean symbols.

If our results are assured we have added at least two brief verbatim fragments to the one previously allowed to have come from the book of Anaximander, the reputed originator of Greek prose. Of these fragments it is not necessary now to speak at length; it is perhaps deserving of mention, however, that in point of style they closely resemble not only the fragment communicated by Simplicius but likewise the fragments of Hecataeus. Of the three the sentence quoted by Simplicius is the most complex; for the most part their structure is exceedingly simple, no elaborate periods being attempted; but there is no want of precision or lucidity. Hecataeus, as far as we can judge, made no advance in this respect; even Herodotus in general constructed his sentences on the same model, only occasionally betraying the influence of fifth century sophists. It would therefore be as proper to speak of Herodotus as primitive as it would of Anaximander. That Simplicius should think the terms used by Anaximander rather 'poetic' is only a compliment to the imaginative vigor of his speech.

Though Anaximander and Hecataeus of course used Ionic forms, the distinctive differences from the Attic have almost entirely vanished in the course of transmission.

II

Our survey of the tradition regarding Anaximander's book shows that it touched on matters not germane to a philosophical treatise, properly so called. This fact raises a variety of questions which are of importance in relation to the history of Greek philosophy; for though Thales is commonly regarded as the originator of this kind of inquiry, we know so little of his scientific work that it is only with his successor Anaximander that we begin with a certain assurance to discern the character and direction of thought cultivated at Miletus, the city which bred the new interests destined to have an illustrious career in the western world.

Were it profitable to express a feeling of regret, perhaps the greatest loss to history might be said to be that which virtually blotted out the story of this ancient city of Miletus, the pride of Ionia. Even the excavations conducted there in recent years have produced almost nothing: one gratefully excepts the headless statue erected by appreciative contemporaries to Anaximander, showing that they valued him even in his lifetime. What we need to remember is that Miletus even in his day had passed the zenith of its power: it is always in the afternoon or evening of a civilization that man turns to reflection on the world, its origin and its destiny. Of the earlier period, in which Miletus ran its feverish course of unexampled activity, there are no written records extant: like the good mother she was, she lived on in her almost countless children, the colonies she had planted. Among the last of these was Apollonia, which Anaximander served as founder.

Thales seems to have lived to an advanced age and to have died about the same time as Anaximander. There is every indication that Simplicius added the reference to the poetic style. See Strabo 1.2,6 C. 18.

In reality Anaximander may quite possibly have derived his form of expression and the suggestion of the cosmic process in question from a curious practice observed in his home, which Strabo reports that they formed the nucleus of a group of men, their fellow-citizens, among whom certain intellectual interests were cultivated. It is perhaps misnaming this circle to call it a school; but it was destined to become the parent of all the 'schools.' One thinks of the circle formed by Franklin at Philadelphia, which eventually became a university: but Franklin had models to copy, while Thales and his fellows pretty certainly had no predecessors who worked in the same spirit.

What, we naturally ask, were the interests which inspired the goodly fellowship at Miletus to organize this first 'college?' They must have been related to the life of the group and of the city; but there is no indication that in the beginning political questions, questions that is concerning the government of Miletus, engaged the attention of the group. They were citizens, of course, and shared the life of the city; but it is as statesmen concerned with larger issues that we hear of them. Thales proposed the unification of Ionia into a federal state; what Anaximander may have done to win the honor bestowed on him we can only conjecture; Hecataeus, one of the last of the 'school,' was prominent as an elder statesman at the time of the Ionian Revolt. But of such political activity, looking to the control of the government of their city, as appears in the circle of Pythagoras, we have not a hint; though it is more than likely that Pythagoras, in this as in other respects, was inspired by the example of the Milesian 'college.' The discussion of the principles to be followed in founding colonies, in which Anaximander at least participated, inevitably led to the consideration of the ideal city; that it was a topic discussed by the Milesian 'school' goes without saying, but is abundantly clear upon reflection, for city-planning and the Utopian schemes of the Greek historico-geographical tradition everywhere lead back to the Milesians of the sixth century. Such ideals quite naturally arose in a city with far-flung colonies and with relations, through Naucratis, with Egypt, which in the entire Greek tradition appears as the Utopia par excellence.

Aside from the direct reports regarding Thales, Anaximander and Anaximenes, who for us at least constitute the Milesian 'school of philosophy,' the best evidence we have regarding that memorable circle comes from our knowledge of the men most influenced by this triad. Leaving out of account those who are said to have had relations with 'the philosophy of Anaximenes,' because their debt is too special, we think necessarily of Pythagoras, Xenophanes and Hecataeus, the three whom, with Hesiod, Heraclitus rebuked for their polymathy, which failed to teach them understanding. This list is not the product of chance; for a clear line, running from Hesiod through Thales and Anaximander, leads us to Pythagoras, the mathematician, to Xenophanes, the rationalist interested in ethnography and history, and to Hecataeus the geographer, historian, and naturalist. Heraclitus is said to have testified to the interest of Thales in astronomy, and Eudemus called him the father of geometry. The latter also, apparently, is responsible for the data we have for Anaximander's ideas regarding the magnitudes and intervals of the heavenly bodies and for the statement that he outlined the subject of geometry.

How these several intellectual interests were cultivated in the Milesian circle, we do not know; but it is not difficult to discover a relation between their studies and the problems which crowded upon the intelligent citizens of Miletus. Thus Thales was credited with a work on nautical astronomy and with various nautical devices natural in the busiest trading center of the Levant, whose sailors went everywhere. Of similar interest was presumably his study of the calendar. As for the pursuit of geometry, its relation to city-planning and to the allotment of lands was well recognized in antiquity; the relation of both astronomy and geometry to geography was no less distinctly seen. The schematic geometrical treatment of the early Ionian (Milesian) maps is known to every student of ancient geography: hence we need not suppose that Eratosthenes first brought geometry to the service of cartography.

In the busy streets of Miletus there met men who had voyaged to Egypt and seen the Ethiopians, snub-nosed and dark of skin, and to Thrace, and knew its blue-eyed and red-haired inhabitants: one could gather there, even without travel, to which every Milesian must have been tempted, the most varied lore about all sorts of strange peoples and their customs. Pretty nearly everything we learn of the 'barbarians' before the close of the fifth century comes ultimately from early Ionian writers. They interested themselves also in the progress of civilization and the steps and 'inventions' whereby it was advanced.

But all this store of information was in the true Greek manner to be somehow set in order and brought into relation to the time and place in which they found themselves. How consciously these early Milesians worked we do not know; but the result of their labors is writ large in the physiognomy of Greek science.

Hesiod occupies a strangely anomalous position in Greek literature. The Homeric epic, at least in its finished form, is acknowledged to be the product of Ionia. After their childhood days, in which the Ionians gave themselves to telling tales of the long ago merely for the delight they took in heroic adventure, ensues an age of almost total eclipse of this extraordinary people, from which it emerges in the sixth century, past its prime and in a measure decadent. When it thus again comes to view it is engaged in writing treatises in prose on scientific themes. Meanwhile, for us, the connecting link between the heroic epic and the sober prose of science appears in Hesiod, not in Ionia, but in the Mother Land, which was, intellectually considered, centuries behind the Greeks of Asia Minor. It is perhaps idle to speculate, but one cannot refrain from asking how this fact is to be explained.

Can we believe that there was really a lapse of consciousness in Ionia and that when the people suddenly awoke, they took the cues of their intellectual life from Greece Proper? Would it not be more reasonable to suppose that the beginnings of Ionian prose lie in that dark age, the general substance of the attempts of the Ionians at reconstructing their past being worked up by Hesiodic poets who borrowed their ideas from contemporary Ionia and the form from the Homeric epic?

If we could assume that the first 'theogonies' and 'catalogues' were in prose, we should be able to account both for their disappearance and for certain characteristics of the Hesiodic poetry itself.

Be that as it may, Miletus in the sixth century has definitively broken with the Hesiodic and Homeric past. It is not in a mood for poetry: the gods have melted away in the cosmos, and genealogies are useful solely as materials from which one may by criticism and combination extract history. Miletus is at a certain point on a map of the earth, which has its assignable place in the cosmos. The Milesian who walks its streets feels himself likewise at a definite point of time, and he sets about reaching backward to fixed points in the past in order to reconstruct a chronology. His immediate data are furnished by family traditions, and an approximate, limited scale is constructed by using the generation as a unit. The absolute scale was not to be found in Greece: Hecataeus discovered it in the immemorial civilization of Egypt with it records running back thousands of years.

The connection between the Greek and Egyptian scales, and therefore the control and placing of Greek dates in relation to the absolute scale, were brought about by certain identifications, no matter how arbitrary they may have been. These are the methods of a thoroughly rational and conscious science: they have been refined in the course of time, and the admissibility and validity of certain data have been more sharply scrutinized; but historical science in all its essentials was achieved in Miletus before the close of the sixth century. This, as historians recognize, is the dawn of the historical period in Greece; and here we first find really historical dates. Dates for a generation or two farther back are approximately correct, as one might expect; beyond that we have, so far as Greek sources are concerned, nothing intrinsically different from the data with which the Milesians themselves had to deal.

This was the crowning achievement of the Milesians, and we are justified in regarding it as the expression of the dominant interest of the Milesian 'school.' To this result the several members of that epoch-making circle made their contributions. Anaximander, as we have seen, concerned himself with geography and history as well as with cosmology. We should like very much to know more about his book; but everything beyond what we have already said must be learned by inference.

There are two classes of facts from which permissible inferences may be drawn regarding the character of Anaximander's book. One consists of the testimony of the ancients regarding it and the opinions of its author. Of a part of these data we have already taken cognizance; others we have still to consider. When we shall have completed the review of the contents of the book, and drawn such inferences from them as appear to be justified, we shall be in position to institute a new inquiry: to wit, whether other works of like character existed, or still exist, from which one may draw further inferences.

Anaximander is generally regarded as a philosopher: hence we will begin with such opinions as seem to justify that title. He dealt, we are told, with the origin of the cosmos. Out of the Infinite it came: into the Infinite it will be resolved. The cosmos is described, and its constituent members are placed in due order with their intervals noted, the earth being at the centre. This world is but one of an infinite number, past, present and still to come. These worlds may be called gods. Certain phenomena of the cosmos are noted and explained. The earth does not lie in the plane of the zodiac, but the latter runs obliquely about it. The nature of sun, moon and stars is set forth, and eclipses are explained. He explains also the origin of the sea and the reason why it is salt, and offers explanations of various meteorological phenomena. Aristotle treats most of these topics in *De caelo*, *De generatione et corruptione*, and *Meteorologica*.

One recurrent note cannot fail to arrest the attention: it is the quest after origins, and the glance ahead, seeking to divine the end. Whence and how the cosmos arose, where it will vanish at last; how the sea originated and became salt, and how in the end it will quite dry up: — these are, one may say, the all-inclusive questions, giving the setting of the whole and providing for matters in detail of lesser importance. Judging by our records, the outlook of Anaximander is in the last analysis historical. It is in keeping with this point of view that, as we have seen in tracing the record of his book, Anaximander displayed an interest in heroic genealogies and in the origin of writing, a question then as now of vital concern to the historian, because the use of writing is the precondition of the existence of records serviceable for history. Of like character are the questions, to which we know Anaximander addressed himself, concerning the origin of land animals and especially of the human species.

That Anaximander concerned himself with geography we know. We have tried to point out the actual, or at any rate the possible, relation to his geographical studies of his pursuit of geometry and his use of the *gnomon*. But this instrument had obvious uses also in determining the calendar, which is the basis of chronology and of history; for history without definite measures of time is impossible. History and geography go necessarily together: in Greece they formed from the beginning a unit, geography being generally treated in excursus in the historical narrative. It was only by Ephorus and Polybius that geography came to be set apart as distinct books, though embodied, as were the earlier geographical excursus, by Aristotle's *Meteorologica*. The importance of Milesian science does not seem to be fully recognized, — probably because he does not often refer to his predecessors by name.

This statement would be paradoxical, were it not for our knowledge of Hecataeus and Herodotus: even where the predominant interest is apparently geographical, the geographical account falls within the historical scheme. In describing countries which furnished no historical clues the status quo of course alone was given. When one tries to form a conception of Anaximander's book, one thinks inevitably of Hecataeus, his successor, who can hardly have remained uninfluenced by his example. As we have before remarked, the traditional titles applied to the work of Hecataeus are numerous; two, however, are clearly inclusive of the rest, (a) *Histories* (or *Genealogies*) and (b) *Tour of the Earth*. In later times these were regarded as separate treatises, but it is far from certain that they were originally and to the mind of their author distinct. Two facts point rather to the conclusion that they were conceived as a unity. First, we know of only one introduction, in which the author gave his name, and that was prefatory to the *Genealogies*. Secondly, the *Tour of the Earth*, being evidently without express mention of its author, was mistakenly assigned to Nesiotes, and therefore the claims of Hecataeus were for a time disputed. The statement sometimes made that the *Tour of the Earth* was composed before the *Histories*, is wholly without foundation. Logically the Tour of the Earth, having regard primarily for the status quo in its author's time, follows the *Genealogies*, which treated of the past. If we assume that Hecataeus composed his treatise as a single work, which was subsequently divided for convenience, the facts known about it are most readily explained. To be sure, we are thus led to postulate in the sixth century an historico-geographical treatise in size comparable perhaps to the *Histories* of Herodotus. To some this may seem incredible: perhaps they shall have to revise their preconceived notions regarding what was possible in sixth century Miletus.

If we ask where in such a treatise, as we suppose Anaximander's to have been, certain questions on which he held opinions may have been discussed, we again look to the models which have come down to us intact. Let us take Herodotus and Strabo as examples. The debt of Herodotus to Hecataeus is acknowledged. We may well suppose that it was the Tour of the Earth to which the fifth century historian was chiefly indebted, though he unquestionably used also the Genealogies. Now Hecataeus clearly gave no cosmology: so far as he interested himself in matters pertaining to meteorology and kindred fields of science, he brought forth his opinions in connection with the description of particular lands, especially of Egypt. After Anaximander the 'school' of Miletus seems to have had a fate similar to that of Aristotle: where the master, in the true encyclopedic fashion, sought to cover the whole field of science, his successors divided the field. There is no evidence that Anaximenes gave any thought to geography and history, and the same is true of those who are brought by tradition in relation to 'the philosophy of Anaximenes'; while Hecataeus, as has already been remarked, neglected cosmology, and devoted himself to history and geography. Herodotus, though with inadequate comprehension of the spirit and the achievements of the Ionians, was inspired by the example of Hecataeus and Dionysius, thus falling roughly in line with their branch of the tradition originating at Miletus.

Another branch of the tradition can be traced through Eratosthenes to Strabo: it is largely indebted, however, to the collateral line which is concerned primarily with history. Geography, as we have previously remarked, had come to occupy a place apart as an independent science. Whether Democritus was at least in part responsible for this innovation we cannot say; certainly Ephorus, by separating his geographical books distinctly from the historical, contributed not a little to this result. Eudoxus certainly conceived his geography as related to his astronomy. In Eratosthenes, as in Strabo, the discussion of the earth, as the subject of geography, is made to follow that of the cosmos. Anaximander had done the same, describing the circles of the celestial bodies with the earth at their centre. Here, then, we have those parts of his treatise to which could be given the titles *Sphere* or *On the Fixed Stars*. This, we may be sure, formed the beginning of his treatise. It is a matter of no small interest, however, that we find not only in Strabo but in Diodorus also a second cosmology introduced in their accounts of Egypt.

This fact can hardly be due to anything else but the force of literary tradition. There were those who had discussed the earth both in relation to the heavens and to the geological history of our planet in connection with Egypt, with which they must have made a beginning. One may plainly see the results of this practice in Herodotus, traces of it being visible throughout the entire geographical tradition. Hecataeus, as we have already remarked, set forth his own geological opinions chiefly in his account of Egypt; but the observations upon which his opinions were based, such as the presence of fossils in the stones of the pyramids, were not new in his day, as we chance to know that Xenophanes had previously made similar observations in other places. There can hardly be a doubt regarding the source of the latter's interest in such evidence, since his relation to the earlier Milesians is unquestionable. How significant these facts are may be seen when one considers another point. Later geographers regularly began their description of the *orbis terrarum* with the Pillars of Hercules, passing clock-wise round the Mediterranean. Now, if it be true, as has been plausibly maintained, that

Hecataeus of Miletus began his *Tour of the Earth* with the Pillars of Hercules, proceeding clock-wise about the *orbis terrarum*, the whole of Europe and Asia (proper) had been traversed before he reached Egypt. That under these circumstances he should have paused at this point to give a detailed account of the earth and its formation would seem to call for an explanation, the need of which is further emphasized by the fact, already mentioned, that even the late historians like Diodorus, and geographers, like Strabo, at this point insert a cosmology.

This phenomenon, hardly to be explained except by the conservatism of literary tradition, raises the question whether Hecataeus, like his successors, was not herein betraying the influence of his predecessors. But of predecessors of Hecataeus in this field we know Anaximander only, unless we should assume that Thales also was in some sense a geographer. For Thales, however, there is no direct evidence whatever. Nevertheless there is a point that deserves consideration in this connection. Almost the sole doctrine attributed to Thales is that all things come from water: which Aristotle and Theophrastus interpret with reference to the origin of life. Now Anaximander likewise expressed opinions regarding the origin of life, animal and human; and he also held that it originated in water, as with the gradual progress of evaporation of the once all-engulfing sea dry land emerged. But not only Herodotus, but the entire Greek tradition, where reference is not had to such myths as that of the creation of man by Prometheus, represent the 'scientific' theory of the origin of life as brought into relation with the swamps of the Nile Delta. There fishes were spontaneously generated; there existed the ideal conditions for the beginnings of life; there was the cradle of the human race and the fountain head of civilization. There, we may with reason assume, Anaximander (and perhaps Thales) laid the scene of the early life history of the earth. But if this were true, the work in which Anaximander set forth his theory of the origin of life would bear a definite relation to the later known works of the historico-geographical tradition. The derivation of the alphabet from Egypt through Danaus proves that Anaximander shared the view which sought in that land of many wonders the beginnings of civilization.

It is quite possible also that many of the explanations of meteorological and other phenomena which Theophrastus and his successors found in Anaximander's book were scattered through it and were offered in connection with various lands or places. Not only the second book of Aristotle's *Meteorologica*, but the various historical and geographical treatises also which survive from antiquity in whole or in part, afford sufficient examples to justify such a theory. It is not necessary to assert that this was true of Anaximander's book; it suffices for our purposes that it may be true. For a consideration of the character of the doxographic record of his opinions will readily show that it affords no presumption whatever regarding the form of his treatise. Through the genius of Professor Diels we are enabled to gather from the welter of late extracts a view of the *Opinions of the Physical Philosophers* of Theophrastus, the disciple and successor of Aristotle, from which ultimately derive most of the statements regarding the doctrines of the early thinkers. That work, as we see, was a systematic account of Greek philosophy arranged under heads following closely the order which Aristotle himself had used in his treatises. Thus the arrangement is that of the Peripatetic historian and bears no necessary relation to the order in which the early 'philosophers' set forth their opinions. What we know, moreover, of the method of Theophrastus, who was wholly under the influence of his master, suggests caution in respect to the 'philosophical,' that is to say especially the metaphysical or ontological, doctrines which he reports; for both Aristotle and Theophrastus were prone to discover in statements intended as descriptions of physical processes a deeper meaning which would bear a metaphysical interpretation.

Now it happens that Theophrastus, following Aristotle, allowed no place in his scheme for matters pertaining directly to history and geography. We cannot, therefore, be surprised that the doxographic tradition contains no hint of Anaximander's services in these directions: they were not germane to the 'physical philosopher' with whom alone Theophrastus was concerned. Strictly speaking, to be sure, this statement is at best a half-truth. Theophrastus, like Aristotle, speaks not of physical philosophers, but of *physikoi* or *physiologoi*, meaning thereby those who discoursed about *physis*. Having elsewhere treated of the latter term I have no intention of taking it up afresh. Suffice it for the present to say that men of the most diverse interests in detail had in the fifth century much to say about *physis* who never found their way into the group recognized as *physikoi* or *physiologoi* by the doxographic tradition. When one considers the members of the group in detail, and the questions which were noted as falling within the purview of the historian of their opinions, one sees that the classification, though intelligible from the point of view of Aristotle's conception of philosophy, is altogether arbitrary as regards the fields of knowledge cultivated by men of science in that day.

Opinions relating, or supposed to relate, to 'material' and 'efficient' causes, to cosmology, to the more important meteorological and terrestrial phenomena, to the gods, to the soul and its faculties, and to the more striking physiological functions, were included; such as concerned the biological sciences, zoology and botany, and the fields of history and geography, were ignored. It is the same process of selection which, at a later stage, determined the choice of those among the writings of Aristotle that should have the honor of a commentary; only in the latter instance the interest of the schools in logic led to the inclusion of the Organon.

The same inconsistency is found in regard to the title *On Nature*. Probably the earliest extant reference to this catch-word as a title occurs in the Hippocratic treatise *On the Old School of Medicine*. Earlier references in the fifth century are to be found in Euripides and elsewhere, but hardly so pointedly or so clearly to titles of treatises. Finally, as in Galen, we find it the generally accepted name. This is no rational classification: it is an omnibus label which gives no guaranty of the contents of any particular work to which it may be applied.

III

We have spoken of the doxographic tradition and noted briefly its scope. Deriving immediately from Theophrastus, it revealed the conception he had of them and of the interests which properly characterized them. He does not expressly call them philosophers, but as such of course he regards them. We have already pointed out how closely the scheme followed the order of topics in the systematic works of Aristotle and have remarked that in substance also, that is to say in his interpretation of the data regarding the early thinkers, Theophrastus (except possibly in a few instances) adhered to the views of his master. This was the more natural because Aristotle himself was wont to report briefly the opinions of his predecessors as furnishing the proper basis for a discussion of the several questions with which he had to deal.

It is almost as if Aristotle had had at hand for the purposes of his lectures a brief digest of the earlier history of philosophy. What Theophrastus did was in effect to expand these pronouncements of his teacher, using where he could the original texts for fuller statements, and criticizing the views reported at greater length. Thus in a real sense the doxographic tradition is essentially Aristotelian. Now with the advance in the critical study of early Greek thought it has become increasingly apparent that Aristotle, with all his advantages and excellences, was not a safe guide for the interpretation of texts.

Great as a systematizer and keen as a critic, he lacked the true historical sense; hence the manifest need of going, so to speak, behind the returns, of checking the Aristotelian account wherever possible by other data. Besides the authentic fragments of the early thinkers, to which the historian will have recourse, other sources of information exist, which it is not now necessary to discuss in detail; but it is of some importance to trace this tradition, which we may rightly call Aristotelian, somewhat farther back.

Behind Aristotle stands Plato, to whom we owe relatively few but precious statements regarding the opinions of his predecessors. Possessing perhaps the keenest intellect known to history, he was endowed likewise with that rarest of all gifts, the faculty of entering sympathetically into the point of view of men from whom he radically differed.

This is what made him the greatest master of the philosophical dialogue, and might have made him the greatest dramatic genius, had he not fallen under the spell of Socrates. Not a slave to system, but following the argument wherever it might lead, two interests — perhaps, rather instincts — alone seemed to govern his thinking and writing, the love of truth and an innate sense of form. From such a man we may expect, as indeed we receive, reports which, when scrutinized with reference to his intention, are transparently true.

Before Plato we do not find in the works of philosophers references to one another which are of such a character as to yield appreciable assistance to the student of their opinions. There is, however, even here something that may be called a tradition: it concerns the very fundamental matter of the conception of the philosopher and of philosophy. We cannot here pause to review the evidence as to the employment of such terms as 'sage,' 'sophist' and 'philosopher'; but so much may be said to be beyond question: whether the old Milesians did or did not use the terms philosopher and philosophy, a change at least came in their employment by Heraclitus and the Pythagoreans. However much indebted both Heraclitus and Pythagoras were to the Milesians, they cannot have failed to perceive that they were making a distinct departure in their points of view and in the matters which chiefly claimed their attention. Of Pythagoras, indeed, we are able to judge solely by later Pythagoreans; as for Heraclitus, he has in his own words so clearly expressed himself as to leave no room for doubt. For him the philosopher, though he must of course know many things, does not attain wisdom by much learning; the wisdom of the philosopher lies in the understanding of the unifying and governing principle. Pythagoras might have said that it lay in learning the mathematical formula for the law.

This new interest is metaphysical, or at all events akin to metaphysics. It does not, so far as I can discover, appear anywhere in the Milesians; but through Socrates, who was equally influenced by Heracliteans and Pythagoreans, this conception of what marks the philosopher and philosophy descended to Plato and to Aristotle, and so shaped the doxographic tradition.

The interests of the Milesians — chronology, descriptive geography, ethnography, ethnic and biological history — could not be included in the scope of philosophy proper. However scientific their methods and aims, they were then and still remain essentially empirical; however much they may in subordinate matters employ mathematics, principles, such as Heraclitus and the Pythagoreans sought, are not to be discovered there. Only in cosmology might one perhaps think to find an exception; but even here we pass from would-be history among the Milesians to mathematical and descriptive astronomy in the Pythogoreans.

From this survey of the doxographic tradition, it becomes apparent that the early Milesians, so far as they appear in it, are out of their element, and in any case could not hope to be represented sympathetically, especially from Aristotle onwards. If they appear at all, it must be in a capacity at least doubtful. Aristotle regarded Thales, Anaximander and Anaximenes as proposing doctrines concerned with ontological principles and with processes of change having metaphysical implications. We have no intention of debating here the question whether in any or all of these matters he was right or wrong: for our purposes it is sufficient to say that in no instance is he certainly right, since the opinions in question are quite susceptible of interpretation with reference to purely physical facts or processes.

The influences which we have so cursorily reviewed gave rise to a body of statements of supposed fact and critical judgments, constituting and perpetuating a literary tradition. Properly it is only from Theophrastus onwards that one may call it doxographic; but for our present purposes we may apply this name to the earlier stages also, in which were framed the conceptions which dominate it to the end. Thanks to the intensive study of Greek philosophy and especially to the illuminating analysis of Professor Diels this particular literary tradition can be traced in the main with great precision. The phenomenon is, however, not at all isolated; for every literary kind has its traditions more or less clearly defined. This becomes at once apparent to the student who surveys any series of books on a given subject: the innovations appear trivial in comparison with the mass of purely traditionary matter and opinion. Mathematics, for obvious, reasons, presents perhaps the best examples; as Sir Thomas Heath has recently said, "elementary geometry is Euclid, however much editors of text-books may try to obscure the fact." These special literary traditions deserve far more attention and critical study than scholars have accorded them.

Now, as we have seen, a considerable field of early scientific thought and interest lies partly or wholly without the scope of the doxographic tradition. Considering the development which can be discerned in Greece from the fifth century onwards we are justified in speaking of it as that of history and geography together, because they were not really separate. To our view this fact is apt to be obscured by the solitary eminence of Thucydides, who breaks the line of continuity and with those whom he immediately inspired forms a group apart. Dealing with a circumscribed area well known to his readers he had no need to digress into geographical descriptions or considerable ethnographic details. But if we disregard Thucydides and his kind, the continuity of the historico-geographical tradition in Greece is palpable.

So evident is the wholesale appropriation of matter from predecessors by successors that an eminent student of ancient history mournfully denounces the procedure as plagiarism. Without concerning ourselves with moral judgments we may content ourselves with signalizing the solid basis of what we call the tradition. Unfortunately there exists for this literary kind no such exhaustive treatise as we possess for the doxographers; but the complexity and the generally fragmentary state of the materials amply explain its absence. Of the historico-geographical tradition we do, however, know enough to be able in most cases to tell whether a given writer belongs to it or not.

Now a survey of our sources of information regarding the earlier Greek thinkers, with whom we are at present chiefly concerned, is worth making for many reasons. We may disregard as sufficiently appraised those which fall to the doxographic tradition; but for Thales and Anaximander we must clearly take account of others. Thus Herodotus refers to the prediction of an eclipse of the sun by Thales, to the report current among the Greeks that he diverted the waters of the Halys and so enabled Croesus to cross, and to his advice to the Ionians to form a federal state in order to maintain their independence; he mentions, besides, the explanation of the Nile floods as due to the Etesian winds, which later writers of the historico-geographical tradition attribute to Thales. We know, then, not to go farther into details nor to pass final judgment in disputable matters, that Thales figured as a man of science in the historico-geographical tradition even before Herodotus. Duly considered this certain fact is of prime importance. It is unfortunate on all accounts that Herodotus is the only extant representative of this branch of literature from the sixth and fifth centuries, — in fact down to the time of Diodorus; all the really representative authors in this kind being known solely through detached quotations or fragmentary reports at second or third hand. For Herodotus, though an accomplished writer and an indispensable source for the Persian Wars, comprehended little of Ionian science, and was never deemed worthy of being accounted a geographer until Strabo, almost as superficial as himself, did him the honor of so regarding him. Furthermore, whether from literary affectation or for other reasons, Herodotus often suppresses names and facts which were obviously known to him. Thus it happens that he is for our purposes as little serviceable as one who dealt with the same subject-matter in the fifth century could possibly be. What can be learned from his book has usually to be wrung from him as from an unwilling witness. Anaximander, who certainly played an important role, he does not even mention: Hecataeus, to whom he owed the whole of his second book, he names a few times only, and then (in the part borrowed from him) in rather clumsy ridicule. Anaximenes and his 'school' are, as we said above, not mentioned at all except in the doxographical tradition, which clearly points to the conclusion that he did not share the historical and geographical interests of the other Milesians.

If now we turn to Anaximander we find a considerable number of sources regarding him which have no real or original connection with the doxographers. Thus, when Aelian reports that Anaximander led in the colonization of Apollonia in Thrace from Miletus, it is obvious that he derived this datum from some work pertaining to history, whether general in character or dealing with biographies of philosophers. There is no reason to connect this source with Theophrastus or any of his kind. To a similar treatise we must look for the source of the statement, already mentioned, and reported by Favorinus, that he set up a dial at Sparta. From the history of astronomy prepared by Eudemus, who like Theophrastus was a disciple of Aristotle, derive in all probability the data given by Pliny as to Anaximander's discovery of the obliquity of the ecliptic and the date he assigned for the heliacal setting of the Pleiades. Certainly Simplicius cites Eudemus as authority for the statement that Anaximander was the first to set forth an opinion regarding the sizes and intervals of the planets. Eudemus of course regarded Anaximander solely from the point of view of the mathematician and astronomer.

But we know that such matters engaged the attention of historians before Eudemus. Herodotus speaks not only of Egyptian mathematic, but also of Thales' prediction of an eclipse; and Hippias of Elis about the same time interested himself in the earlier history of mathematics. To what source Plutarch owed his reference to Anaximander's theory of the origin of man from fishes it is not possible to say. He as well as Censorinus may have derived their information from the doxographers; but there is reason to believe that there was an even earlier tradition on this question among the historians who treated of Egypt.

The data regarding Anaximander's map we have already traced back to Eratosthenes and his geographical treatise. From him derive the statements of Agathemerus and Strabo as well as the other extant references. But one naturally asks whether Eratosthenes had access to a map unquestionably belonging to Anaximander. This possibility cannot be denied; but in view of the evidence that even in Herodotus' day there existed numerous Ionian maps, and of the great probability that charts were both multiplied and modified almost at will, it cannot be regarded as very likely. But, under such circumstances, one must ask, Where did Eratosthenes find the information which justified his statements regarding the charts of Anaximander and Hecataeus? The reasonable answer is surely that they were referred to by historical and geographical writers now lost to us but accessible to him. This is made all but certain by the confident tone in which the charts of Anaximander, Hecataeus and Damastes are mentioned. Statements such as we find in Agathemerus, who depends on Eratosthenes, presuppose a critical discussion of maps and accompanying texts with clear distinctions drawn between the several contributions and indebtedness of geographers in chronological order; and these geographers cannot, as in Herodotus, have been left unnamed or thrown together under the collective title of 'Ionians.' Thus we have every reason for postulating even before Eratosthenes a literature dealing with the progress of geography, even if, as is perhaps most likely, it did not take the form of disinterested learned comparison, but consisted of the works of successive geographers who took cognizance of the opinions and charts of their predecessors. Just such criticism is in fact abundant in Strabo, drawn in good part (with express citations) from his predecessors.

In other words, there must have existed before Eratosthenes a geographical tradition in all essentials like that which we know from Strabo existed after his time. It is to this tradition, then, that we owe the record of Anaximander's map. As we have seen, Eratosthenes did not know enough of Anaximander's book to be sure that it was genuine. His own treatise marked the beginning of a new epoch; for it was the first in which a serious, if somewhat too confident, effort was made to describe and chart the inhabited earth on the basis of the newly established shape and dimensions of the earth. We know from Strabo that Hipparchus at many points recurred to the old maps for things which Eratosthenes had discarded. This is hardly explicable except on the hypothesis that the procedure of Eratosthenes was characterized by a radical departure from tradition, which his keen critic could not justify. Such being the case, we can readily believe that Eratosthenes was not an altogether sympathetic student of the earlier geographers.

In the first flush of enthusiasm over the new geography the old was naturally neglected. It was only after a generation or two had passed that the texts of Anaximander and Hecataeus were again brought forth from the archives and studied with intelligent interest by Demetrius of Scepsis and Apollodorus, while Hipparchus, like Eratosthenes but apparently in greater measure, displayed a keen interest in the ancient charts. Thus the geographical tradition was assured of a continuity, which for a moment seemed threatened. This continuous tradition makes it possible even now in part to prove, in part to divine, the character of Anaximander's book.

However much prose literature may or may not have existed in Ionia before the days of Anaximander, his book is for us at once the earliest known prose treatise and the earliest known literary document, whether in verse or prose, of the scientific interests of Ionia. As such it naturally possesses a peculiar fascination for us, and we could wish to know far more about it than the grudging record vouchsafes. It is perhaps possible even yet by a close scrutiny of the whole early tradition to gather certain further data in detail regarding his opinions and the structure of his chart; but of the economy and spirit of Anaximander's book we seem with our present resources to be able to learn no more than we have above set forth. A part even of this is of course not susceptible of strict proof; but we have endeavored to conduct our inquiry with due regard to the evidence and the principles which must be observed in historical studies. Though Anaximander was apparently a name not uncommon in Miletus, we do not meet it elsewhere; and the literary tradition seems to have recorded two persons only of that name as authors of books. We have therefore to choose between them when it is a question of assigning a datum attributed simply to 'Anaximander'; and the result of our inquiry is what one might reasonably have expected. The name 'Anaximander' must have suggested to the Greek the great Milesian of the sixth century as naturally as the name 'Jefferson' or 'Washington' suggests to an American the well-known personages of our own history. That another writer of the same name and born in the same city was known is indeed clear from the record; but the sole reference to him outside the entries of a biographical and bibliographical nature is of a sort to lead naturally to his identification, even though he is not expressly called 'Anaximander the Younger.'

Anaximander's book must be seen in its true perspective, that is to say, in relation to the tradition of which it was a part. Whether it stood at the head of the series or itself had predecessors, we do not certainly know; but of its successors we may discover enough to discern in part the lines of connection. From Anaximander onward we can trace several streams of tradition growing in volume and progressively differentiating themselves until they give rise to quite distinct and special sciences. One takes on the form of cosmogony or cosmology and a study of the microcosm, the latter developing into scientific medicine; another begins as history with a geographical appendix, which in time constitutes a science apart. Mathematics and cosmography, fructified by a new interest born partly of Orphic and other religious speculations, give rise to new points of view and to questions which in their development eventuate in metaphysics or ontology, and determine the history of philosophy, as they shape the doxographic tradition. The latter, though dominated by alien interests, depends perforce on the historico-geographic tradition for the necessary data regarding the beginnings of Ionian science, since Aristotle clearly did not possess a copy of a book by Thales, if such a book ever existed. Regarding Anaximander's book Aristotle seems to have known little or nothing at first hand: his opinions regarding the Infinite and the reason why the earth keeps its central position he clearly did not understand, and in the latter case he certainly attributed to the Milesian an explanation utterly alien to his thought.

That Theophrastus perpetuated the blunder is certain and significant. Meanwhile the central interest of the early Milesians was ruled out as not germane to philosophy, and the best record of their thought derives from other branches of the tradition. In conclusion let us attempt to frame a picture of this ancient book. In compass it cannot have been large, if the statement of Diogenes Laertius, which in this particular is probably drawn from either Apollodorus or Posidonius, is true; for he reports that Anaximander gave "a summary exposition of his opinions." In spirit and intention it was historical, purporting to sketch the life-history of the cosmos from the moment of its emergence from infinitude to the author's own time, and looking forward to the death and dissolution not only of the earth and its inhabitants but also of this and all particular worlds. This being so the exposition naturally followed the order of chronological sequence, recounting first the origin of the world and of the earth, proceeding with the origin of life and the evolution of species capable of living on land as the once all engulfing sea gradually allowed dry land to appear, the origin of human life, probably in Egypt, and the spread of the race and its civilization. Heroic genealogies bridged the interval between the beginnings and the disposition of the peoples and their habitats in Anaximander's time, which were, however briefly, sketched in his book as well as figured on his chart.

In this portion of his treatise, presumably, occurred some at least of the explanations which he gave of certain outstanding natural phenomena, such as earthquakes, and such strictly historical data as the old Milesian saw fit to give. They would most naturally concern the royal houses, not improbably linked up with Heracles, of the great powers of Asia, the Lydians and the Medes.

Such a book, however significant to one whose antiquarian or broadly historical interest enabled him to detect in it the germs of future great developments, was of course destined to be speedily antiquated and thus ignored by the vulgar. The greatest wonder is that it did not disappear without a trace, as Theophrastus believed, probably with good reason, that many still earlier books had done; for until institutional libraries began to be formed in the days of Plato and Aristotle books, except such great favorites as the major poets, must have had an extremely precarious existence. The schools of philosophy took an interest in Anaximander's book in virtue of a part of its contents and because it was the earliest of its kind that came to their knowledge; geographers sought out, if not his authentic map, at least such information regarding it as might be gleaned from later writers in the same field; finally, at the very height of Alexandrian criticism, Apollodorus, qualified as no other was by training and interest to assess its worth, had the good fortune to retrieve it from obscurity, and the grace to use it in a way to reveal its true scope and character. The doxographic tradition, no doubt, called it a treatise *On Nature*, which sufficiently characterized it in part; someone possessed of a truer perspective, and regarding the whole book in the light of its conclusion called it a *Tour of the Earth*, unless — as is indeed possible — the distinctly geographical portion of the book had become detached from the beginning and so led for a time a life divorced, in which case the latter title may have been originally given to the separate part. In any case, the fortunes of Anaximander's book would seem to have been strikingly similar to the fortunes experienced by the work of his successor, Hecataeus.

The School of Miletus

By John Marshall

Thales

For several centuries prior to the great Persian invasions of Greece, perhaps the very greatest and wealthiest city of the Greek world was Miletus. Situate about the centre of the Ionian coasts of Asia Minor, with four magnificent harbours and a strongly defensible position, it gathered to itself much of the great overland trade, which has flowed for thousands of years eastward and westward between India and the Mediterranean; while by its great fleets it created a new world of its own along the Black Sea coast. Its colonies there were so numerous that Miletus was named 'Mother of Eighty Cities.' From Abydus on the Bosphorus, past Sinope, and so onward to the Crimea and the Don, and thence round to Thrace, a busy community of colonies, mining, manufacturing, ship-building, corn-raising, owned Miletus for their mother-city. Its marts must therefore have been crowded with merchants of every country from India to Spain, from Arabia to Russia; the riches and the wonders of every clime must have become familiar to its inhabitants. And fitly enough, therefore, in this city was born the first notable Greek geographer, the first constructor of a map, the first observer of natural and other curiosities, the first recorder of varieties of custom among various communities, the first speculator on the causes of strange phenomena,—Hecataeus. His work is in great part lost, but we know a good deal about it from the frequent references to him and it in the work of his rival and follower, Herodotus.

The city naturally held a leading place politically as well as commercially. Empire in our sense was alien to the instincts of the Greek race; but Miletus was for centuries recognised as the foremost member of a great commercial and political league, the political character of the league becoming more defined, as first the Lydian and then the Persian monarchy became an aggressive neighbour on its borders.

It was in this active, prosperous, enterprising state, and at the period of its highest activity, that Thales, statesman, practical engineer, mathematician, philosopher, flourished. Without attempting to fix his date too closely, we may take it that he was a leading man in Miletus for the greater part of the first half of the sixth century before Christ. We hear of an eclipse predicted by him, of the course of a river usefully changed, of shrewd and profitable handling of the market, of wise advice in the general councils of the league. He seems to have been at once a student of mathematics and an observer of nature, and withal something having analogy with both, an inquirer or speculator into the origin of things. To us nowadays this suggests a student of geology, or physiography, or some such branch of physical science; to Thales it probably rather suggested a theoretical inquiry into the simplest thinkable aspect of things as existing. "Under what form known to us," he would seem to have asked, "may we assume an identity in all known things, so as best to cover or render explicable the things as we know them?" The 'beginning' of things (for it was thus he described this assumed identity) was not conceived by him as something which was long ages before, and which had ceased to be; rather it meant the reality of things now. Thales then was the putter of a question, which had not been asked expressly before, but which has never ceased to be asked since. He was also the formulator of a new meaning for a word; the word 'beginning' (Greek *arche*) got the meaning of 'underlying reality' and so of 'ending' as well. In short, he so dealt with a word, on the surface of it implying time, as to eliminate the idea of time, and suggest a method of looking at the world, more profound and far-reaching than had been before imagined.

It is interesting to find that the man who was thus the first philosopher, the first observer who took a metaphysical, non-temporal, analytical view of the world, and so became the predecessor of all those votaries of 'other-world' ways of thinking,—whether as academic idealist, or 'budge doctor of the Stoic fur,' or Christian ascetic or what not, whose ways are such a puzzle to the 'hard-headed practical man,'—was himself one of the shrewdest men of his day, so shrewd that by common consent he was placed foremost in antiquity among the Seven Sages, or seven shrewd men, whose practical wisdom became a world's tradition, enshrined in anecdote and crystallised in proverb.

The chief record that we possess of the philosophic teaching of Thales is contained in an interesting notice of earlier philosophies by Aristotle, the main part of which as regards Thales runs as follows:

"The early philosophers as a rule formulated the originative principle of all things under some material expression. By the originative principle or element of things they meant that of which all existing things are composed, that which determines their coming into being, and into which they pass on ceasing to be. Where these philosophers differed from each other was simply in the answer which they gave to the question what was the nature of this principle, the differences of view among them applying both to the number, and to the character, of the supposed element or elements.

"Thales, the pioneer of this philosophy, maintained that Water was the originative principle of all things. It was doubtless in this sense that he said that the earth rested on water. What suggested the conception to him may have been such facts of observation, as that all forms of substance which promote life are moist, that heat itself seems to be conditioned by moisture, that the life-producing seed in all creatures is moist, and so on."

Other characteristics of water, it is elsewhere suggested, may have been in Thales' mind, such as its readiness to take various shapes, its convertibility from water into vapour or ice, its ready mixture with other substances, and so forth. What we have chiefly to note is, that the more unscientific this theory about the universe may strike us as being, the more completely out of accord with facts now familiar to everybody, the more striking is it as marking a new mood of mind, in which unity, though only very partially suggested or discoverable by the senses, is preferred to that infinite and indefinite variety and difference which the senses give us at every moment.

There is here the germ of a new aspiration, of a determination not to rest in the merely momentary and different, but at least to try, even against the apparent evidence of the senses, for something more permanently intelligible. As a first suggestion of what this permanent underlying reality may be, Water might very well pass. It is probable that even to Thales himself it was only a symbol, like the figure in a mathematical proposition, representing by the first passable physical phenomenon which came to hand, that ideal reality underlying all change, which is at once the beginning, the middle, and the end of all. That he did not mean Water, in the ordinary prosaic sense, to be identical with this, is suggested by some other sayings of his.

"Thales," says Aristotle elsewhere, "thought the whole universe was full of gods."

"All things," he is recorded as saying, "have a soul in them, in virtue of which they move other things, and are themselves moved, even as the magnet, by virtue of its life or soul, moves the iron." Without pushing these fragmentary utterances too far, we may well conclude that whether Thales spoke of the soul of the universe and its divine indwelling powers, or gods, or of water as the origin of things, he was only vaguely symbolising in different ways an idea as yet formless and void, like the primeval chaos, but nevertheless, like it, containing within it a promise and a potency of greater life hereafter.

Anaximander

Our information with respect to thinkers so remote as these men is too scanty and too fragmentary, to enable us to say in what manner or degree they influenced each other. We cannot say for certain that any one of them was pupil or antagonist of another. They appear each of them, one might say for a moment only, from amidst the darkness of antiquity; a few sayings of theirs we catch vaguely across the void, and then they disappear. There is not, consequently, any very distinct progression or continuity observable among them, and so far therefore one has to confess that the title 'School of Miletus' is a misnomer. We have already quoted the words of Aristotle in which he classes the Ionic philosophers together, as all of them giving a material aspect of some kind to the originative principle of the universe. But while this is a characteristic observable in some of them, it is not so obviously discoverable in the second of their number, Anaximander.

This philosopher is said to have been younger by one generation than Thales, but to have been intimate with him. He, like Thales, was a native of Miletus, and while we do not hear of him as a person, like Thales, of political eminence and activity, he was certainly the equal, if not the superior, of Thales in mathematical and scientific ability. He is said to have either invented or at least made known to Greece the construction of the sun-dial. He was associated with Hecataeus in the construction of the earliest geographical charts or maps; he devoted himself with some success to the science of astronomy. His familiarity with the abstractions of mathematics perhaps accounts for the more abstract form, in which he expressed his idea of the principle of all things.

To Anaximander this principle was, as he expressed it, the infinite; not water nor any other of the so-called elements, but a different thing from any of them, something hardly namable, out of whose formlessness the heavens and all the worlds in them came to be. And by necessity into that same infinite or indefinite existence, out of which they originally emerged, did every created thing return. Thus, as he poetically expressed it, "Time brought its revenges, and for the wrong-doing of existence all things paid the penalty of death."

The momentary resting-place of Thales on the confines of the familiar world of things, in his formulation of Water as the principle of existence, is thus immediately removed. We get, as it were, to the earliest conception of things as we find it in Genesis; before the heavens were, or earth, or the waters under the earth, or light, or sun, or moon, or grass, or the beast of the field, when the "earth was without form, and void, and darkness was upon the face of the deep." Only, be it observed, that while in the primitive Biblical idea this formless void precedes in time an ordered universe, in Anaximander's conception this formless infinitude is always here, is in fact the only reality which ever is here, something without beginning or ending, underlying all, enwrapping all, governing all.

To modern criticism this may seem to be little better than verbiage, having, perhaps, some possibilities of poetic treatment, but certainly very unsatisfactory if regarded as science. But to this we have to reply that one is not called upon to regard it as science. Behind science, as much to-day when our knowledge of the details of phenomena is so enormously increased, as in the times when science had hardly begun, there lies a world of mystery which we cannot pierce, and yet which we are compelled to assume. No scientific treatise can begin without assuming Matter and Force as data, and however much we may have learned about the relations of forces and the affinities of things, Matter and Force as such remain very much the same dim infinities, that the originative 'Infinite' was to Anaximander.

It is to be noted, however, that while modern science assumes necessarily two correlative data or originative principles,—Force, namely, as well as Matter,—Anaximander seems to have been content with the formulation of but one; and perhaps it is just here that a kinship still remains between him and Thales and other philosophers of the school. He, no more than they, seems to have definitely raised the question, How are we to account for, or formulate, the principle of difference or change? What is it that causes things to come into being out of, or recalls them back from being into, the infinite void? It is to be confessed, however, that our accounts on this point are somewhat conflicting. One authority actually says that he formulated motion as eternal also. So far as he attempted to grasp the idea of difference in relation to that of unity, he seems to have regarded the principle of change or difference as inhering in the infinite itself. Aristotle in this connection contrasts his doctrine with that of Anaxagoras, who formulated two principles of existence—Matter and Mind. Anaximander, he points out, found all he wanted in the one.

As a mathematician Anaximander must have been familiar in various aspects with the functions of the Infinite or Indefinable in the organisation of thought. To the student of Euclid, for example, the impossibility of adequately defining any of the fundamental elements of the science of geometry—the point, the line, the surface—is a familiar fact. In so far as a science of geometry is possible at all, the exactness, which is its essential characteristic, is only attainable by starting from data which are in themselves impossible, as of a point which has no magnitude, of a line which has no breadth, of a surface which has no thickness. So in the science of abstract number the fundamental assumptions, as that 1=1, x=x, etc., are contradicted by every fact of experience, for in the world as we know it, absolute equality is simply impossible to discover; and yet these fundamental conceptions are in their development most powerful instruments for the extension of man's command over his own experiences. Their completeness of abstraction from the accidents of experience, from the differences, qualifications, variations which contribute so largely to the personal interests of life, this it is which makes the abstract sciences demonstrative, exact, and universally applicable. In so far, therefore, as we are permitted to grasp the conception of a perfectly abstract existence prior to, and underlying, and enclosing, all separate existences, so far also do we get to a conception which is demonstrative, exact, and universally applicable throughout the whole world of knowable objects.

Such a conception, however, by its absolute emptiness of content, does not afford any means in itself of progression; somehow and somewhere a principle of movement, of development, of concrete reality, must be found or assumed, to link this ultimate abstraction of existence to the multifarious phenomena of existence as known. And it was, perhaps, because Anaximander failed to work out this aspect of the question, that in the subsequent leaders of the school movement, rather than mere existence, was the principle chiefly insisted upon.

Before passing, however, to these successors of Anaximander, some opinions of his which we have not perhaps the means of satisfactorily correlating with his general conception, but which are not without their individual interest, may here be noted. The word husk or bark (Greek *phloios*) seems to have been a favourite one with him, as implying and depicting a conception of interior and necessary development in things. Thus he seems to have postulated an inherent tendency or law in the infinite, which compelled it to develop contrary characters, as hot and cold, dry and moist. In consequence of this fundamental tendency an envelope of fire, he says, came into being, encircling another envelope of air, which latter in turn enveloped the sphere of earth, each being like the 'husk' of the other, or like the bark which encloses the tree. This concentric system he conceives as having in some way been parted up into various systems, represented by the sun, the moon, the stars, and the earth. The last he figured as hanging in space, and deriving its stability from the inherent and perfect balance or relation of its parts.

Then, again, as to the origin of man, he seems to have in like manner taught a theory of development from lower forms of life. In his view the first living creatures must have come into being in moisture (thus recalling the theory of Thales). As time went on, and these forms of life reached their fuller possibilities, they came to be transferred to the dry land, casting off their old nature like a husk or bark. More particularly he insists that man must have developed out of other and lower forms of life, because of his exceptional need, under present conditions, of care and nursing in his earlier years. Had he come into being at once as a human creature he could never have survived.

The analogies of these theories with modern speculations are obvious and interesting. But without enlarging on these, one has only to say in conclusion that, suggestive and interesting as many of these poor fragments, these disjecti membra poetae, are individually, they leave us more and more impressed with a sense of incompleteness in our knowledge of Anaximander's theory as a whole. It may be that as a consistent and perfected system the theory never was worked out; it may be that it never was properly understood.

Anaximenes

This philosopher was also a native of Miletus, and is said to have been a hearer or pupil of Anaximander. As we have said, the tendency of the later members of the school was towards emphasising the motive side of the supposed underlying principle of nature, and accordingly Anaximenes chose Air as the element which best represented or symbolised that principle. Its fluidity, readiness of movement, wide extension, and absolute neutrality of character as regards colour, taste, smell, form, etc., were obvious suggestions. The breath also, whose very name to the ancients implied an identity with the life or soul, was nothing but air; and the identification of Air with Life supplied just that principle of productiveness and movement, which was felt to be necessary in the primal element of being. The process of existence, then, he conceived as consisting in a certain concentration of this diffused life-giving element into more or less solidified forms, and the ultimate separation and expansion of these back into the formless air again. The contrary forces previously used by Anaximander—heat and cold, drought and moisture—are with Anaximenes also the agencies which institute these changes.

This is pretty nearly all that we know of Anaximenes. So far as the few known facts reveal him, we can hardly say that except as supplying a step towards the completer development of the motive idea in being, he greatly adds to the chain of progressive thought.

Heraclitus

Although not a native of Miletus, but of Ephesus, Heraclitus, both by his nationality as an Ionian and by his position in the development of philosophic conceptions, falls naturally to be classed with the philosophers of Miletus. His period may be given approximately as from about 560 to 500 B.C., though others place him a generation later. Few authentic particulars have been preserved of him. We hear of extensive travels, of his return to his native city only to refuse a share in its activities, of his retirement to a hermit's life. He seems to have formed a contrast to the preceding philosophers in his greater detachment from the ordinary interests of civic existence; and much in his teaching suggests the ascetic if not the misanthrope. He received the nickname of 'The Obscure,' from the studied mystery in which he was supposed to involve his teaching. He wrote not for the vulgar, but for the gifted few. 'Much learning makes not wise' was the motto of his work; the man of gift, of insight, that man is better than ten thousand. He was savage in his criticism of other writers, even the greatest. Homer, he said, and Archilochus too, deserved to be hooted from the platform and thrashed. Even the main purport of his writings was differently interpreted. Some named his work 'The Muses,' as though it were chiefly a poetic vision; others named it 'The sure Steersman to the Goal of Life'; others, more prosaically, 'A Treatise of Nature.'

The fundamental principle or fact of being Heraclitus formulated in the famous dictum, 'All things pass.' In the eternal flux or flow of being consisted its reality; even as in a river the water is ever changing, and the river exists as a river only in virtue of this continual change; or as in a living body, wherein while there is life there is no stability or fixedness; stability and fixedness are the attributes of the unreal image of life, not of life itself. Thus, as will be observed, from the material basis of being as conceived by Thales, with only a very vague conception of the counter-principle of movement, philosophy has wheeled round in Heraclitus to the other extreme; he finds his permanent element in the negation of permanence; being or reality consists in never 'being' but always 'becoming,' not in stability but in change.

This eternal movement he pictures elsewhere as an eternal strife of opposites, whose differences nevertheless consummate themselves in finest harmony. Thus oneness emerges out of multiplicity, multiplicity out of oneness; and the harmony of the universe is of contraries, as of the lyre and the bow. War is the father and king and lord of all things. Neither god nor man presided at the creation of anything that is; that which was, is that which is, and that which ever shall be; even an ever-living Fire, ever kindling and ever being extinguished.

Thus in Fire, as an image or symbol of the underlying reality of existence, Heraclitus advanced to the furthest limit attainable on physical lines, for the expression of its essentially motive character. That this Fire was no more than a symbol, suggested by the special characteristics of fire in nature,—its subtlety, its mobility, its power of penetrating all things and devouring all things, its powers for beneficence in the warmth of living bodies and the life-giving power of the sun,—is seen in the fact that he readily varies his expression for this principle, calling it at times the Thunderbolt, at others the eternal Reason, or Law, or Fate. To his mental view creation was a process eternally in action, the fiery element descending by the law of its being into the cruder forms of water and earth, only to be resolved again by upward process into fire; even as one sees the vapour from the sea ascending and melting into the aether. As a kindred vapour or exhalation he recognised the Soul or Breath for a manifestation of the essential element. It is formless, ever changing with every breath we take, yet it is the constructive and unifying force which keeps the body together, and conditions its life and growth. At this point Heraclitus comes into touch with Anaximenes. In the act of breathing we draw into our own being a portion of the all-pervading vital element of all being; in this universal being we thereby live and move and have our consciousness; the eternal and omnipresent wisdom becomes, through the channels of our senses, and especially through the eyes, in fragments at least our wisdom. In sleep we are not indeed cut off wholly from this wisdom; through our breathing we hold as it were to its root; but of its flower we are then deprived. On awaking again we begin once more to partake according to our full measure of the living thought; even as coals when brought near the fire are themselves made partakers of it, but when taken away again become quenched.

Hence, in so far as man is wise, it is because his spirit is kindled by union with the universal spirit; but there is a baser, or, as Heraclitus termed it, a moister element also in him, which is the element of unreason, as in a drunken man. And thus the trustworthiness or otherwise of the senses, as the channels of communication with the divine, depends on the dryness or moistness,—or, as we should express it, using, after all, only another metaphor,—on the elevation or baseness of the spirit that is within. To those whose souls are base and barbarous, the eternal movement, the living fire, is invisible; and thus what they do see is nothing but death. Immersed in the mere appearances of things and their supposed stability, they, whether sleeping or waking, behold only dead forms; their spirits are dead.

For the guidance of life there is no law but the common sense, which is the union of those fragmentary perceptions of eternal law, which individual men attain, in so far as their spirits are dry and pure. Of absolute knowledge human nature is not capable, but only the Divine. To the Eternal, therefore, alone all things are good and beautiful and just, because to Him alone do things appear in their totality. To the human partial reason some things are unjust and others just. Hence life, by reason of the limitations involved in it, he sometimes spoke of as the death of the soul, and death as the renewal of its life. And so, in the great events of man's life and in the small, as in the mighty circle of the heavens, good and evil, life and death, growth and decay, are but the systole and diastole, the outward and inward pulsation, of an eternal good, an eternal harmony. Day and night, winter and summer, war and peace, satiety and hunger—each conditions the other, all are part of God. It is sickness that makes health good and sweet, hunger that gives its pleasure to feeding, weariness that makes sleep a good.

This vision of existence in its eternal flux and interchange, seems to have inspired Heraclitus with a contemplative melancholy. In the traditions of later times he was known as the weeping philosopher. Lucian represents him as saying, "To me it is a sorrow that there is nothing fixed or secure, and that all things are thrown confusedly together, so that pleasure and pain, knowledge and ignorance, the great and the small, are the same, ever circling round and passing one into the other in the sport of time." "Time," he says elsewhere, "is like a child that plays with the dice." The highest good, therefore, for mortals is that clarity of perception in respect of oneself and all that is, whereby we shall learn to apprehend somewhat of the eternal unity and harmony, that underlies the good and evil of time, the shock and stress of circumstance and place. The highest virtue for man is a placid and a quiet constancy, whatever the changes and chances of life may bring. It is the pantheistic apathy.

The sadder note of humanity, the note of Euripides and at times of Sophocles, the note of Dante and of the Tempest of Shakespeare, of Shelley and Arnold and Carlyle,—this note we hear thus early and thus clear, in the dim and distant utterances of Heraclitus. The mystery of existence, the unreality of what seems most real, the intangibility and evanescence of all things earthly,—these thoughts obscurely echoing to us across the ages from Heraclitus, have remained, and always will remain, among the deepest and most insistent of the world's thoughts, in its sincerest moments and in its greatest thinkers.

The Eleatics:

Xenophanes, Parmenides, Zeno and Melissus

By John Marshall

Xenophanes

Xenophanes was a native of Colophon, one of the Ionian cities of Asia Minor, but having been forced at the age of twenty-five to leave his native city owing to some political revolution, he wandered to various cities of Greece, and ultimately to Zancle and Catana, Ionian colonies in Sicily, and thence to Elea or Velia, a Greek city on the coast of Italy. This city had, like Miletus, reached a high pitch of commercial prosperity, and like it also became a centre of philosophic teaching. For there Xenophanes remained and founded a school, so that he and his successors received the name of Eleatics. His date is uncertain; but he seems to have been contemporary with Anaximander and Pythagoras, and to have had some knowledge of the doctrine of both. He wrote in various poetic measures, using against the poets, and especially against Homer and Hesiod, their own weapons, to denounce their anthropomorphic theology. If oxen or lions had hands, he said, they would have fashioned gods after their likeness which would have been as authentic as Homer's. As against these poets, and the popular mythology, he insisted that God must be one, eternal, incorporeal, without beginning or ending. As Aristotle strikingly expresses it, "He looked forth over the whole heavens and said that God is one, that that which is one is God." The favourite antitheses of his time, the definite and the indefinite, movable and immovable, change-producing and by change produced—these and such as these, he maintained, were inapplicable to the eternally and essentially existent. In this there was no partition of organs or faculties, no variation or shadow of turning; the Eternal Being was like a sphere, everywhere equal; everywhere self-identical.

His proof of this was a logical one; the absolutely self-existent could not be thought in conjunction with attributes which either admitted any external influencing Him, or any external influenced by Him. The prevailing dualism he considered to be, as an ultimate theory of the universe, unthinkable and therefore false. Outside the Self-existent there could be no second self-existent, otherwise each would be conditioned by the existence of the other, and the Self-existent would be gone. Anything different from the Self-existent must be of the non-existent, i.e. must be nothing.

One can easily see in these discussions some adumbration of many theological or metaphysical difficulties of later times, as of the origin of evil, of freewill in man, of the relation of the created world to its Creator. If these problems cannot be said to be solved yet, we need not be surprised that Xenophanes did not solve them. He was content to emphasise that which seemed to him to be necessary and true, that God was God, and not either a partner with, or a function of, matter.

At the same time he recognised a world of phenomena, or, as he expressed it, a world of guesswork or opinion (Greek *doxa*). As to the origin of things within this sphere he was ready enough to borrow from the speculations of his predecessors. Earth and water are the sources from which we spring; and he imagined a time when there was neither sea nor land, but an all-pervading slough and slime; nay, many such periods of inundation and emergence had been, hence the sea-shells on the tops of mountains and the fossils in the rocks. Air and fire also as agencies of change are sometimes referred to by him; anticipations in fact are visible of the fourfold classification of the elements which was formally made by some of his successors.

Parmenides

The pupil and successor of Xenophanes was Parmenides, a native of Elea. In a celebrated dialogue of Plato bearing the name of this philosopher he is described as visiting Socrates when the latter was very young. "He was then already advanced in years, very hoary, yet noble to look upon, in years some sixty and five." Socrates was born about 479 B.C. The birth of Parmenides might therefore, if this indication be authentic, be about 520. He was of a wealthy and noble family, and able therefore to devote himself to a learned leisure. Like his master he expounded his views in verse, and fragments of his poem of considerable length and importance have been preserved. The title of the work was *Peri Phueos—Of Nature*.

The exordium of the poem is one of some grandeur. The poet describes himself as soaring aloft to the sanctuary of wisdom where it is set in highest aether, the daughters of the Sun being his guides; under whose leading having traversed the path of perpetual day and at length attained the temple of the goddess, he from her lips received instruction in the eternal verities, and had shown to him the deceptive guesses of mortals. "'Tis for thee," she says, "to hear of both,—to have disclosed to thee on the one hand the sure heart of convincing verity, on the other hand the guesses of mortals wherein is no ascertainment. Nevertheless thou shalt learn of these also, that having gone through them all thou may'st see by what unsureness of path must he go who goeth the way of opinion. From such a way of searching restrain thou thy thought, and let not the much-experimenting habit force thee along the path wherein thou must use thine eye, yet being sightless, and the ear with its clamorous buzzings, and the chattering tongue. 'Tis by Reason that thou must in lengthened trial judge what I shall say to thee."

Thus, like Xenophanes, Parmenides draws a deep division between the world of reason and the world of sensation, between probative argument and the guess-work of sense-impressions. The former is the world of Being, the world of that which truly is, self-existent, uncreated, unending, unmoved, unchanging, ever self-poised and self-sufficient, like a sphere. Knowledge is of this, and of this only, and as such, knowledge is identical with its object; for outside this known reality there is nothing. In other words, Knowledge can only be of that which is, and that which is alone can know. All things which mortals have imagined to be realities are but words; as of the birth and death of things, of things which were and have ceased to be, of here and there, of now and then.

It is obvious enough that in all this, and in much more to the same effect reiterated throughout the poem, we have no more than a statement, in various forms of negation, of the inconceivability by human reason of that passage from being as such, to that world of phenomena which is now, but was not before, and will cease to be,—from being to becoming, from eternity to time, from the infinite to the finite (or, as Parmenides preferred to call it, from the perfect to the imperfect, the definite to the indefinite). In all this Parmenides was not contradicting such observed facts as generation, or motion, or life, or death; he was talking of a world which has nothing to do with observation; he was endeavouring to grasp what was assumed or necessarily implied as a prior condition of observation, or of a world to observe.

What he and his school seem to have felt was that there was a danger in all this talk of water or air or other material symbol, or even of the indefinite or characterless as the original of all,—the danger, namely, that one should lose sight of the idea of law, of rationality, of eternal self-centred force, and so be carried away by some vision of a gradual process of evolution from mere emptiness to fulness of being. Such a position would be not dissimilar to that of many would-be metaphysicians among evolutionists, who, not content with the doctrine of evolution as a theory in science, an ordered and organising view of observed facts, will try to elevate it into a vision of what is, and alone is, behind the observed facts. They fail to see that the more blind, the more accidental, so to speak, the process of differentiation may be; the more it is shown that the struggle for existence drives the wheels of progress along the lines of least resistance by the most commonplace of mechanical necessities, in the same proportion must a law be posited behind all this process, a reason in nature which gathers up the beginning and the ending. The protoplasmic cell which the imagination of evolutionists places at the beginning of time as the starting-point of this mighty process is not merely this or that, has not merely this or that quality or possibility, it is; and in the power of that little word is enclosed a whole world of thought, which is there at the first, remains there all through the evolutions of the protoplasm, will be there when these are done, is in fact independent of time and space, has nothing to do with such distinctions, expresses rather their ultimate unreality. So far then as Parmenides and his school kept a firm grip on this other-world aspect of nature as implied even in the simple word is, or be, so far they did good service in the process of the world's thought. On the other hand, he and they were naturally enough disinclined, as we all are disinclined, to remain in the merely or mainly negative or defensive. He would not lose his grip of heaven and eternity, but he would fain know the secrets of earth and time as well. And hence was fashioned the second part of his poem, in which he expounds his theory of the world of opinion, or guess-work, or observation.

In this world he found two originative principles at work, one pertaining to light and heat, the other to darkness and cold. From the union of these two principles all observable things in creation come, and over this union a God-given power presides, whose name is Love. Of these two principles, the bright one being analogous to Fire, the dark one to Earth, he considered the former to be the male or formative element, the latter the female or passive element; the former therefore had analogies to Being as such, the latter to Non-being. The heavenly existences, the sun, the moon, the stars, are of pure Fire, have therefore an eternal and unchangeable being; they are on the extremest verge of the universe, and corresponding to them at the centre is another fiery sphere, which, itself unmoved, is the cause of all motion and generation in the mixed region between. The motive and procreative power, sometimes called Love, is at other times called by Parmenides Necessity, Bearer of the Keys, Justice, Ruler, etc.

But while in so far as there was union in the production of man or any other creature, the presiding genius might be symbolised as Love; on the other hand, since this union was a union of opposites (Light and Dark), Discord or Strife also had her say in the union. Thus the nature and character in every creature was the resultant of two antagonistic forces, and depended for its particular excellence or defect on the proportions in which these two elements—the light and the dark, the fiery and the earthy—had been commingled.

No character in Greek antiquity, at least in the succession of philosophic teachers, held a more honoured position than Parmenides. He was looked on with almost superstitious reverence by his fellow-countrymen. Plato speaks of him as his "Father Parmenides," whom he "revered and honoured more than all the other philosophers together." To quote Professor Jowett in his introduction to Plato's dialogue Parmenides, he was "the founder of idealism and also of dialectic, or in modern phraseology, of metaphysics and of logic." Of the logical aspect of his teaching we shall see a fuller exemplification in his pupil and successor Zeno; of his metaphysics, by way of summing up what has been already said, it may be remarked that its substantial excellence consists in the perfect clearness and precision with which Parmenides enunciated as fundamental in any theory of the knowable universe the priority of Existence itself, not in time merely or chiefly, but as a condition of having any problem to inquire into. He practically admits that he does not see how to bridge over the partition between Existence in itself and the changeful, temporary, existing things which the senses give us notions of. But whatever the connection may be, if there is a connection, he is convinced that nothing would be more absurd than to make the data of sense in any way or degree the measure of the reality of existence, or the source from which existence itself comes into being.

On this serenely impersonal position he took his stand; we find little or nothing of the querulous personal note so characteristic of much modern philosophy. We never find him asking, "What is to become of me in all this?" "What is my position with regard to this eternally-existing reality?"

Of course this is not exclusively a characteristic of Parmenides, but of the time. The idea of personal relation to an eternal Rewarder was only vaguely held in historical times in Greece. The conception of personal immortality was a mere pious opinion, a doctrine whispered here and there in secret mystery; it was not an influential force on men's motives or actions. Thought was still occupied with the wider universe, the heavens and their starry wonders, and the strange phenomena of law in nature. In the succession of the seasons, the rising and setting, the fixities and aberrations, of the heavenly bodies, in the mysteries of coming into being and passing out of it, in these and other similar marvels, and in the thoughts which they evoked, a whole and ample world seemed open for inquiry. Men and their fate were interesting enough to men, but as yet the egotism of man had not attempted to isolate his destiny from the general problem of nature. To the crux of philosophy as it appeared to Parmenides in the relation of being as such to things which seem to be, modernism has appended a sort of corollary, in the relation of being as such to my being. Till the second question was raised its answer, of course, could not be attempted. But all those who in modern times have said with Tennyson—

Thou wilt not leave us in the dust:
Thou madest man, he knows not why;
He thinks he was not made to die;
And Thou hast made him: Thou art just,

may recognise in Parmenides a pioneer for them. Without knowing it, he was fighting the battle of personality in man, as well as that of reality in nature.

Zeno

The third head of the Eleatic school was Zeno. He is described by Plato in the Parmenides as accompanying his master to Athens on the visit already referred to (see above, p. 34), and as being then "nearly forty years of age, of a noble figure and fair aspect." In personal character he was a worthy pupil of his master, being, like him, a devoted patriot. He is even said to have fallen a victim to his patriotism, and to have suffered bravely the extremest tortures at the hands of a tyrant Nearchus rather than betray his country.

His philosophic position was a very simple one. He had nothing to add to or to vary in the doctrine of Parmenides. His function was primarily that of an expositor and defender of that doctrine, and his particular pre-eminence consists in the ingenuity of his dialectic resources of defence. He is in fact pronounced by Aristotle to have been the inventor of dialectic or systematic logic.

The relation of the two is humorously expressed thus by Plato (Jowett, Plato, vol. iv. p. 128); "I see, Parmenides, said Socrates, that Zeno is your second self in his writings too; he puts what you say in another way, and would fain deceive us into believing that he is telling us what is new. For you, in your poems, say, All is one, and of this you adduce excellent proofs; and he, on the other hand, says, There is no many; and on behalf of this he offers overwhelming evidence." To this Zeno replies, admitting the fact, and adds: "These writings of mine were meant to protect the arguments of Parmenides against those who scoff at him, and show the many ridiculous and contradictory results which they suppose to follow from the affirmation of the One. My answer is an address to the partisans of the many, whose attack I return with interest by retorting upon them that their hypothesis of the being of many if carried out appears in a still more ridiculous light than the hypothesis of the being of one."

The arguments of Zeno may therefore be regarded as strictly arguments in kind; quibbles if you please, but in answer to quibbles. The secret of his method was what Aristotle calls Dichotomy—that is, he put side by side two contradictory propositions with respect to any particular supposed real thing in experience, and then proceeded to show that both these contradictories alike imply what is inconceivable. Thus "a thing must consist either of a finite number of parts or an infinite number." Assume the number of parts to be finite. Between them there must either be something or nothing. If there is something between them, then the whole consists of more parts than it consists of. If there is nothing between them, then they are not separated, therefore they are not parts; therefore the whole has no parts at all; therefore it is nothing. If, on the other hand, the number of parts is infinite, then, the same kind of argument being applied, the magnitude of the whole is by infinite successive positing of intervening parts shown to be infinite; therefore this one thing, being infinitely large, is everything.

Take, again, any supposed fact, as that an arrow moves. An arrow cannot move except in space. It cannot move in space without being in space. At any moment of its supposed motion it must be in a particular space. Being in that space, it must at the time during which it is in it be at rest. But the total time of its supposed motion is made up of the moments composing that time, and to each of these moments the same argument applies; therefore either the arrow never was anywhere, or it always was at rest.

Or, again, take objects moving at unequal rates, as Achilles and a tortoise. Let the tortoise have a start of any given length, then Achilles, however much he excel in speed, will never overtake the tortoise. For, while Achilles has passed over the originally intervening space, the tortoise will have passed over a certain space, and when Achilles has passed over this second space the tortoise will have again passed over some space, and so on ad infinitum; therefore in an infinite time there must always be a space, though infinitely diminishing, between the tortoise and Achilles, i.e. the tortoise must always be at least a little in front.

These will be sufficient to show the kind of arguments employed by Zeno. In themselves they are of no utility, and Zeno never pretended that they had any. But as against those who denied that existence as such was a datum independent of experience, something different from a mere sum of isolated things, his arguments were not only effective, but substantial. The whole modern sensational or experiential school, who derive our 'abstract ideas,' as they are called, from 'phenomena' or 'sensation,' manifest the same impatience of any analysis of what they mean by phenomena or sensation, as no doubt Zeno's opponents manifested of his analyses. As in criticising the one, modern critics are ready with their answer that Zeno's quibbles are simply "a play of words on the well-known properties of infinities," so they are quick to tell us that sensation is an "affection of the sentient organism"; ignoring in the first case the prior question where the idea of infinity came from, and in the second, where the idea of a sentient organism came from.

Indirectly, as we shall see, Zeno had a great effect on subsequent philosophies by the development of a process of ingenious verbal distinction, which in the hands of so-called sophists and others became a weapon of considerable, if temporary, power.

Melissus

The fourth and last of the Eleatic philosophers was Melissus, a native of Samos. His date may be fixed as about 440 B.C. He took an active part in the politics of his native country, and on one occasion was commander of the Samian fleet in a victorious engagement with the Athenians, when Samos was being besieged by Pericles. He belongs to the Eleatic school in respect of doctrine and method, but we have no evidence of his ever having resided at Elea, nor any reference to his connection with the philosophers there, except the statement that he was a pupil of Parmenides. He developed very fully what is technically called in the science of Logic the Dilemma. Thus, for example, he begins his treatise *On Existence* or *On Nature* thus: "If nothing exists, then there is nothing for us to talk about. But if there is such a thing as existence it must either come into being or be ever-existing. If it come into being, it must come from the existing or the non-existing. Now that anything which exists, above all, that which is absolutely existent, should come from what is not, is impossible. Nor can it come from that which is. For then it would be already, and would not come into being. That which exists, therefore, comes not into being; it must therefore be ever-existing."

By similar treatment of other conceivable alternatives he proceeds to show that as the existent had no beginning so it can have no ending in time. From this, by a curious transition which Aristotle quotes as an example of loose reasoning, he concludes that the existent can have no limit in space either. As being thus unlimited it must be one, therefore immovable (there being nothing else into which it can move or change), and therefore always self-identical in extent and character. It cannot, therefore, have any body, for body has parts and is not therefore one.

Being incapable of change one might perhaps conclude that the absolutely existing being is incapable of any mental activity or consciousness. We have no authority for assuming that Melissus came to this conclusion; but there is a curious remark of Aristotle's respecting this and previous philosophers of the school which certain critics have made to bear some such interpretation. He says: "Parmenides seems to hold by a Unity in thought, Melissus by a Material unity. Hence the first defined the One as limited, the second declared it to be unlimited. Xenophanes made no clear statement on this question; he simply, gazing up to the arch of heaven, declared, The One is God."

But the difference between Melissus and his master can hardly be said to be a difference of doctrine; point for point, they are identical. The difference is a difference of vision or mental picture as to this mighty All which is One. Melissus, so to speak, places himself at the centre of this Universal being, and sees it stretching out infinitely, unendingly, in space and in time. Its oneness comes to him as the sum of these infinities. Parmenides, on the other hand, sees all these endless immensities as related to a centre; he, so to speak, enfolds them all in the grasp of his unifying thought, and as thus equally and necessarily related to a central unity he pronounces the All a sphere, and therefore limited. The two doctrines, antithetical in terms, are identical in fact. The absolutely unlimited and the absolutely self-limited are only two ways of saying the same thing.

This difference of view or vision Aristotle in the passage quoted expresses as a difference between thought (Greek *logos*) and matter (Greek *hule*). This is just a form of his own radical distinction between Essence and Difference, Form and Matter, of which much will be said later on. It is like the difference between Deduction and Induction; in the first you start from the universal and see within it the particulars; in the second you start from the particulars and gather them into completeness and reality in a universal. The substance remains the same, only the point of view is different. To put the matter in modern mathematical form, one might say, The universe is to be conceived as a sphere (Parmenides) of infinite radius (Melissus). Aristotle is not blaming Melissus or praising Parmenides. As for Xenophanes, Aristotle after his manner finds in him the potentiality of both. He is prior both to the process of thought from universal to particular, and to that from particular to universal. He does not argue at all; his function is Intuition. "He looks out on the mighty sky, and says, The One is God."

Melissus applied the results of his analysis in an interesting way to the question already raised by his predecessors, of the trustworthiness of sensation. His argument is as follows: "If there were many real existences, to each of them the same reasonings must apply as I have already used with reference to the one existence. That is to say, if earth really exists, and water and air and iron and gold and fire and things living and things dead; and black and white, and all the various things whose reality men ordinarily assume,— if all these really exist, and our sight and our hearing give us facts, then each of these as really existing must be what we concluded the one existence must be; among other things, each must be unchangeable, and can never become other than it really is. But assuming that sight and hearing and apprehension are true, we find the cold becoming hot and the hot becoming cold; the hard changes to soft, the soft to hard; the living thing dies; and from that which is not living, a living thing comes into being; in short, everything changes, and what now is in no way resembles what was. It follows therefore that we neither see nor apprehend realities.

"In fact we cannot pay the slightest regard to experience without being landed in self-contradictions. We assume that there are all sorts of really existing things, having a permanence both of form and power, and yet we imagine these very things altering and changing according to what we from time to time see about them. If they were realities as we first perceived them, our sight must now be wrong. For if they were real, they could not change. Nothing can be stronger than reality. Whereas to suppose it changed, we must affirm that the real has ceased to be, and that that which was not has displaced it."

To Melissus therefore, as to his predecessors, the world of sense was a world of illusion; the very first principles or assumptions of which, as of the truthfulness of the senses and the reality of the various objects which we see, are unthinkable and absurd.

The weakness as well as the strength of the Eleatic position consisted in its purely negative and critical attitude. The assumptions of ordinary life and experience could not stand for a moment when assailed in detail by their subtle analysis. So-called facts were like a world of ghosts, which the sword of truth passed through without resistance. But somehow the sword might pierce them through and through, and show by all manner of arguments their unsubstantiality, but there they were still thronging about the philosopher and refusing to be gone. The world of sense might be only illusion, but there the illusion was. You could not lay it or exorcise it by calling it illusion or opinion. What was this opinion? What was the nature of its subject matter? How did it operate? And if its results were not true or real, what was their nature? These were questions which still remained when the analysis of the idea of absolute existence had been pushed to its completion. These were the questions which the next school of philosophy attempted to answer. After the Idealists, the Realists; after the philosophy of mind, the philosophy of matter.

The Pre-Socratics

By George Grote

PLATONIC REPUBLIC — ABSTRACT.

The Republic is the longest of all the Platonic dialogues, except the dialogue *De Legibus*. It consists of ten books, each of them as long as any one of the dialogues which we have passed in review. Partly from its length — partly from its lofty pretensions as the great constructive work of Plato — I shall give little more than an abstract of it in the present chapter, and shall reserve remark and comment for the succeeding.

Declared theme of the *Republic* — Expansion and multiplication of the topics connected with it.

The professed subject is — What is Justice? Is the just man happy in or by reason of his justice? whatever consequences may befall him? Is the unjust man unhappy by reason of his injustice? But the ground actually travelled over by Socrates, from whose mouth the exposition proceeds, is far more extensive than could have been anticipated from this announced problem. An immense variety of topics, belonging to man and society, is adverted to more or less fully. A theory of psychology or phrenology generally, is laid down and advocated: likewise a theory of the Intellect, distributed into its two branches:

1. Science, with the Platonic Forms or Ideas as Realities corresponding to it;

2. Opinion, with the fluctuating semi-realities or pseudo-realities, which form its object.

A sovereign rule, exercised by philosophy, is asserted as indispensable to human happiness. The fundamental conditions of a good society, as Plato conceived it, are set forth at considerable length, and contrasted with the social corruptions of various existing forms of government. The outline of a perfect education, intellectual and emotional, is drawn up and prescribed for the ruling class: with many accompanying remarks on the objectionable tendencies of the popular and consecrated poems. The post-existence, as well as the pre-existence of the soul, is affirmed in the concluding books.

As the result of the whole, Plato emphatically proclaims his conviction, that the just man is happy in and through his justice, quite apart from all consideration of consequences — yet that the consequences also will be such as to add to his happiness, both during life as well as after death: and the unjust man unhappy in and through his injustice.

The dramatic introduction of the dialogue (which is described as held during the summer, immediately after the festival of the Bendideia in Peiraeus), with the picture of the aged Kephalus and his views upon old age, is among the richest and most spirited in the Platonic works: but the discussion does not properly begin until Kephalus retires, leaving it to be carried on by Socrates with Polemarchus, Glaukon, Adeimantus, and Thrasymachus.

"Old age has its advantages to reasonable men (says Kephalus). If I have lost the pleasures of youth, I have at the same time lost the violent desires which then overmastered me. I now enjoy tranquillity and peace. Without doubt, this is in part owing to my wealth. But the best that wealth does for me is, that it enables me to make compensation for deceptions and injustice, practised on other men in my younger days — and to fulfil all vows made to the Gods. An old man who is too poor to render such atonement for past falsehood and injustice, becomes uneasy in his mind as death approaches; he begins to fear that the stories about Hades, which he has heard and ridiculed in his youth, may perhaps prove true."

"Is that your explanation of justice (asks Socrates): that it consists in telling truth, and rendering to every one what you have had from him?" The old man Kephalus here withdraws; Polemarchus and the others prosecute the discussion. "The poet Simonides (says Polemarchus) gives an explanation like to that which you have stated — when he affirms, That just dealing consists in rendering to every man what is owing to him."

"I do not know what Simonides means," replies Socrates. "He cannot mean that it is always right to tell the truth, or always right to give back a deposit. If my friend, having deposited arms with me, afterwards goes mad, and in that state demands them back, it would not be right in me either to restore the arms, or to tell the truth, to a man in that condition. Therefore to say that justice consists in speaking truth and in giving back what we have received, cannot be a good definition."

Polemarchus here gives a peculiar meaning to the phrase of Simonides: a man owes good to his friends — evil to his enemies: and he ought to pay back both. Upon this Socrates comments.

Socrates here remarks that the precepts — Speak truth; Restore what has been confided to you — ought not to be considered as universally binding. Sometimes justice, or those higher grounds upon which the rules of justice are founded, prescribe that we should disobey the precepts. Socrates takes this for granted, as a matter which no one will dispute; and it is evident that what Plato had here in his mind was, the obvious consideration that to tell the truth or restore a weapon deposited, to one who had gone mad, would do no good to any one, and might do immense mischief: thus showing that general utility is both the foundation and the limiting principle of all precepts respecting just and unjust. That this is present to the mind of Plato appears evident from his assuming the position as a matter of course; it is moreover Socratic, as we see by the *Memorabilia* of Xenophon.

But Plato, in another passage of the *Republic*, clothes this Socratic doctrine in a language and hypothesis of his own. He sets up Forms or Ideas, per se. The Just, — The Unjust, — The Honourable, — The Base, &c. He distinguishes each of these from the many separate manifestations in which it is specialised. The Form, though one reality in itself, appears manifold when embodied and disguised in these diversified accompaniments. It remains One and Unchanged, the object of Science and universal infallible truth; but each of its separate manifestations is peculiar to itself, appears differently to different minds, and admits of no higher certainty than fallible opinion. Though the Form of Justice always remains the same, yet its subordinate embodiments ever fluctuate; there is no given act nor assemblage of acts which is always just. Every just act (see *Republic*) is liable under certain circumstances to become unjust; or to be invaded and overclouded by the Form of Injustice. The genuine philosopher will detect the Form of Justice wherever it is to be found, in the midst of accompaniments however discrepant and confused, over all which he will ascend to the region of universal truth and reality. The unphilosophical mind cannot accomplish this ascent, nor detect the pure Form, nor even recognise its real existence: but sees nothing beyond the multiplicity of diverse particular cases in which it is or appears to be embodied. Respecting these particular cases there is no constant or universal truth, no full science. They cannot be thrown into classes to which the superior Form constantly and unconditionally adheres. They are midway between reality and non-reality: they are matters of opinion more or less reasonable, but not of certain science or unconditional affirmation. Among mankind generally, who see nothing of true and absolute Form, the received rules and dogmas respecting the Just, the Beautiful, &c., are of this intermediate and ambiguous kind: they can neither be affirmed universally, nor denied universally; they are partly true, partly false, determinable only by opinion in each separate case. Plato, *Repub.*

Of the distinction here drawn in general terms by Plato, between the pure unchangeable Form, and the subordinate classes of particulars in which that Form is or appears to be embodied, the reasoning above cited respecting truth-telling and giving back a deposit is an example.

S. — Simonides meant to say (you tell me) that Justice consists in rendering benefits to your friends, evil to your enemies: that is, in rendering to each what is proper and suitable. But we must ask him farther — Proper and suitable — how? in what cases? to whom? The medical art is that which renders what is proper and suitable, of nourishment and medicaments for the health of the body: the art of cookery is that which renders what is proper and suitable, of savoury ingredients for the satisfaction of the palate. In like manner, the cases must be specified in which justice renders what is proper and suitable — to whom, how, or what?

P. — Justice consists in doing good to friends, evil to enemies.

S. — Who is it that is most efficient in benefiting his friends and injuring his enemies, as to health or disease?

P. — It is the physician.

S. — Who, in reference to the dangers in navigation by sea?

P. — The steersman.

S. — In what matters is it that the just man shows his special efficiency, to benefit friends and hurt enemies?

P. — In war: as a combatant for the one and against the other.

S. — To men who are not sick, the physician is of no use nor the steersman, to men on dry land: Do you mean in like manner, that the just man is useless to those who are not at war?

P. — No: I do not mean that. Justice is useful in peace also.

S. — So also is husbandry, for raising food — shoemaking, for providing shoes. Tell me for what want or acquisition justice is useful during peace?

P. — It is useful for the common dealings and joint transactions between man and man.

S. — When we are engaged in playing at draughts, the good player is our useful co-operator: when in laying bricks and stones, the skilful mason: much more than the just man. Can you specify in what particular transactions the just man has any superior usefulness as a co-operator?

P. — In affairs of money, I think.

S. — Surely not in the employment of money. When you want to buy a horse, you must take for your assistant, not the just man, but one who knows horses: so also, if you are purchasing a ship. What are those modes of jointly employing money, in which the just man is more useful than others?

P. — He is useful when you wish to have your money safely kept.

S. — That is, when your money is not to be employed, but to lie idle: so that when your money is useless, then is the time when justice is useful for it.

P. — So it seems.

S. — In regard to other things also, a sickle, a shield, a lyre when you want to use them, the pruner, the hoplite, the musician, must be invoked as co-operators: justice is useful only when you are to keep them unused. In a word, justice is useless for the use of any thing, and useful merely for things not in use. Upon this showing, it is at least a matter of no great worth.

The just man, being good for keeping property guarded, must also be good for stealing property — Analogies cited.

But let us pursue the investigation (continues Socrates). In boxing or in battle, is not he who is best in striking, best also in defending himself? In regard to disease, is not he who can best guard himself against it, the most formidable for imparting it to others? Is not the general who watches best over his own camp, also the most effective in surprising and over-reaching the enemy? In a word, whenever a man is effective as a guard of any thing, is he not also effective as a thief of it?

P. — Such seems the course of the discussion.

S. — Well then, the just man turns out to be a sort of thief, like the Homeric Autolykus. According to the explanation of Simonides, justice is a mode of thieving, for the profit of friends and damage of enemies.

P. — It cannot be so. I am in utter confusion. Yet I think still that justice is profitable to friends, and hurtful to enemies.

Justice consists in doing good to friends, evil to enemies — But how, if a man mistakes who his friends are, and makes friends of bad men?

S. — Whom do you call friends: those whom a man believes to be good, — or those who really are good, whether he believes them to be so or not: and the like, in reference to enemies?

P. — I mean those whom he believes to be good. It is natural that he should love them and that he should hate those whom he believes to be evil.

S. — But is not a man often mistaken in this belief?

P. — Yes: often.

S. — In so far as a man is mistaken, the good men are his enemies, and the evil men his friends. Justice, therefore, on your showing, consists in doing good to the evil men, and evil to the good men.

P. — So it appears.

S. — Now good men are just, and do no wrong to any one. It is therefore just, on your explanation, to hurt those who do no wrong.

P. — Impossible! that is a monstrous doctrine.

S. — You mean, then, that it is just to hurt unjust men, and to benefit just men?

P. — Yes; that is something better.

S. — It will often happen, therefore, when a man misjudges about others, that justice will consist in hurting his friends, since they are in his estimation the evil men: and in benefiting his enemies, since they are in his estimation the good men. Now this is the direct contrary of what Simonides defined to be justice.

Justice consists in doing good to your friend, if really a good man: hurt to your enemy, with the like proviso. Socrates affirms that the just man will do no hurt to any one. Definition of Simonides rejected.

"We have misconceived the meaning of Simonides (replies Polemarchus). He must have meant that justice consists in benefiting your friend, assuming him to be a good man: and in hurting your enemy, assuming him to be an evil man." Socrates proceeds to impugn the definition in this new sense. He shows that justice does not admit of our hurting any man, either evil or good. By hurting the evil man, we only make him more evil than he was before. To do this belongs not to justice, but to injustice. The definition of justice — That it consists in rendering benefit to friends and hurt to enemies — is not suitable to a wise man like Simonides, but to some rich potentate like Periander or Xerxes, who thinks his own power irresistible.

Thrasymachus takes up the dialogue — Repulsive portrait drawn of him.

At this turn of the dialogue, when the definition given by Simonides has just been refuted, Thrasymachus breaks in, and takes up the conversation with Socrates. He is depicted as angry, self-confident to excess, and coarse in his manners even to the length of insult. The portrait given of him is memorable for its dramatic vivacity, and is calculated to present in an odious point of view the doctrines which he advances: like the personal deformities which Homer heaps upon Thersites in the *Iliad*. But how far it is a copy of the real man, we have no evidence to inform us.

In the contrast between Socrates and Thrasymachus, Plato gives valuable hints as to the conditions of instructive colloquy.

"What nonsense is all this!" (exclaims Thrasymachus). "Do not content yourself with asking questions, Socrates, which you know is much easier than answering: but tell us yourself what Justice is: give us a plain answer: do not tell us that it is what is right — or profitable — or for our interest — or gainful — or advantageous: for I will not listen to any trash like this."

"Be not so harsh with us, Thrasymachus" (replies Socrates, in a subdued tone). "If we have taken the wrong course of inquiry, it is against our own will. You ought to feel pity for us rather than anger."

"I thought" (rejoined Thrasymachus, with a scornful laugh) "that you would have recourse to your usual pretence of ignorance, and would decline answering."

S. — How can I possibly answer, when you prescribe beforehand what I am to say or not to say? If you ask men — How much is twelve? and at the same time say — Don't tell me that it is twice six, or three times four, or four times three — how can any man answer your question?

T. — As if the two cases were similar!

S. — Why not similar? But even though they be not similar, yet if the respondent thinks them so, how can he help answering according as the matter appears to him, whether we forbid him or not?

T. — Is that what you intend to do? Are you going to give me one of those answers which I forbade?

S. — Very likely I may, if on consideration it appears to me the proper answer.

T. — What will you say if I show you another answer better than all of them? What penalty will you then impose upon yourself?

S. — What penalty? — why, that which properly falls upon the ignorant. It is their proper fate to learn from men wiser than themselves: that is the penalty which I am prepared for.

Definition given by Thrasymachus — Justice is that which is advantageous to the more powerful. Comments by Socrates. What if the powerful man mistakes his own advantage?

After a few more words, in the same offensive and insolent tone ascribed to him from the beginning, Thrasymachus produces his definition of Justice:— "Justice is that which is advantageous to the more powerful". Some comments from Socrates bring out a fuller explanation, whereby the definition stands amended:— "Justice is that which is advantageous to the constituted authority, or to that which holds power, in each different community: monarchy, oligarchy, or democracy, as the case may be. Each of these authorities makes laws and ordinances for its own interest: declares what is just and unjust: and punishes all citizens who infringe its commands. Justice consists in obeying these commands. In this sense, justice is everywhere that which is for the interest or advantage of the more powerful."

"I too believe" (says Socrates) "that justice is something advantageous, in a certain sense. But whether you are right in adding these words — 'to the more powerful' — is a point for investigation. Assuming that the authorities in each state make ordinances for their own advantage, you will admit that they sometimes mistake, and enact ordinances tending to their own disadvantage. In so far as they do this, justice is not that which is advantageous, but that which is disadvantageous, to the more powerful. Your definition therefore will not hold."

Correction by Thrasymachus — if the Ruler mistakes, he is pro tanto no Ruler — The Ruler, qua Ruler — qua Craftsman — is infallible.

Thrasymachus might have replied to this objection by saying, that he meant what the superior power conceived to be for its own advantage, and enacted accordingly, whether such conception was correct or erroneous. This interpretation, though indicated by a remark put into the mouth of Kleitophon, is not farther pursued. But in the reply really ascribed to Thrasymachus, he is made to retract what he had just before admitted — that the superior authority sometimes commits mistakes. In so far as a superior or a ruler makes mistakes (Thrasymachus says), he is not a superior. We say, indeed, speaking loosely, that the ruler falls into error, just as we say that the physician or the steersman falls into error. The physician does not err quâ physician, nor the steersman quâ steersman. No craftsman errs quâ craftsman. If he errs, it is not from his craft, but from want of knowledge: that is, from want of craft. What the ruler, as such, declares to be best for himself, and therefore enacts, is always really best for himself: this is justice for the persons under his rule.

To this subtle distinction, Socrates replies by saying (in substance), "If you take the craftsman in this strict meaning, as representing the abstraction Craft, it is not true that his proceedings are directed towards his own interest or advantage. What he studies is, the advantage of his subjects or clients, not his own. The physician, as such, has it in view to cure his patients: the steersman, to bring his passengers safely to harbour: the ruler, so far forth as craftsman, makes laws for the benefit of his subjects, and not for his own. If obedience to these laws constitutes justice, therefore, it is not true that justice consists in what is advantageous to the superior or governing power. It would rather consist in what is advantageous to the governed."

Thrasymachus is now represented as renouncing the abstraction above noted, and reverting to the actualities of life. "Such talk is childish!" (he exclaims, with the coarseness imputed to him in this dialogue). "Shepherds and herdsmen tend and fatten their flocks and herds, not for the benefit of the sheep and oxen, but for the profit of themselves and the proprietors. So too the genuine ruler in a city: he regards his subjects as so many sheep, looking only to the amount of profit which he can draw from them.

Justice is, in real truth, the good of another; it is the profit of him who is more powerful and rules — the loss of those who are weaker and must obey. It is the unjust man who rules over the multitude of just and well-meaning men. They serve him because he is the stronger: they build up his happiness at the cost of their own. Everywhere, both in private dealing and in public function, the just man is worse off than the unjust. I mean by the unjust, one who has the power to commit wrongful seizure on a large scale. You may see this if you look at the greatest injustice of all — the case of the despot, who makes himself happy while the juster men over whom he rules are miserable. One who is detected in the commission of petty crimes is punished, and gets a bad name: but if a man has force enough to commit crime on the grand scale, to enslave the persons of the citizens, and to appropriate their goods — instead of being called by a bad name, he is envied and regarded as happy, not only by the citizens themselves, but by all who hear him named. Those who blame injustice, do so from the fear of suffering it, not from the fear of doing it. Thus then injustice, in its successful efficiency, is strong, free, and over-ruling, as compared with justice. Injustice is profitable to a man's self: justice (as I said before) is what is profitable to some other man stronger than he."

Thrasymachus is described as laying down this position in very peremptory language, and as anxious to depart immediately after it, if he had not been detained by the other persons present. His position forms the pivot of the subsequent conversation. The two opinions included in it — (That justice consists in obedience yielded by the weak to the orders of the strong, for the advantage of the strong — That injustice, if successful, is profitable and confers happiness: justice the contrary) — are disputed, both of them, by Socrates as well as by Glaukon.

Socrates is represented as confuting and humiliating Thrasymachus by various arguments, of which the two first at least are more subtle than cogent. He next proceeds to argue that injustice, far from being a source of strength, is a source of weakness — That any community of men, among whom injustice prevails, must be in continual dispute; and therefore incapable of combined action against others — That a camp of mercenary soldiers or robbers, who plunder every one else, must at least observe justice among themselves — That if they have force, this is because they are unjust only by halves: that if they were thoroughly unjust, they would also be thoroughly impotent — That the like is true also of an individual separately taken, who, so far as he is unjust, is in a perpetual state of hatred and conflict with himself, as well as with just men and with the Gods: and would thus be divested of all power to accomplish any purpose.

Having thus shown that justice is stronger than injustice, Socrates next offers an argument to prove that it is happier or confers more happiness than injustice. The conclusion of this argument is — That the just man is happy, and the unjust miserable. Thrasymachus is confuted, and retires humiliated from the debate. Yet Socrates himself is represented as dissatisfied with the result. "At the close of our debate" (he says) "I find that I know nothing about the matter. For as I do not know what justice is, I can hardly expect to know whether it is a virtue or not; nor whether the man who possesses it is happy or not happy."

Glaukon intimates that he is not satisfied with the proof, though he agrees in the opinion expressed by Socrates. Tripartite distribution of Good — To which of the three heads does Justice belong?

Here Glaukon enters the lists, intimating that he too is dissatisfied with the proof given by Socrates, that justice is every way better than injustice: though he adopts the conclusion, and desires much to hear it fully demonstrated.

"You know" (he says), "Socrates, that there are three varieties of Good — 1. Good, per se, and for its own sake (apart from any regard to ulterior consequences): such as enjoyment and the innocuous pleasures. 2. Good both in itself, and by reason of its ulterior consequences: such as full health, perfect vision, intelligence, &c. 3. Good, not in itself, but altogether by reason of its consequences: such as gymnastic training, medical treatment, professional business, &c. Now in which of these branches do you rank Justice?"

S. — I rank it in the noblest — that is — in the second branch: which is good both in itself, and by reason of its consequences.

G. — Most persons put it in the third branch: as being in itself difficult and laborious, but deserving to be cultivated in consequence of the reward and good name which attaches to the man who is reputed just.

S. — I know that this is the view taken by Thrasymachus and many others: but it is not mine.

G. — Neither is it mine.

Yet still I think that you have not made out your case against Thrasymachus, and that he has given up the game too readily. I will therefore re-state his argument, not at all adopting his opinion as my own, but simply in order to provoke a full refutation of it from you, such as I have never yet heard from any one. First, I shall show what his partisans say as to the nature and origin of justice. Next, I shall show that all who practise justice, practise it unwillingly; not as good per se, but as a necessity. Lastly, I shall prove that such conduct on their part is reasonable. If these points can be made out, it will follow that the life of the unjust man is much better than that of the just.

Pleading of Glaukon. Justice is in the nature of a compromise for all — a medium between what is best and what is worst.

The case, as set forth first by Glaukon, next by Adeimantus, making themselves advocates of Thrasymachus — is as follows. "To do injustice, is by nature good: to suffer injustice is by nature evil: but the last is greater as an evil, than the first as a good: so that when men have tasted of both, they find it advantageous to agree with each other, that none shall either do or suffer injustice. These agreements are embodied in laws; and what is prescribed by the law is called lawful and just. Here you have the generation and essence of justice, which is intermediate between what is best and what is worst: that is, between the power of committing injustice with impunity, and the liability to suffer injustice without protection or redress. Men acquiesce in such compromise, not as in itself good, but because they are too weak to commit injustice safely. For if any man were strong enough to do so, and had the dispositions of a man, he would not make such a compromise with any one: it would be madness in him to do so.

"That men are just, only because they are too weak to be unjust, will appear if we imagine any of them, either the just or the unjust, armed with full power and impunity, such as would be conferred by the ring of Gyges, which rendered the wearer invisible at pleasure. If the just man could become thus privileged, he would act in the same manner as the unjust: his temper would never be adamantine enough to resist the temptations which naturally prompt every man to unlimited satisfaction of his desires. Such temptations are now counteracted by the force of law and opinion; but if these sanctions were nullified, every man, just or unjust, would seize every thing that he desired, without regard to others. When he is just, he is so not willingly, but by compulsion. He chooses that course not as being the best for him absolutely, but as the best which his circumstances will permit.

"To determine which of the two is happiest, the just man or the unjust, let us assume each to be perfect in his part, and then compare them. The unjust man must be assumed to have at his command all means of force and fraud, so as to procure for himself the maximum of success; i.e., the reputation of being a just man, along with all the profitable enormities of injustice. Against him we will set the just man, perfect in his own simplicity and righteousness; a man who cares only for being just in reality, and not for seeming to be so. We shall suppose him, though really just, to be accounted by every one else thoroughly unjust. It is only thus that we can test the true value of his justice: for if he be esteemed just by others, he will be honoured and recompensed, so that we cannot be sure that his justice is not dictated by regard to these adventitious consequences. He must be assumed as just through life, yet accounted by every one else unjust, and treated accordingly: while the unjust man, with whom we compare him, is considered and esteemed by others as if he were perfectly just. Which of the two will have the happiest life? Unquestionably the unjust man. He will have all the advantages derived from his unscrupulous use of means, together with all that extrinsic favour and support which proceeds from good estimation on the part of others: he will acquire superior wealth, which will enable him both to purchase partisans, and to offer costly sacrifices ensuring to him the patronage of the Gods. The just man, on the contrary, will not only be destitute of all these advantages, but will be exposed to a life of extreme suffering and torture. He will learn by painful experience that his happiness depends, not upon being really just, but upon being accounted just by others."

Pleading of Adeimantus on the same side. He cites advice given by fathers to their sons, recommending just behaviour by reason of its consequences.

Here Glaukon concludes. Adeimantus now steps in as second counsel on the same side, to the following effect: "Much yet remains to be added to the argument. To make it clearer, we must advert to the topics insisted on by those who oppose Glaukon — those who panegyrise justice and denounce injustice. A father, who exhorts his sons to be just, says nothing about the intrinsic advantages of justice per se: he dwells upon the beneficial consequences which will accrue to them from being just. Through such reputation they will obtain from men favours, honours, commands, prosperous alliances — from the Gods, recompenses yet more varied and abundant. If, on the contrary, they commit injustice, they will be disgraced and ill-treated among men, severely punished by the Gods.

Such are the arguments whereby a father recommends justice, and dissuades injustice, he talks about opinions and after consequences only, he says nothing about justice or injustice in themselves. Such are the allegations even of those who wish to praise and enforce justice.

But there are others, and many among them, who hold an opposite language, proclaiming unreservedly that temperance and justice are difficult to practise — injustice and intemperance easy and agreeable, though law and opinion brand them as disgraceful. These men affirm that the unjust life is for the most part more profitable than the just. They are full of panegyrics towards the wealthy and powerful, however unprincipled; despising the poor and weak, whom nevertheless they admit to be better men.

They even say that the Gods themselves entail misery upon many good men, and confer prosperity on the wicked. Then there come the prophets and jugglers, who profess to instruct rich men, out of many books, composed by Orpheus and Musaeus, how they may by appropriate presents and sacrifices atone for all their crimes and die happy.

"When we find that the case is thus stated respecting justice, both by its panegyrists and by its enemies — that the former extol it only from the reputation which it procures, and that the latter promise to the unjust man, if clever and energetic, a higher recompense than any such reputation can obtain for him — what effect can we expect to be produced on the minds of young men of ability, station, and ambition? What course of life are they likely to choose? Surely they will thus reason: A just life is admitted to be burdensome — and it will serve no purpose, unless I acquire, besides, the reputation of justice in the esteem of others. Now the unjust man, who can establish such reputation, enjoys the perfection of existence. My happiness turns not upon the reality, but upon the seeming: upon my reputation with others.

Such reputation then it must be my aim to acquire. I must combine the real profit of injustice with the outside show and reputation of justice. Such combination is difficult: but all considerable enterprises are difficult: I must confederate with partisans to carry my point by force or fraud. If I succeed, I attain the greatest prize to which man can aspire. I may be told that the Gods will punish me; but the same poets, who declare the existence of the Gods, assure me also that they are placable by prayer and sacrifice: and the poets are as good authority on the one point as on the other.

Such" (continues Adeimantus) "will be the natural reasoning of a powerful, energetic, aspiring, man. How can we expect that such a man should prefer justice, when the rewards of injustice on its largest scale are within his reach?

Unless he be averse to injustice, from some divine peculiarity of disposition — or unless he has been taught to abstain from it by the acquisition of knowledge, — he will treat the current encomiums on justice as ridiculous. No man is just by his own impulse. Weak men or old men censure injustice, because they have not force enough to commit it with success: which is proved by the fact than any one of them who acquires power, immediately becomes unjust as far as his power reaches.

"The case as I set it forth" (pursues Adeimantus) "admits of no answer on the ground commonly taken by those who extol justice and blame injustice, from the earliest poets down to the present day. What they praise is not justice per se, but the reputation which the just man obtains, and the consequences flowing from it. What they blame is not injustice per se, but its results. They never commend, nor even mention, justice as it exists in and moulds the internal mind and character of the just man; even though he be unknown, misconceived and detested, by Gods as well as by men. Nor do they ever talk of the internal and intrinsic effects of injustice upon the mind of the unjust man, but merely of his ulterior prospects. They never attempt to show that injustice itself, in the mind of the unjust man, is the gravest intrinsic evil: and justice in the mind of the just man, the highest intrinsic good: apart from consequences on either side. If you had all held this language from the beginning, and had impressed upon us such persuasion from our childhood, there would have been no necessity for our keeping watch upon each other to prevent injustice. Every man would have been the best watch upon himself, through fear lest by becoming unjust he might take into his own bosom the gravest evil.

Whoever reads this, will see that Plato does not intend (as most of his commentators assert) that the arguments which Socrates combats in the Republic were the invention of Protagoras, Prodikus, and other Sophists of the Platonic century.

Adeimantus calls upon Socrates to recommend and enforce Justice on its own grounds, and to explain how Justice in itself benefits the mind of the just man.

"Here therefore is a deficiency in the argument on behalf of justice, which I call upon you, Socrates, who have employed all your life in these meditations, to supply. You have declared justice to be good indeed for its consequences, but still more of a good from its own intrinsic nature. Explain how it is good, and how injustice is evil, in its own intrinsic nature: what effect each produces on the mind, so as to deserve such an appellation. Omit all notice of consequences accruing to the just or unjust man, from the opinion, favourable or otherwise, entertained towards him by others. You must even go farther: you must suppose that both of them are misconceived, and that the just man is disgraced and punished as if he were unjust — the unjust man honoured and rewarded as if he were just. This is the only way of testing the real intrinsic value of justice and injustice, considered in their effects upon the mind. If you expatiate on the consequences — if you regard justice as in itself indifferent, but valuable on account of the profitable reputation which it procures, and injustice as in itself profitable, but dangerous to the unjust man from the hostile sentiment and damage which it brings upon him — the real drift of your exhortation will be, to make us aspire to be unjust in reality, but to aim at maintaining a reputation of justice along with it. In that line of argument you will concede substantially the opinion of Thrasymachus — That justice is another man's good, the advantage of the more powerful: and injustice the good or profit of the agent, but detrimental to the weaker."

With the invocation here addressed to Socrates, Adeimantus concludes his discourse. Like Glaukon, he disclaims participation in the sentiments which the speech embodies. Both of them, professing to be dissatisfied with the previous refutation of Thrasymachus by Socrates, call for a deeper exposition of the subject. Both of them then enunciate a doctrine, resembling partially, though not entirely, that of Thrasymachus — but without his offensive manner, and with superior force of argument. They propose it as a difficult problem, which none but Socrates can adequately solve. He accepts the challenge, though with apparent diffidence: and we now enter upon his solution, which occupies the remaining eight books and a half of the Republic. All these last books are in fact expository, though in the broken form of dialogue. The other speakers advance scarce any opinions for Socrates to confute, but simply intervene with expressions of assent, or doubt, or demand for farther information.

Statement of the question as it stands after the speeches of Glaukon and Adeimantus. What Socrates undertakes to prove.

I here repeat the precise state of the question, which is very apt to be lost amidst the mæanderings of a Platonic dialogue.

First, What is Justice? Socrates had declared at the close of the first book, that he did not know what Justice was; and that therefore he could not possibly decide, whether it was a virtue or not:— nor whether the possessor of it was happy or not.

Secondly, To which of the three classes of good things does Justice belong? To the second class — i. e. things good per se, and good also in their consequences? Or to the third class — i. e. things not good per se, but good only in their consequences? Socrates replies (in the beginning of the second book) that it belongs to the second class.

Evidently, these two questions cannot stand together. In answering the second, Socrates presupposes a certain determination of the first; inconsistent with that unqualified ignorance, of which he had just made profession. Socrates now professes to know, not merely that Justice is a good, but to what class of good things it belongs. The first question has thus been tacitly dropped without express solution, and has given place to the second. Yet Socrates, in providing his answer to the second, includes implicitly an answer to the first, so far as to assume that Justice is a good thing, and proceeds to show in what way it is good.

Some say that Justice is good (i.e. that it ensures, or at least contributes to, the happiness of the agent), but not per se: only in its ulterior consequences. Taken per se, it imposes privation, loss, self-denial; diminishing instead of augmenting the agent's happiness. But taken along with its results, this preliminary advance is more than adequately repaid; since without it the agent would not obtain from others that reciprocity of justice, forbearance, and good treatment without which his life would be intolerable.

If this last opinion be granted, Glaukon argues that Justice would indeed be good for weak and middling agents, but not for men of power and energy, who had a good chance of extorting the benefit without paying the antecedent price. And Thrasymachus, carrying this view still farther, assumes that there are in every society men of power who despotise over the rest; and maintains that Justice consists, for the society generally, in obeying the orders of these despots. It is all gain to the strong, all loss to the weak. These latter profit by it in no other way than by saving themselves from farther punishment or ill usage on the part of the strong.

Socrates undertakes to maintain the opposite — That Justice is a good per se, ensuring the happiness of the agent by its direct and intrinsic effects on the mind: whatever its ulterior consequences may be. He maintains indeed that these ulterior consequences are also good: but that they do not constitute the paramount benefit, or the main recommendation of Justice: that the good of Justice per se is much greater. In this point of view, Justice is not less valuable and necessary to the strong than to the weak. He proceeds to show, what Justice is, and how it is beneficial per se to the agent, apart from consequences: also, what Injustice is, and how it is injurious to the agent per se, apart from consequences.

He begins by affirming the analogy between an entire city or community, and each individual man or agent. There is justice (he says) in the entire city — and justice in each individual man. In the city, the characteristics of Justice are stamped in larger letters or magnified, so as to be more easily legible. We will therefore first read them in the city, and then apply the lesson to explain what appears in smaller type in the individual man. We will trace the steps by which a city is generated, in order that we may see how justice and injustice spring up in it.

It is in this way that Plato first conducts us to the formation of a political community. A parallel is assumed between the entire city and each individual man: the city is a man on a great scale — the man is a city on a small scale. Justice belongs both to one and to the other. The city is described and analysed, not merely as a problem for its own sake, but in order that the relation between its constituent parts may throw light on the analogous constituent parts, which are assumed to exist in each individual man

Fundamental principle, to which communities of mankind owe their origin — Reciprocity of want and service between individuals — No individual can suffice to himself.

The fundamental principle (Socrates affirms) to which cities or communities owe their origin, is, existence of wants and necessities in all men. No single man is sufficient for himself: every one is in want of many things, and is therefore compelled to seek communion or partnership with neighbours and auxiliaries. Reciprocal dealings begin: each man gives to others, and receives from others, under the persuasion that it is better for him to do so.

Common needs, helplessness of individuals apart, reciprocity of service when they are brought together — are the generating causes of this nascent association. The simplest association, comprising the mere necessaries of life, will consist only of four or five men: the husbandman, builder, weaver, shoemaker, &c. It is soon found advantageous to all, that each of these should confine himself to his own proper business: that the husbandman should not attempt to build his own house or make his own shoes, but should produce corn enough for all, and exchange his surplus for that of the rest in their respective departments. Each man has his own distinct aptitudes and dispositions; so that he executes both more work and better work, by employing himself exclusively in the avocation for which he is suited. The division of labour thus becomes established, as reciprocally advantageous to all. This principle soon extends itself: new wants arise: the number of different employments is multiplied. Smiths, carpenters, and other artisans, find a place: also shepherds and herdsmen, to provide oxen for the farmer, wool and hides for the weaver and the shoemaker. Presently a farther sub-division of labour is introduced for carrying on exchange and distribution: markets are established: money is coined: foreign merchants will import and export commodities: dealers, men of weak body, and fit for sedentary work, will establish themselves to purchase wholesale the produce brought by the husbandman, and to sell it again by retail in quantities suitable for distribution. Lastly, the complement of the city will be made up by a section of labouring men who do jobs for hire: men of great bodily strength, though not adding much to the intelligence of the community.

It is remarkable that in this first outline of the city Plato recognises only free labour, not slave labour.

Moderate equipment of a sound and healthy city — Few wants.

Such is the full equipment of the sound and healthy city, confined to what is simple and necessary. Those who compose it will have sufficient provision of wheat and barley, for loaves and cakes — of wine to drink —

of clothing and shoes — of houses for shelter, and of myrtle and yew twigs for beds. They will enjoy their cheerful social festivals, with wine, garlands, and hymns to the Gods. They will take care not to beget children in numbers greater than their means, knowing that the consequence thereof must be poverty or war. [48] They will have, as condiment, salt and cheese, olives, figs, and chestnuts, peas, beans, and onions. They will pass their lives in peace, and will die in a healthy old age, bequeathing a similar lot to their children. Justice and injustice, which we are seeking for, will be founded on a certain mode of mutual want and dealing with each other.

You feed your citizens, Socrates (observes Glaukon), as if you were feeding pigs. You must at least supply them with as many sweets and condiments as are common at Athens: and with beds and tables besides.

Enlargement of the city — Multiplied wants and services. First origin of war and strife with neighbours — It arises out of these multiplied wants.

I understand you (replies Socrates): you are not satisfied with a city of genuine simplicity: you want a city luxurious and inflated. Well then — we will suppose it enlarged until it comprehends all the varieties of elegant and costly enjoyment: gold, silver, and ivory: musicians and painters in their various branches: physicians: and all the crowd of attendants required for a society thus enlarged. Such extension of consumption will carry with it a numerous population, who cannot be maintained from the lands belonging to the city. We shall be obliged to make war upon our neighbours and seize some of their lands. They too will do the same by us, if they have acquired luxurious habits. Here we see the first genesis of war, with all its consequent evils: springing from the acquisition of wealth, beyond the limit of necessity. Having war upon our hands, we need soldiers, and a considerable camp of them. Now war is essentially a separate craft and function, requiring to be carried on by persons devoted to it, who have nothing else to do. We laid down from the beginning, that every citizen ought to confine himself exclusively to that business for which he was naturally fit; and that no one could be allowed to engage in two distinct occupations. This rule is above all things essential for the business of war. The soldier must perform the duties of a soldier, and undertake no others.

Separate class of soldiers or Guardians. One man cannot do well more than one business. Character required in the Guardians — Mildness at home with pugnacity against enemies.

The functions of these soldiers are more important than those of any one else. Upon them the security of the whole community depends. They are the Guardians of the city: or rather, those few seniors among them, who are selected from superior merit and experience, and from a more perfect education to exercise command, are the proper Guardians: while the remaining soldiers are their Auxiliaries. These Guardians, or Guardians and their Auxiliaries, must be first chosen with the greatest care, to ensure that they have appropriate natural dispositions: next, their training and education must be continued as well as systematic. Appropriate natural dispositions are difficult to find: for we require the coincidence of qualities which are rarely found together. The Auxiliaries must be mild and gentle towards their fellow citizens, passionate and fierce towards enemies. They must be like generous dogs, full of kindness towards those whom they know, angrily disposed towards those whom they do not know.

Peculiar education necessary, musical as well as gymnastical.

Assuming children of these dispositions to be found, we must provide for them the best training and education. The training must be twofold: musical, addressed to the mind: gymnastical, addressed to the body — pursuant to the distribution dating from ancient times. Music includes all training by means of words or sounds: speech and song, recital and repetition, reading and writing, &c.

This appeal of Plato to antiquity and established custom deserves notice.

Musical education, by fictions as well as by truth. Fictions addressed to the young: the religious legends now circulating are often pernicious: censorship necessary.

The earliest training of every child begins from the stories or fables which he hears recounted: most of which are false, though some among them are true. We must train the child partly by means of falsehood, partly by means of truth: and we must begin first with the falsehood. The tenor of these fictions, which the child first hears, has a powerful effect in determining his future temper and character. But such fictions as are now currently repeated, will tend to corrupt his mind, and to form in him sentiments and opinions adverse to those which we wish him to entertain in after life. We must not allow the invention and circulation of stories at the pleasure of the authors: we must establish a censorship over all authors; licensing only such of their productions as we approve, and excluding all the rest, together with most of those now in circulation.

The fables told by Homer, Hesiod, and other poets, respecting the Gods and Heroes, are in very many cases pernicious, and ought to be suppressed. They are not true; and even were they true, ought not to be mentioned before children. Stories about battles between the Gods and the Giants, or quarrels among the Gods themselves, are mischievous, whether intended as allegories or not: for young hearers cannot discriminate the allegorical from the literal.

I am no poet (continues the Platonic Socrates), nor can I pretend to compose legends myself: but I shall lay down a type of theological orthodoxy, to which all the divine legends in our city must conform. Every poet must proclaim that the Gods are good, and therefore cannot be the cause of anything except good. No poet can be allowed to describe the Gods (according to what we now read in Homer and elsewhere) as dispensing both good and evil to mankind. The Gods must be announced as causes of all the good which exists, but other causes must be found for all the evil: the Gods therefore are causes of comparatively few things, since bad things are far more abundant among us than good. No poetical tale can be tolerated which represents the Gods as assuming the forms of different persons, and going about to deceive men into false beliefs. Falsehood is odious both to Gods and to men: though there are some cases in which it is necessary as a precaution against harm, towards enemies, or even towards friends during seasons of folly or derangement. But none of these exceptional circumstances can apply to the Gods.

The Guardians must not fear death. No terrible descriptions of Hades must be presented to them: no intense sorrow, nor violent nor sensual passion, must be recounted either of Gods or Heroes.

It is indispensable to inspire these youthful minds with courage, and to make them fear death as little as possible. But the terrific descriptions, given by the poets, of Hades and the underworld, are above all things likely to aggravate the fear of death. Such descriptions must therefore be interdicted, as neither true nor useful. Even if poetically striking, they are all the more pernicious to be listened to by youths whom we wish to train up as spirited free-men, fearing enslavement more than death.

We must also prohibit the representations of intense grief and distress, imputed by Homer to Heroes or Gods, to Achilles, Priam, or Zeus, for the death of friends and relatives. A perfectly reasonable man will account death no great evil, either for himself or for his friend: he will be, in a peculiar degree, sufficient to himself for his own happiness, and will therefore endure with comparative equanimity the loss of friends, relatives, or fortune. We must teach youth to be ashamed of indulging in immoderate grief or in violent laughter. We must teach them also veracity and temperance, striking out all those passages in Homer which represent the Gods or Heroes as incontinent, sensual, furiously vindictive, reckless of obligation, or money-loving. The poets must either not recount such proceedings at all, or must not ascribe them to Gods and Heroes.

We have thus prescribed the model to which all poets must accommodate their narratives respecting Gods and Heroes. We ought now to set out a similar model for their narratives respecting men. But this is impossible, until our present investigation is brought to a close: because one of the worst misrepresentations which the poets give of human affairs, is, when they say that there are many men unjust, yet happy — just, yet still miserable:— that successful injustice is profitable, and that justice is a benefit to other persons, but a loss to the agent. We affirm that this is a misrepresentation; but we cannot assume it as such at present, since the present enquiry is intended to prove that it is so.

From the substance of these stories we pass to the style and manner. The poet will recount either in his own person, by simple narrative: or he will assume the characters and speak in the names of others, thus making his composition imitative. He will imitate every diversity of character, good and bad, wise and foolish. This however cannot be tolerated in our city. We can permit no imitation except that of the reasonable and virtuous man. Every man in our city exercises one simple function: we have no double-faced or many-faced citizens. We shall respectfully dismiss the poet who captivates us by variety of characters, and shall be satisfied with the dry recital of simple stories useful in their tendency, expressing the feeling of the reasonable man and no other.

Rhythm and Melody regulated. None but simple and grave music allowed: only the Dorian and Phrygian moods, with the lyre and harp.

We must farther regulate the style of the Odes and Songs, consistent with what has been already laid down. Having prescribed what the sense of the words must be, we must now give directions about melody and rhythm. We shall permit nothing but simple music, calculated less to please the ear, than to inspire grave, dignified, and resolute sentiment. We shall not allow either the wailing Lydian, or the soft and convivial Ionic mood: but only the Phrygian and Dorian moods. Nor shall we tolerate either the fife, or complicated stringed instruments: nothing except the lyre and harp, with the panspipe for rural abodes. The rhythm or measure must also be simple, suitable to the movements of a calm and moderate man. Both good rhythm, graceful and elegant speaking, and excellence of sense, flow from good and virtuous dispositions, tending to inspire the same dispositions in others: just as bad rhythm, ungraceful and indecorous demeanour, defective proportion, &c., are companions of bad speech and bad dispositions.

Contrasts of this kind pervade not only speech and song, but also every branch of visible art: painting, architecture, weaving, embroidery, pottery, and even the natural bodies of animals and plants. In all of them we distinguish grace and beauty, the accompaniments of a good and sober disposition — from ungracefulness and deformity, visible signs of the contrary disposition. Now our youthful Guardians, if they are ever to become qualified for their functions, must be trained to recognise and copy such grace and beauty. [68] For this purpose our poets, painters, architects, and artisans, must be prohibited from embodying in their works any ungraceful or unseemly type. None will be tolerated as artists, except such as can detect and embody the type of the beautiful. Our youth will thus insensibly contract exclusive familiarity, both through the eye and through the ear, with beauty in its various manifestations: so that their minds will be brought into harmonious preparation for the subsequent influence of beautiful discourse.

This indeed (continues Socrates) is the principal benefit arising from musical tuition, that the internal mind of a youth becomes imbued with rhythm and harmony. Hence he learns to commend and be delighted with the beautiful, and to hate and blame what is ugly; before he is able to render any reason for his sentiments: so that when mature age arrives, his sentiments are found in unison with what reason enjoins, and already predisposed to welcome it. He becomes qualified to recognise the Forms of Temperance, Courage, Liberality, Magnanimity, and their embodiments in particular persons. To a man brought up in such sentiments, no spectacle can be so lovely as that of youths combining beauty of mental disposition with beauty of exterior form. He may indeed tolerate some defects in the body, but none in the mind. His love, being genuine and growing out of musical and regulated contemplations, will attach itself to what is tempered and beautiful; not to the intense pleasures of sense, which are inconsistent with all temperance. Such will be the attachments subsisting in our city, and such is the final purpose of musical training — To generate love of the Beautiful.

We next proceed to gymnastic training, which must be simple, for the body — just as our musical training was simple for the mind. We cannot admit luxuries and refinements either in the one or in the other. Our gymnastics must impart health and strength to the body, as our music imparts sobriety to the mind. We shall require few courts of justice and few physicians. Where many of either are needed, this is a proof that ill-regulated minds and diseased bodies abound. It would be a disgrace to our Guardians if they could not agree on what is right and proper among themselves, without appealing to the decision of others. Physicians too are only needed for wounds or other temporary and special diseases. We cannot admit those refinements of the medical art, and that elaborate nomenclature and classification of diseases, which the clever sons of Aesculapius have invented, in times more recent than Aesculapius himself.

He knew, but despised, such artifices; which, having been devised chiefly by Herodikus, serve only to keep alive sickly and suffering men — who are disqualified for all active duty through the necessity of perpetual attention to health, — and whose lives are worthless both to themselves and to the city. In our city, every man has his distinct and special function, which he is required to discharge. If he be disqualified by some temporary ailment, the medical art will be well employed in relieving and restoring him to activity: but he has no leisure to pass his life as a patient under cure, and if he be permanently unfit to fill his place in the established cycle of duties, his life ought not to be prolonged by art, since it is useless to himself and useless to the city also. Our medical treatment for evils of the body, and our judicial treatment for evils of the mind, must be governed by analogous principles. Where body and mind are sound at bottom, we must do our best to heal temporary derangements: but if a man has a body radically unsound, he must be suffered to die — and if he has a mind unsound and incurable, he must be put to death by ourselves.

Value of Gymnastic in imparting courage to the mind — Gymnastic and Music necessary to correct each other.

Gymnastic training does some good in strengthening the body, but it is still more serviceable in imparting force and courage to the mind. As regards the mind, gymnastic and music form the indispensable supplement one to the other. Gymnastic by itself makes a man's nature too savage and violent: he acquires no relish for knowledge, comes to hate discourse, and disdains verbal persuasion. On the other hand, music by itself makes him soft, cowardly, and sensitive, unfit for danger or hardship. The judicious combination of the two is the only way to form a well-balanced mind and character.

Such must be the training, from childhood upwards, of these Guardians and Auxiliaries of our city. We must now select from among these men themselves, a few to be Governors or chief Guardians; the rest serving as auxiliaries. The oldest and best of them must be chosen for this purpose, those who possess in the greatest perfection the qualities requisite for Guardians. They must be intelligent, capable, and solicitous for the welfare of the city. Now a man is solicitous for the welfare of that which he loves. He loves those whose interests he believes to be the same as his own; those whose well-being he believes to coincide with his own well-being — the contrary, with the contrary. The Guardians chosen for Chiefs must be those who are most thoroughly penetrated with such sympathy; who have preserved most tenaciously throughout all their lives the resolution to do every thing which they think best for the city, and nothing which they do not think to be best for it. They must be watched and tested in temptations pleasurable as well as painful, to see whether they depart from this resolution. The elders who have best stood such trial, must be named Governors. These few will be the chief Guardians or Rulers: the remaining Guardians will be their auxiliaries or soldiers, acting under their orders.

Fundamental creed required to be planted in the minds of all the citizens respecting their breed and relationship.

Here then our city will take its start; the body of Guardians marching in arms under the orders of their Chiefs, and encamping in a convenient acropolis, from whence they may best be able to keep order in the interior and to repel foreign attack. But it is indispensable that both they and the remaining citizens should be made to believe a certain tale, — which yet is altogether fictitious and of our own invention. They must be told that they are all earthborn, sprung from the very soil which they inhabit: all therefore brethren, from the same mother Earth: the auxiliaries or soldiers, born with their arms and equipments. But there was this difference (we shall tell them) between the different brethren. Those fit for Chiefs or Rulers, were born with a certain mixture of gold in their constitution: those fit for soldiers or Guardians simply, with a like mixture of silver: the remainder, with brass or iron. In most individual cases, each of these classes will beget an offspring like themselves. But exceptions will sometimes happen, in which the golden man will have a child of silver, or brass, — or the brazen or iron man, a child of nobler metal than his own. Now it is of the last importance that the Rulers should keep watch to preserve the purity of these breeds. If any one of their own children should turn out to be of brass or iron, they must place him out among the husbandmen or artisans: if any of the brazen or iron men should chance to produce a child of gold, they must receive him among themselves, since he belongs to them by his natural constitution. Upon the maintenance of these distinct breeds, each in its appropriate function, depends the entire fate of the city: for an oracle has declared that it will perish, if ever iron or brazen men shall become its Guardians.

How is such a fiction to be accredited in the first instance? Difficulty extreme, of first beginning; but if once accredited, it will easily transmit itself by tradition.

It is indispensable (continues Socrates) that this fiction should be circulated and accredited, as the fundamental, consecrated, unquestioned, creed of the whole city, from which the feeling of harmony and brotherhood among the citizens springs. But how can we implant such unanimous and unshaken belief, in a story altogether untrue? Similar fables have often obtained implicit credence in past times: but no such case has happened of late, and I question whether it could happen now. The postulate seems extravagant: do you see by what means it could be realised? — I see no means (replies Glaukon) by which the fiction could be first passed off and accredited, among these men themselves: but if it were once firmly implanted, in any one generation, I do not doubt that their children and descendants would inherit and perpetuate it. We must be satisfied with thus much (replies Socrates): assuming the thing to be done, and leaving the process of implanting it to spontaneous and oracular inspiration. I now proceed with the description of the city.

The Rulers and their auxiliaries the body of Guardians must be lodged in residences, sufficient for shelter and comfort, yet suitable for military men, and not for tradesmen. Every arrangement must be made for rendering them faithful guardians of the remaining citizens. It would be awful indeed, if they were to employ their superior strength in oppressing instead of protecting the flock entrusted to them. To ensure their gentleness and fidelity, the most essential guarantee is to be found in the good musical and gymnastic training which they will have received. But this alone will not suffice. All the conditions of their lives must be so determined, that they shall have the least possible motive for committing injustice towards the other citizens.

None of them must have any separate property of his own, unless in special case of proved necessity: nor any house or store cupboard from which others are excluded. They must receive, from the contributions of the remaining citizens, sufficient subsistence for the health and comfort of military men, but nothing beyond. They must live together in their camp or barrack, and dine together at a public mess-table. They must not be allowed either to possess gold and silver, or to drink in cups of those metals, or to wear them as appendages to clothing, or even to have them under the same roof. They must be told, that these metals, though not forbidden to the other citizens, are forbidden to them, because they have permanently inherent in their mental constitution the divine gold and silver, which would be corrupted by intermixture with human.

If the Guardians fail in these precautions, and acquire private interests, the city will be ruined.

If these precautions be maintained, the Guardians may be secure themselves, and may uphold in security the entire city. But if the precautions be relinquished — if the Guardians or Soldiers acquire separate property in lands, houses, and money — they will then become householders and husbandmen instead of Guardians or Soldiers: hostile masters, instead of allies and protectors to their fellow-citizens. They will hate their fellow-citizens, and be hated by them in return: they will conspire against them, and will be themselves conspired against. In this manner they will pass their lives, dreading their enemies within far more than their enemies without. They, and the whole city along with them, will be perpetually on the brink of destruction.

Complete unity of the city, every man performing his own special function.
But surely (remarks Adeimantus), according to this picture, your Guardians or Soldiers, though masters of all the city, will be worse off than any of the other citizens. They will be deprived of those means of happiness which the others are allowed to enjoy. Perhaps they will (replies Socrates): yet I should not be surprised if they were to be the happiest of all. Be that as it may, however, my purpose is, not to make them especially happy, but to make the whole city happy. The Guardians can enjoy only such happiness as consists with the due performance of their functions as Guardians. Every man in our city must perform his appropriate function, and must be content with such happiness as his disposition will admit, subject to this condition. [88] In regard to all the citizens without exception, it must be the duty of the Guardians to keep out both riches and poverty, both of which spoil the character of every one. No one must be rich, and no one must be poor. In case of war, the constant discipline of our soldiers will be of more avail than money, in making them efficient combatants against other cities. Moreover, other cities are divided against themselves: each is many cities, and not one: poor and rich are at variance with each other, and various fractions of each of these classes against other fractions. Our city alone, constituted as I propose, will be really and truly One. It will thus be the greatest of all cities, even though it have only one thousand fighting men. It may be permitted to increase, so long as it will preserve its complete unity, but no farther. Farthermore, each of our citizens is one and not many: confined to that special function for which he is qualified by his nature.

The maintenance of the city depends upon that of the habits, character, and education of the Guardians.

It will devolve upon our Guardians to keep up this form of communion unimpaired; and they will have no difficulty in doing so, as long as they maintain their own education and training unimpaired. No change must be allowed either in the musical or gymnastic training: especially not in the former, where changes are apt to creep in, with pernicious effect. Upon this education depends the character and competence of the Guardians. They will provide legislation in detail, which will be good, if their general character is good — bad, on the contrary supposition. If their character and the constitution of the city be defective at the bottom, it is useless for us to prescribe regulations of detail, as we would do for sick men. The laws in detail cannot be good, while the general constitution of the city is bad. Those teachers are mistaken who exhort us to correct the former, but to leave the latter untouched.

Religious legislation — Consult the Delphian Apollo.

In regard to religious legislation — the raising of temples, arrangement of sacrifices, &c. — we must consult Apollo at Delphi, and obey what he directs. We know nothing ourselves about these matters, nor is there any other authority equally trustworthy.

Our city is now constituted and peopled (continues Socrates). We mast examine it, and see where we can find Justice and Injustice — reverting to our original problem, which was, to know what each of them was, and which of the two conferred happiness. Now assuming our city to be rightly constituted, it will be perfectly good: that is, it will be wise, courageous, temperate, and just. These four constituents cover the whole: accordingly, if we can discover and set out Wisdom, Courage, and Temperance — that which remains afterwards will be Justice.

First, we can easily see where Wisdom resides. The city includes in itself a great variety of cognitions, corresponding to all the different functions in which its citizens are employed. But it is not called wise, from its knowledge of husbandry, or of brazier's and carpenter's craft: since these are specialties which cover only a small fraction of its total proceedings. It is called wise, or well-advised, from that variety of intelligence or cognition which directs it as a whole, in its entire affairs: that is, the intelligence possessed by the chief Guardians or Rulers. Now the number of persons possessing this variety of intelligence is smaller than the number of those who possess any other variety. The wisdom of the entire city resides in this very small presiding fraction, and in them alone.

Next, we can also discern without difficulty in what fraction of the city Courage resides. The city is called courageous from the valour of those Guardians or Soldiers upon whom its defence rests. These men will have learnt, in the course of their training, what are really legitimate objects of fear, and what are not legitimate objects of fear. To such convictions they will resolutely adhere, through the force of mind implanted by their training, in defiance of all disturbing impulses. It is these right convictions, respecting the legitimate objects of fear, which I (says Socrates) call true political courage, when they are designedly inculcated and worked in by regular educational authority: when they spring up without any rational foundation, as in animals or slaves, I do not call them Courage. The Courage of the entire city thus resides in its Guardians or Soldiers.

Thirdly, wherein resides the Temperance of the city? Temperance implies a due relation, proportion, or accord, between different elements. The temperate man is called superior to himself: but this expression, on first hearing, seems unmeaning, since the man must also be inferior to himself. But the expression acquires a definite meaning, when we recognise it as implying that there are in the same man's mind better and worse elements: and that when the better rules over the worse, he is called superior to himself, or temperate — when the worse rules over the better, he is called inferior to himself, or intemperate. Our city will be temperate, because the better part of it, though smaller in number, rules over the worse and inferior part, numerically greater. The pleasures, pains, and desires of our few Rulers, which are moderate and reasonable, are preponderant: controuling those of the Many, which are miscellaneous, irregular, and violent. And this command is exercised with the perfect consent and good-will of the subordinates. The Many are not less willing to obey than the Few to command. There is perfect unanimity between them as to the point — Who ought to command, and who ought to obey? It is this unanimity which constitutes the temperance of the city: which thus resides, not in any one section of the city, like Courage and Wisdom, but in all sections alike: each recognising and discharging its legitimate function.

There remains only Justice for us to discover. Wherein does the Justice of the city reside? Not far off. Its justice consists in that which we pointed out at first as the fundamental characteristic of the city, when we required each citizen to discharge one function, and one alone — that for which he was best fitted by nature. That each citizen shall do his own work, and not meddle with others in their work — that each shall enjoy his own property, as well as do his own work — this is true Justice. It is the fundamental condition without which neither temperance, nor courage, nor wisdom could exist; and it fills up the good remaining after we have allowed for the effects of the preceding three.100 All the four are alike indispensable to make up the entire Good of the city: Justice, or each person (man, woman, freeman, slave, craftsman, guardian) doing his or her own work — Temperance, or unanimity as to command and obedience between Chiefs, Guardians, and the remaining citizens — Courage, or the adherence of the Guardians to right reason, respecting what is terrible and not terrible — Wisdom, or the tutelary superintendence of the Chiefs, who protect each person in the enjoyment of his own property.

As justice consists in each person doing his own work, and not meddling with that of another — so injustice occurs, when a person undertakes the work of another instead of his own, or in addition to his own. The mischief is not great, when such interference takes place only in the subordinate functions: when, for example, the carpenter pretends to do the work of the shoemaker, or vice versâ; or when either of them undertake both. But the mischief becomes grave and deplorable, when a man from the subordinate functions meddles with the higher — when a craftsman, availing himself of some collateral support, wealth or party or strength, thrusts himself into the functions of a soldier or auxiliary — or when the Guardian, by similar artifice, usurps the functions of a Chief — or when any one person combines these several functions all at once in himself. Herein consists the true injustice, ruinous to the city: when the line of demarcation is confounded between these three classes — men of business, Guardians, Chiefs. That each of these classes should do its own work, is Justice: that either of them should meddle with the work of the rest, and especially that the subordinate should meddle with the business of the superior, is Injustice, with ruin following in its train. It is from these opposite characteristics that the titles Just or Unjust will be rightfully bestowed upon our city.

Analogy of the city to the individual — Each man is tripartite, having in his mind Reason, Energy, Appetite. These three elements are distinct, and often conflicting.

We must now apply, as we undertook to do, the analogy of the city to the individual. The just man, so far forth as justice is concerned, cannot differ from the just city. He must therefore have in his own individual mind three distinct parts, elements, or classes, corresponding to the three classes above distinguished in the city. But is it the fact that there are in each man three such mental constituents — three different classes, sorts, or varieties, of mind?

To settle this point as it ought to be settled, would require a stricter investigation than our present dialogue will permit: but we may contribute something towards it. It is manifest that there exist different individuals in whom reason, energy (courage or passion), and appetite, are separately and unequally developed: thus in the Thracians there is a predominance of energy or courage — in the Phœnicians of appetite — in the Athenians, of intellect or reason. The question is, whether we employ one and the same mind for all the three — reason, energy, and appetite; or whether we do not employ a different mind or portion of mind, when we exercise reason — another, when we are under the influence of energy — and a third, when we follow appetite.

To determine this question, we must consider that the same thing cannot at the same time do or suffer opposites, in the same respect and with reference to the same thing. The same thing or person cannot at the same time, and in the same respect, both stand still and move. This may be laid down as an universal truth: but since some may not admit it to be so, we will at any rate assume it as an hypothesis. Now in reference to the mind, we experience at the same time various movements or affections contrary to each other: assent and dissent — desire and aversion — the attracting any thing to ourselves, and the repelling it from ourselves: each of these is different from and contrary to the other. As a specimen of desires, we will take thirst. When a man is in this condition, his mind desires nothing else but to drink; and strains entirely towards that object. If there be any thing which drags back his mind when in this condition, it must be something different from that which pulls him forward and attracts him to drink. That which attracts him, and that which repels him, cannot be the same: just as when the archer at the same time pulls his bow towards him and pushes it away from him, it is one of his hands that pulls and another that pushes. Now it often happens that a man athirst refuses to drink: there is something within him that prompts him to drink, and something still more powerful that forbids him. These two cannot be the same: one of them is different from the other: that which prompts is appetite, that which forbids is reason. The rational element of the mind is in like manner something different or distinguishable from all the appetites, which tend towards repletion and pleasure.

Here then we have two distinct species, forms, or kinds, existing in the mind. Besides these two, however, there is a third, distinct from both: Energy, Passion, Courage, which neither belongs to Appetite nor to individual Reason. Each of these three acts apart from, and sometimes in contrariety to, each of the others. There are thus three distinct elements or varieties of mind in the individual — Reason, Energy, Appetite: corresponding to the three constituent portions of the city — The Chiefs or Rulers — The Guardians or Soldiers — The Craftsmen, or the remaining Community. The Wisdom of the city resides in its Elders: that of the individual in his Reason. The Courage of the city resides in its Guardians or Soldiers: that of the individual in his Energy. But in the city as well as in the individual, it is the right and privilege of the rational element to exercise command, because it alone looks to the welfare and advantage of the whole compound: it is the duty of the two other elements — the energetic and the appetitive — to obey. It is moreover the special function of the Guardians in the city to second the Chiefs in enforcing obedience upon the Craftsmen: so also in the individual, it is the special function of Energy or Courage to second Reason in controlling Appetite.

A man is just when these different parts of his mind exercise their appropriate functions without hindrance.

These special functions of the separate parts being laid down, Justice as well as Temperance will appear analogous in the individual and in the city. Both Justice and Temperance reside in all the parts equally: not in one of them exclusively, as Wisdom and Courage reside. Justice and Temperance belong to the subordinate as well as to the dominant parts. Justice exists when each of the parts performs its own function, without encroaching on the function of the others: Temperance exists when all the parts are of one opinion as to the title of the higher or rational element to exercise command.

A man as well as a city is just, when each of his three sorts or varieties of mind confines itself to its own legitimate function: when Reason reigns over and controuls the other two, and when Energy seconds Reason in controuling Appetite. Such a man will not commit fraud, theft, treachery, perjury, or any like proceedings. On the contrary, injustice exists when the parts are in conflict with each other: when either of them encroaches on the function of the other: or when those parts which ought to be subordinate rise in insurrection against that which ought to be superior.

Justice is in the mind what health is in the body, when the parts are so arranged as to controul and be controuled pursuant to the dictates of nature. Injustice is in the mind what disease is in the body, when the parts are so arranged as to controul and be controuled contrary to the dictates of nature. Virtue is thus the health, beauty, good condition of the mind: Vice is the disease, ugliness, weakness, of the mind.

Original question now resumed — Does Justice make a man happy, and Injustice make him miserable, apart from all consequences? Answer — Yes.

Having thus ascertained the nature of justice and injustice, we are now in a condition (continues Socrates) to reply to the question proposed for investigation — Is it profitable to a man to be just and to do justice per se, even though he be not known as just either by Gods or men, and may thus be debarred from the consequences which would ensue if he were known? Or is it profitable to him to be unjust, if he can contrive to escape detection and punishment? We are enabled to answer the first question in the affirmative, and the second question in the negative. As health is the greatest good, and sickness the greatest evil, of body: so Justice is the greatest good, and injustice the greatest evil, of mind. No measure of luxury, wealth, or power, could render life tolerable, if we lost our bodily health: no amount of prosperity could make life tolerable, without mental health or justice. As bodily health is good per se, and sickness evil per se, even apart from its consequences: so justice also is good in itself, and injustice evil in itself, apart from its consequences.

Glaukon requires farther explanation about the condition of the Guardians, in regard to sexual and family ties.

Socrates now assumes the special question of the dialogue to be answered, and the picture of the just or perfect city, as well as of the just or perfect individual, to be completed. He is next proceeding to set forth the contrasts to this picture — that is, the varieties of injustice, or the various modes of depravation and corruption — when he is arrested by Polemarchus and Adeimantus: who call upon him to explain more at large the position of the body of Guardians or Soldiers in the city, in regard to women, children, and the family.

Men and women will live together and perform the duties of Guardians alike — They will receive the same gymnastic and musical training.

In reply, Socrates announces his intention to make such provision as will exclude separate family ties, as well as separate property, among these Guardians. The Guardians will consist both of men and women. The women will receive the same training, both musical and gymnastical, as the men. They will take part both in the bodily exercises of the palæstra, in the military drill, and in the combats of war. Those who deride these naked exercises as preposterous for the female sex, should be reminded (Socrates says) that not long ago it was considered unseemly among the Greeks (as it still is among many of the barbari) for men to expose their naked bodies in the palæstra: but such repugnance has been overpowered by the marked usefulness of the practice: the Kretans first setting the example, next the Lacedæmonians; lastly all other Greeks doing the same.

We maintain the principle which we laid down in the beginning, that one person should perform only one duty — that for which he is best qualified. But there is no one function, or class of functions, for which women as such are peculiarly qualified, or peculiarly disqualified. Between women generally, and men generally, in reference to the discharge of duties, there is no other difference, except that men are superior to women in every thing: the best women will be on a level only with the second-best men, but they will be superior to all men lower than the second best. But among women, as among men, there are great individual differences: one woman is fit for one duty, another for another: and in our city, each must be employed for the duty suitable to her individual disposition. Those who are best qualified by nature for the office of Guardians, must be allotted to that office: they must discharge it along with the men, and must be trained for it by the same education as the men, musical and gymnastical.

If an objector accuses us of proposing arrangements contrary to nature, we not only deny the force of the objection, but we retort the charge. We affirm that the arrangements now existing in society, which restrict all women to a limited number of domestic and family functions, are contrary to nature — and that ours are founded upon the genuine and real dictates of nature. The only difference admissible between men and women, in the joint discharge of the functions of Guardians, is, that the easier portion of such functions must in general be assigned to women, and the more difficult to men, in consequence of the inferiority of the feminine nature.

These intermingled male and female Guardians, in the discharge of their joint functions, will live together in common barracks and at common mess-tables. There must be no separate houses or separate family-relations between them. All are wives or husbands of all: no youth must know his own father, no mature man must know his own son: all the mature men and women are fathers or mothers of all the younger: all of the same age are brothers and sisters. We do not intend, however, that the copulation between them shall take place in a promiscuous and arbitrary manner: we shall establish laws to regulate the intermarriages and breeding. We must copy the example of those who regulate the copulation of horses, dogs, and other animals: we must bring together those who will give existence to the best offspring. We must couple, as often as we can, the men who are best, with the women who are best, both in mind and body; and the men who are least good, with the women who are least good. We must bring up the offspring of the former couples — we must refuse to bring up the offspring of the latter. And such results must be accomplished by underhand arrangements of the Elder Chiefs; so as to be unknown to every one else, in order to prevent discontent and quarrel among the body of the Guardians. These Elders will celebrate periodical festivals, in which they will bring together the fitting brides and bridegrooms, under solemn hymns and sacrifices. They must regulate the number of marriages in such manner as to keep the total list of Guardians as much as possible without increase as well as without diminution.

The Elders must make an artful use of the lot, so that these couplings shall appear to every one else the effect of chance. Distinguished warriors must be rewarded with a larger licence of copulation with different women, which will produce the farther advantage of having as many children as possible born from their procreation. All the children as soon as born must be consigned to the Chiefs or Elders, male and female, who will conceal in some convenient manner those who are born either from the worst couples or with any bodily imperfection: while they place the offspring of the best couples in special outbuildings under the charge of nurses. Those mothers who are full of milk will be brought here to give suck, but every precaution will be taken that none of them shall know her own child: wet-nurses will also be provided in addition, to ensure a full supply: but all the care of the children will devolve on the public nurses, not on the mothers.

Regulations about age, for procreation — Children brought up under public authority.

The age for such intermarriages, destined to be procreative for the benefit of the city, must be from thirty to fifty-five, for men — from twenty to forty, for women. No man or woman, above or below these limits of age, will be allowed to meddle with the function of intermarriage and procreation for the public; which function must always be conducted under superintendence of the authorities, with proper sacrifice and prayers to the Gods. Nor will any man, even within the licensed age, be allowed to approach any woman except by assignment from the authorities. If any infringement of this law should occur, the offspring arising from it will be pronounced spurious and outcast. But when the above limits of age are passed, both men and women may have intercourse with whomsoever they please, except fathers with daughters or sons with mothers: under condition, however, that no offspring shall be born from such intercourse, or that if any offspring be born, it shall be exposed.

How is the father to know his own daughter (it is asked), or the son his own mother? They cannot know (replies Socrates): but each couple will consider every child born in the seventh month or tenth month after their marriage, as their child, and will address him or her by the appellation of son or daughter. The fathers and mothers will be fathers and mothers of all the children born at that time: the sons and daughters will be in filial relation to all the couples brought together at the given antecedent period

Perfect communion of sentiment and interest among the Guardians — Causes of pleasure and pain the same to all, like parts of the same organism.

The main purpose of such regulations, in respect to family as in respect to property, is to establish the fullest communion between all the Guardians, male and female — and to eliminate as much as possible the feeling of separate interest in any fraction of them. The greatest evil to any city is, that which pulls it to pieces and makes it many instead of one: the greatest good to it is that which binds it together and makes it one. Now what is most efficacious in binding it together, is, community of the causes of pleasure and pain: when each individual feels pleasure from the same causes and on the same occasions as all the rest, and pain in like manner. On the other hand, when the causes of pleasure and pain are distinct, this tends to dissolution; and becomes fatal if the opposition is marked, so that some individuals are much delighted, and others much distressed, under the same circumstances. That city is the best arranged, wherein all the citizens pronounce the words Mine and Not Mine, with reference to the same things: when they coalesce into an unity like the organism of a single individual. To him a blow in the finger is a blow to the whole man: so also in the city, pleasure or pain to any one citizen ought to communicate itself by sympathy as pleasure and pain to all.

Now the Guardians under our regulations will present as much as possible this community of Mine and Not Mine, as well as of pleasures and pains — and this exclusion of the separate individual Mine and Not Mine, as well as of separate pleasures and pains. No individual among them will have either separate property or separate family relationship: each will have both one and the other in common with the rest. No one will have property of his own to be increased, nor a family of his own to be benefited, apart from the rest: all will be as much as possible common recipients of pleasure and pain. All the ordinary causes of dispute and litigation will thus be excluded. If two Guardians of the same age happen to quarrel, they must fight it out: this will discharge their wrath and prevent worse consequences — while at the same time it will encourage attention to gymnastic excellence.

But no younger Guardian will raise his hand against an older Guardian, whom he is taught to reverence as his father, and whom every one else would protect if attacked. If the Guardians maintain harmony among themselves, they will easily ensure it among the remaining inhabitants. Assured of sufficient but modest comforts, the Guardians will be relieved from all struggles for the maintenance of a family, from the arts of trade, and from subservience to the rich.

They will escape all these troubles, and will live a life happier than the envied Olympic victor: for they will gain the victory in an enterprise more illustrious than he undertakes, and they will receive from their fellow-citizens fuller maintenance and higher privilege than what is awarded to him, as well as honours after death. Their lives are not to be put in comparison with those of the farmer or the shoemaker. They must not indeed aspire to any happiness incompatible with their condition and duty as Guardians. But that condition will itself involve the highest happiness. And if any silly ambition prompts them to depart from it, they will assuredly change for the worse.

Such is the communion of sexes which must be kept up for the duties of Guardians, and for the exigencies of military defence. As in other races of animals, males and females must go out to fight, and each will inspire the other with bravery. The children must be taken out on horseback to see the encounters from a distance, so that they may be kept clear of danger, yet may nevertheless be gradually accustomed to the sight of it. If any one runs away from the field, he must be degraded from the rank of Guardian to that of husbandman or craftsman. If any man suffers himself to be taken prisoner, he is no loss: the enemy may do what they choose with him. When any one distinguishes himself in battle, he shall be received on his return by garlands and by an affectionate welcome from the youth. Should he be slain in battle, he shall be recognised as having become a Dæmon or Demigod (according to the Hesiodic doctrine), and his sepulchre shall be honoured by appropriate solemnities.

In carrying on war, our Guardians will observe a marked difference in their manner of treating Hellenic enemies and barbaric enemies. They will never enslave any Hellenic city, nor hold any Hellenic person in slavery. They will never even strip the body of an Hellenic enemy, except so far as to take his arms. They will never pile up in their temples the arms, nor burn the houses and lands, of Hellenic enemies. They will always keep in mind the members of the Hellenic race as naturally kindred with each other, and bound to aid each other in mutual defence, against Barbaric aliens who are the natural enemies of all of them. They will not think themselves authorised to carry on war as Hellens now do against each other, except when their enemies are Barbaric.

Question — How is the scheme practicable? It is difficult, yet practicable on one condition — That philosophy and political power should come into the same hands.

The task which you impose (says Socrates) is one of great difficulty: even if you grant me, what must be granted, that every reality must fall short of its ideal type. One condition, and one only, is essential to render it practicable: a condition which you may ridicule as preposterous, but which, though not probable, is certainly supposable. Either philosophers must acquire the ruling power, or else the present rulers of mankind must themselves become genuine philosophers. In one or other of these two ways philosophy and political power must come into the into the same hands. Unless such condition be fulfilled, our city can never be made a reality, nor can there ever be any respite of suffering to the human race.

The supremacy which you claim for philosophers (replies Glaukon), will be listened to with repugnance and scorn. But at least you must show who the philosophers are, on whose behalf you invoke such supremacy. You must show that it belongs to them by nature both to pursue philosophy, and to rule in the various cities: and that by nature also, other men ought to obey them as well as to abstain from philosophy.

Characteristic marks of the philosopher — He contemplates and knows Entia or unchangeable Forms, as distinguished from fluctuating particulars or Fientia.

The first requisite for a philosopher (replies Socrates) is, that he shall love and pursue eagerly every sort of knowledge or wisdom, without shrinking from labour for such purpose. But it is not sufficient that he should be eager about hearing tragedies or learning the minor arts. Other men, accomplished and curious, are fond of hearing beautiful sounds and discourses, or of seeing beautiful forms and colours. But the philosopher alone can see or distinguish truth. It is only he who can distinguish the genuine Form or Idea, in which truth consists, from the particular embodiments in which it occurs. These Forms or Ideas exist, eternal and unchangeable. Since Pulchrum is the opposite of Turpe, they must be two, and each of them must be One: the same about Just and Unjust, Good and Evil; each of these is a distinct Form or Idea, existing as One and Unchangeable by itself, but exhibiting itself in appearance as manifold, diverse, and frequently changing, through communion with different objects and events, and through communion of each Form with others. Now the accomplished, but unphilosophical, man cannot see or recognise this Form in itself. He can see only the different particular cases and complications in which it appears embodied. None but the philosopher can contemplate each Form by itself, and discriminate it from the various particulars in conjunction with which it appears. Such philosophers are few in number, but they are the only persons who can be said truly to live. Ordinary and even accomplished men — who recognise beautiful things, but cannot recognise Beauty in itself, nor even follow an instructor who points it out to them — pass their lives in a sort of dream or reverie: for the dreamer, whether asleep or awake, is one who believes what is similar to another thing to be not merely similar, but to be the actual thing itself.

The philosopher alone, who embraces in his mind the one and unchangeable Form or Idea, along with, yet distinguished from, its particular embodiments, possesses knowledge or science. The unphilosophical man, whose mind embraces nothing higher than variable particulars, does not know — but only opines, or has opinions.

Ens alone can be known — Non-Ens is unknowable. That which is midway between Ens and Non-Ens (particulars) is matter only of opinion. Ordinary men attain nothing beyond opinion.

This latter, the unphilosophical man, will not admit what we say. Accordingly, we must prove it to him. You cannot know without knowing Something: that is, Some Ens: for Non-Ens cannot be known. That which is completely and absolutely Ens, is completely and absolutely cognizable: that which is Non-Ens and nowhere, is in every way uncognizable. If then there be anything which is at once Ens and Non-Ens, it will lie midway between these two: it will be something neither absolutely and completely cognizable, nor absolutely and completely uncognizable: it belongs to something between ignorance and science. Now science or knowledge is one thing, its object is, complete Ens.

Opinion is another thing, its object also is different. Knowing and Opining belong, like Sight and Hearing, to the class of Entia called Powers or Faculties, which we and others possess, and by means of which — that is, by means of one or other of them — we accomplish everything that we do accomplish. Now no one of these powers or faculties has either colour or figure, whereby it may be recognised or distinguished from others. Each is known and distinguished, not by what it is in itself, but by what it accomplishes, and by the object to which it has special relation. That which has the same object and accomplishes the same result, I call the same power or faculty: that which has a different object, and accomplishes a different result, I call a different power or faculty. Now Knowing, Cognition, Science, is one of our faculties or powers, and the strongest of all: Opining is another, and a different one. A marked distinction between the two is, that Knowing or Cognition is infallible — Opining is fallible.

Since Cognition is one power or faculty, and Opining another — the object of one must be different from the object of the other. But the object of Cognition is, the Complete Ens: the object of Opining must therefore be, not the Complete Ens, but something different from it. What then is the object of Opining? It is not Complete Ens, but it is still Something. It is not Non-Ens, or Nothing; for Non-Ens or Nothing is not thinkable or opinable: you cannot think or opine, and yet think or opine nothing. Whoever opines or thinks, must opine or think something. Ens is the object of Cognition, Non-Ens is the object of non-Cognition or Ignorance: Opination or Opinion is midway between Cognition and Ignorance, darker than the former, but clearer than the latter. The object of opination is therefore something midway between Ens and Non-Ens.

But what is this Something, midway between Ens and Particulars Non-Ens, and partaking of both — which is the object of Opination? To make out this, we must revert to the case of the unphilosophical man. We have described him, as not believing in the existence of the Form or Idea of Beauty, or Justice per se; not enduring to hear it spoken of as a real Ens and Unum; not knowing anything except of the many diverse particulars, beautiful and just. We must remind him that every one of these particular beautiful things will appear repulsive also: every one of these just and holy particulars, will appear unjust and unholy also. He cannot refuse to admit that each of them will appear under certain circumstances beautiful and ugly, just and unjust, holy and unholy. In like manner, every particular double will appear also a half: every light thing will appear heavy: every little thing great. Of each among these many particulars, if you can truly predicate any one quality about it, you may with equal truth predicate the opposite quality also. Each of them both is, and is not, the substratum of all these different and opposite qualities. You cannot pronounce them to be either one or the other, with fixity and permanence: they are at once both and neither.

Here then we find the appropriate object of Opination: that which is neither Ens nor Non-Ens, but something between both. Particulars are the object of Opination, as distinguished from universal Entities, Forms, or Ideas, which are the object of Cognition. The many, who disbelieve or ignore the existence of these Forms, and whose minds dwell exclusively among particulars — cannot know, but only opine. Their usages and creeds, as to beautiful, just, honourable, float between positive Ens and Non-Ens. It is these intermediate fluctuations which are caught up by their opining faculty, intermediate as it is between Cognition and Ignorance. It is these also, the objects of Opination, which they love and delight in: they neither recognise nor love the objects of Cognition or Knowledge. They are lovers of opinion and its objects, not lovers of Knowledge. The philosopher alone recognises and loves Knowledge and the objects of Knowledge. His mind dwells, not amidst the fluctuating, diverse, and numerous particulars, but in contemplation of the One, Universal, permanent, unchangeable, Form or Idea.

The philosopher will be ardent for all varieties of knowledge — His excellent moral attributes — He will be trained to capacity for active life.

Here is the characteristic difference (continues Socrates) which you required me to point out, between the philosopher and the unphilosophical man, however accomplished. The philosopher sees, knows, and contemplates, the One, Real, unchangeable, Form or Idea: the unphilosophical man knows nothing of this Form per se, and sees only its multifarious manifestations, each perpetually variable and different from all the rest. The philosopher, having present to his mind this type — and approximating to it, as far as may be, the real institutions and practices — will be the person most competent to rule our city: especially as his education will give him farthermore — besides such familiarity with the Form or Type — as large a measure of experience, and as much virtue, as can fall to the lot of the unphilosophical man. The nature and disposition of the true philosopher, if improved by education, will include all the virtue and competence of the practical man. The philosopher is bent on learning everything which can make him familiar with Universal Forms and Essences in their pure state, not floating amidst the confusion of generated and destroyed realities: and with Forms and Essences little as well as great, mean as well as sublime. Devoted to knowledge and truth — hating falsehood — he has little room in his mind for the ordinary desires: he is temperate, indifferent to money, free from all meanness or shabbiness. A man like him, whose contemplations stretch over all time and all essence, thinks human life a small affair, and has no fear of death. He will be just, mild in his demeanour, quick in apprehension, retentive in memory, elegant in his tastes and movements. All these excellences will be united in the philosophers to whom we confide the rule of our city.

Adeimantus does not dispute the conclusion, but remarks that it is at variance with actual facts — Existing philosophers are either worthless pretenders, or when they are good, useless.

It is impossible, Socrates (remarks Adeimantus), to answer in the negative to your questions. Nevertheless we who hear and answer, are not convinced of the truth of your conclusion. Unskilled as we are in the interrogatory process, we feel ourselves led astray little by little at each successive question; until at length, through the accumulated effect of such small deviations, we are driven up into a corner without the power of moving, like a bad player at draughts defeated by one superior to himself. Here in this particular case your conclusion has been reached by steps to which we cannot refuse assent. Yet if we look at the facts, we see something quite the reverse as to the actual position of philosophers. Those who study philosophy, not simply as a branch of juvenile education but as a continued occupation throughout life, are in most cases strange creatures, not to say thoroughly unprincipled: while the few of them who are most reasonable, derive nothing from this pursuit which you so much extol, except that they become useless in their respective cities.

Socrates admits the fact to be so — His simile of the able steersman on shipboard, among a disobedient crew.

Yes (replies Socrates), your picture is a correct one. The position of true and reasonable philosophers, in their respective cities, is difficult and uncomfortable. Conceive a ship on her voyage, under the management of a steersman distinguished for force of body as well as for skill in his craft, but not clever in dealing with, or acting upon other men. Conceive the seamen all quarrelling with each other to get possession of the rudder; each man thinking himself qualified to steer, though he has never learnt it — nor had any master in it — nor even believes it to be teachable, but is ready to massacre all who affirm that it is teachable.

Imagine, besides, these seamen importuning the qualified steersman to commit the rudder to them, each being ready to expel or kill any others whom he may prefer to them: and at last proceeding to stupify with wine or drugs the qualified steersman, and then to navigate the vessel themselves according to their own views; feasting plentifully on the stores. These men know nothing of what constitutes true and able steersmanship. They extol, as a perfect steersman, that leader who is most efficacious, either by persuasion or force, in seizing the rudder for them to manage: they despise as useless any one who does not possess this talent. They never reflect that the genuine steersman has enough to do in surmounting the dangers of his own especial art, and in watching the stars and the winds: and that if he is to acquire technical skill and practice adequate to such a purpose, he cannot at the same time possess skill and practice in keeping his hold of the rudder whether the crew are pleased with him or not. Such being the condition of the ship and the crew, you see plainly that they will despise and set aside the true steersman as an useless proser and star-gazer.

The uselessness of the true philosopher is the fault of the citizen, who will not invoke his guidance.

Now the crew of this ship represent the citizens and leaders of our actual cities: the steersman represents the true philosopher. He is, and must be, useless in the ship: but his uselessness is the fault of the crew and not his own. It is not for the true steersman to entreat permission from the seamen, that they will allow him to command; nor for the wise man to solicit employment at the doors of the rich. It is for the sick man, whether he be poor or rich, to ask for the aid of the physician; and for every one who needs to be commanded, to invoke the authority of the person qualified to command. No man really qualified will submit to ask command as a favour.

Thus, Adeimantus (continues Socrates), I have dealt with the first part of your remark, that the true philosopher is an useless man in cities as now constituted: I have shown you this is not his fault — that it could not be otherwise, — and that a man even of the highest aptitude, cannot enjoy reputation among those whose turn of mind is altogether at variance with his own.

I shall now deal with your second observation — That while even the best philosophers are useless, the majority of those who cultivate philosophy are worthless men, who bring upon her merited discredit. I admit that this also is correct; but I shall prove that philosophy is not to be blamed for it.

You will remember the great combination of excellent dispositions, intellectual as well as moral, which I laid down as indispensable to form the fundamental character of the true philosopher. Such a combination is always rare. Even under the best circumstances philosophers must be very few. But these few stand exposed, in our existing cities, to such powerful causes of corruption, that they are prevented from reaching maturity, except by some happy accident. First, each one of those very qualities, which, when combined, constitute the true philosopher, — serves as a cause of corruption, if it exists by itself and apart from the rest. Next, what are called good things, or external advantages, act in the same manner — such as beauty, strength, wealth, powerful connections, &c.

Again, the stronger a man's natural aptitudes and the greater his external advantages, — the better will he become under favourable circumstances, the worse will he become, if circumstances are unfavourable. Heinous iniquity always springs from a powerful nature perverted by bad training: not from a feeble nature, which will produce no great effects either for good or evil. Thus the eminent predispositions, — which, if properly improved, would raise a man to the highest rank in virtue, — will, if planted in an unfavourable soil, produce a master-mind in deeds of iniquity, unless counteracted by some providential interposition.

Mistake of supposing that such perversion arises from the Sophists. Irresistible effect of the public opinion generally, in tempting or forcing a dissenter into orthodoxy.

The multitude treat these latter as men corrupted by the Sophists. But this is a mistake. Neither Sophists nor other private individuals produce mischief worth mentioning. It is the multitude themselves, utterers of these complaints, who are the most active Sophists and teachers: it is they who educate and mould every individual, man and woman, young and old, into such a character as they please. When they are assembled in the public assembly or the dikastery, in the theatre or the camp — when they praise some things and blame others, with vociferation and vehemence echoed from the rocks around — how irresistible will be the impression produced upon the mind of a youth who hears them! No private training which he may have previously received can hold out against it. All will be washed away by this impetuous current of multitudinous praise or blame, which carries him along with it. He will declare honourable or base the same things as they declare to be so: he will adopt the character, and follow the pursuits, which they enjoin. Moreover, if he resists such persuasive influence, these multitudinous teachers and Sophists have stronger pressure in store for him. They punish the disobedient with disgrace, fine, and even death. What other Sophist, or what private exhortation, can contend successfully against teachers such as these? Surely none. The attempt to do so is insane. There neither is, nor has been, nor will be, any individual human disposition educated to virtue in opposition to the training of the multitude: I say human, as distinguished from divine, of which I make exception: for in the existing state of society, any individual who is preserved from these ascendant influences to acquire philosophical excellence, owes his preservation to the divine favour.

The Sophists and other private teachers accept the prevalent orthodoxy, and conform their teaching to it.

Moreover, though the multitude complain of these professional teachers as rivals, and decry them as Sophists — yet we must recollect that such teachers inculcate only the opinions received among the multitude themselves, and extol these same opinions as wisdom. The teachers know nothing of what is really honourable and base, — good and evil, — just and unjust. They distribute all these names only with reference to the opinions of the multitude:— pronouncing those things which please the multitude to be good, and those which displease to be evil, — without furnishing any other rational account. They call things necessary by the name of just and honourable; not knowing the material difference between what is good and what is necessary, nor being able to point out that difference to others. Thus preposterous are the teachers, who count it wisdom to suit the taste and feelings of the multitude, whether in painting or in music or in social affairs. For whoever lives among them, publicly exhibiting either poetry or other performances private or official, thus making the multitude his masters beyond the strict limits of necessity — the consequence is infallible, that he must adapt his works to that which they praise. But whether the works which he executes are really good and honourable, he will be unable to render any tolerable account.

The people generally hate philosophy — A youth who aspires to it will be hated by the people, and persecuted even by his own relatives.

It is therefore the multitude, or the general voice of society — not the Sophists or private teachers, mere echoes of that general voice — which works upon and moulds individuals. Now the multitude cannot tolerate or believe in the existence of those Universals or Forms which the philosopher contemplates. They know only the many particulars, not the One Universal. Incapable of becoming philosophers themselves, they look upon the philosopher with hatred: and this sentiment is adopted by all those so-called philosophers who seek to please them. Under these circumstances, what chance is there that those eminent predispositions, which we pointed out as the foundation of the future philosopher, can ever be matured to their proper result? A youth of such promise, especially if his body be on a par with his mind, will be at once foremost among all his fellows. His relatives and fellow-citizens, eager to make use of him for their own purposes, and anxious to appropriate to themselves his growing force, will besiege him betimes with solicitations and flatteries. Under these influences, if we assume him to be rich, well born, and in a powerful city, he will naturally become intoxicated with unlimited hopes and ambition; fancying himself competent to manage the affairs of all governments, and giving himself the empty airs of a lofty potentate.

If there be any one to give him a quiet hint that he has not yet acquired intelligence, nor can acquire it without labour — he will turn a deaf ear. But suppose that such advice should by chance prevail, in one out of many cases, so that the youth alters his tendencies and devotes himself to philosophy — what will be the conduct of those who see, that they will thereby be deprived of his usefulness and party-service, towards their own views? They will leave no means untried to prevent him from following the advice, and even to ruin the adviser, by private conspiracy and judicial prosecution.

It is impossible that the young man can really turn to philosophy, against obstructions thus powerful. You see that those very excellences and advantages, which form the initial point of the growing philosopher, become means and temptations for corrupting him. The best natures, rare as they always are, become thus not only ruined, but turned into instruments of evil. For the same men (as I have already said) who, under favourable training, would have done the greatest good, become perpetrators of the greatest evil, if they are badly placed. Small men will do nothing important, either in the one way or the other.

The really great minds are thus driven away from the path of philosophy — which is left to empty pretenders.

It is thus that the path of philosophy is deserted by those who ought to have trodden it, and who pervert their exalted powers to unworthy objects. That path — being left vacant, yet still full of imposing titles and pretensions, and carrying a show of superior dignity as compared with the vulgar professions — becomes invaded by interlopers of inferior worth and ability, who quit their own small craft, and set up as philosophers. Such men, poorly endowed by nature, and debased by habits of trade, exhibit themselves, in their self-assumed exaltation as philosophers, like a slave recently manumitted, who has put on new clothes and married his master's daughter. Having intruded themselves into a career for which they are unfit, they cannot produce any grand or genuine philosophical thoughts, or any thing better than mere neat sophisms, pleasing to the ear. Through them arises the discredit which is now attached to philosophers.

Rare cases in which a highly qualified philosopher remains — Being at variance with public opinion, he can achieve nothing, and is lucky if he can obtain safety by silence.

Amidst such general degradation of philosophy, some few and rare cases are left, in which the pre-eminent natures qualified for philosophy remain by some favourable accident uncorrupted. One of these is Theages, who would have been long ago drawn away from philosophy to active politics, had he not been disqualified by bad health. The restraining Daemon, peculiar to myself (says Socrates), is another case. Such an exceptional man, having once tasted the sweetness and happiness of philosophy, embraces it as an exclusive profession. He sees that the mass of society are wrongheaded — that scarce any one takes wholesome views on social matters — that he can find no partisans to aid him in upholding justice — that while he will not take part in injustice, he is too weak to contend single-handed against the violence of all, and would only become a victim to it without doing any good either to the city or to his friends — like a man who has fallen among wild beasts. On these grounds he stands aloof in his own separate pursuit, like one sheltering himself under a wall against a hurricane of wind and dust. Witnessing the injustice committed by all around, he is content if he can keep himself clear and pure from it during his life here, so as to die with satisfaction and good hopes.

The philosopher must have a community suitable to him, and worthy of him.

True (replies Socrates) — yet nevertheless he can perform no great achievement, unless he meets with a community suited to him. Amidst such a community he will himself rise to greatness, and will preserve the public happiness as well as his own. But there exists no such community anywhere, at the present moment. Not one of those now existing is worthy of a philosophical disposition: which accordingly becomes perverted, and degenerates into a different type adapted to its actual abode, like exotic seed transported to a foreign soil. But if this philosophical disposition were planted in a worthy community, so as to be able to assert its own superior excellence, it would then prove itself truly divine, leaving other dispositions and pursuits behind as merely human.

It must be such a community as Socrates has been describing — But means must be taken to keep up a perpetual succession of philosophers as Rulers.

You mean by a worthy community (observes Adeimantus), such an one as that of which you have been drawing the outline? — I do (replies Socrates): with this addition, already hinted but not explained, that there must always be maintained in it a perpetual supervising authority representing the scheme and purpose of the primitive lawgiver. This authority must consist of philosophers: and the question now arises — difficult but indispensable — how such philosophers are to be trained up and made efficient for the good of the city.

Proper manner of teaching philosophy — Not to begin at a very early age.

The plan now pursued for imparting philosophy is bad. Some do not learn it at all: and even to those who learn it best, the most difficult part (that which relates to debate and discourse) is taught when they are youths just emerging from boyhood, in the intervals of practical business and money-getting.

After that period, in their mature age, they abandon it altogether; they will scarcely so much as go to hear an occasional lecture on the subject, without any effort of their own: accordingly it has all died out within them, when they become mature in years. This manner of teaching philosophy ought to be reversed. In childhood and youth, instruction of an easy character and suitable to that age ought to be imparted; while the greatest care is taken to improve and strengthen the body during its period of growth, as a minister and instrument to philosophy. As age proceeds, and the mind advances to perfection, the mental exercises ought to become more difficult and absorbing. Lastly, when the age of bodily effort passes away, philosophy ought to become the main and principal pursuit.

If the multitude could once see a real, perfect, philosopher, they could not fail to love him: but this never happens.

Most people will hear all this (continues Socrates) with mingled incredulity and repugnance. We cannot wonder that they do so: for they have had no experience of one or a few virtuously trained men ruling in a city suitably prepared. Such combination of philosophical rulers within a community adapted to them, we must assume to be realised. Though difficult, it is noway impracticable: and even the multitude will become reconciled to it, if you explain to them mildly what sort of persons we mean by philosophers. We do not mean such persons as the multitude now call by that name; interlopers in the pursuit, violent in dispute and quarrel with each other, and perpetually talking personal scandal. The multitude cannot hate a philosophical temper such as we depict, when they once come to know it — a man who, indifferent to all party disputes, dwells in contemplation of the Universal Forms, and tries to mould himself and others into harmony with them.

Such a philosopher will not pretend to make regulations, either for a city or for an individual, until he has purified it thoroughly. He will then make regulations framed upon the type of the Eternal Forms — Justice, Temperance, Beauty — adapting them as well as he can to human exigencies. The multitude, when they know what is really meant, will become perfectly reconciled to it. One single prince, if he rises so as to become a philosopher, and has a consenting community, will suffice to introduce the system which we have been describing. So fortunate an accident can undoubtedly occur but seldom; yet it is not impossible, and one day or other it will really occur.

Course of training in the Platonic city, for imparting philosophy to the Rulers. They must be taught to ascend to the Idea of Good. But what is Good?

I must now (continues Socrates) explain more in detail the studies and training through which these preservers Rulers of our city, the complete philosophers, must be created. The most perfect among the Guardians, after having been tested by years of exercises and temptations of various kinds, will occupy that distinguished place. Very few will be found uniting those distinct and almost incompatible excellences which qualify them for the post. They must give proof of self-command against pleasures as well as pains, and of competence to deal with the highest studies. But what are the highest studies? What is the supreme object of knowledge? It is the Idea of

Good — the Form of Good: to the acquisition of which our philosophers must be trained to ascend, however laborious and difficult the process may be. Neither justice nor any thing else can be useful or profitable, unless we superadd to them a knowledge of the Idea of Good: without this, it would profit us nothing to possess all other knowledge.

Ancient disputes upon this point, though every one yearns after Good. Some say Intelligence; some say Pleasure. Neither is satisfactory.

Now as to the question, What Good is? there are great and long-standing disputes. Every mind pursues Good, and does every thing for the sake of it — yet without either knowledge or firm assurance what Good is, and consequently with perpetual failure in deriving benefit from other acquisitions. Most people say that Pleasure is the Good: an ingenious few identify Intelligence with the Good. But neither of these explanations is satisfactory. For when a man says that Intelligence is the Good, our next question to him must be, What sort of Intelligence do you mean? — Intelligence of what? To this he must reply, Intelligence of the Good: which is absurd, since it presumes us to know already what the Good is — the very point which he is pretending to elucidate. Again, he who contends that Pleasure is the Good, is forced in discussion to admit that there are such things as bad pleasures: in other words, that pleasure is sometimes good, sometimes bad. From these doubts and disputes about the real nature of good, we shall require our philosophical Guardians to have emancipated themselves, and to have attained a clear vision. They will be unfit for their post it they do not well know what the Good is, and in what manner just or honourable things come to be good. Our city will have received its final consummation, when it is placed under the superintendence of one who knows what the Good is.

Adeimantus asks what Socrates says. Socrates says that he can not answer: but he compares it by a metaphor to the Sun.

But tell me, Socrates (asks Adeimantus), what do you conceive the Good to be — Intelligence or Pleasure, or any other thing different from these? I do not profess to know (replies Socrates), and cannot tell you. We must decline the problem, What Good itself is? as more arduous than our present impetus will enable us to reach. Nevertheless I will partially supply the deficiency by describing to you the offspring of Good, very like its parent. You will recollect that we have distinguished the Many from the One: the many just particulars, beautiful particulars, from the One Universal Idea or Form, Just per se, Beautiful per se. The many particulars are seen but not conceived: the one Idea is conceived, but not seen. We see the many particulars through the auxiliary agency of light, which emanates from the Sun, the God of the visible world. Our organ and sense of vision are not the Sun itself, but they are akin to the Sun in a greater degree than any of our other senses. They imbibe their peculiar faculty from the influence of the Sun. The Sun furnishes to objects the power of being seen, and to our eyes the power of seeing: we can see no colour unless we turn to objects enlightened by its rays. Moreover it is the Sun which also brings about the generation, the growth, and the nourishment, of these objects, though it is itself out of the limits of generation: it generates and keeps them in existence, besides rendering them visible.

Now the Sun is the offspring and representative of the Idea of Good: what the Sun is in the sensible and visible world, the Idea of Good is in the intelligible or conceivable world. As the Sun not only brings into being the objects of sense, but imparts to them the power of being seen so the Idea of Good brings into being the objects of conception or cognition, imparts to them the power of being known, and to the mind the power of knowing them. It is from the Idea of Good that all knowledge, all truth, and all real essence spring. Yet the Idea of Good is itself extra-essential; out of or beyond the limits of essence, and superior in beauty and dignity both to knowledge and to truth; which are not Good itself, but akin to Good, as vision is akin to the Sun.

The Idea of Good rules the ideal or intelligible world, as the Sun rules the sensible or visible world.

Here then we have two distinct regions or genera; one, the conceivable or intelligible, ruled by the Idea of Good — the other the visible, ruled by the Sun, which is the offspring of Good. Now let us subdivide each of these regions or *genera*, into two portions. The two portions of the visible will be — first, real objects, visible such as animals, plants, works of art, &c. — second, the images or representations of these, such as shadows, reflexions in water or in mirrors, &c. The first of these two subdivisions will be greatly superior in clearness to the second: it will be distinguished from the second as truth is distinguished from not-truth. Matter of knowledge is in the same relation to matter of opinion, as an original to its copy. Next, the conceivable or intelligible region must be subdivided into two portions, similarly related one to the other: the first of these portions will be analogous to the real objects of vision, the second to the images or representations of these objects: the first will thus be the Forms, Ideas, or Realities of Conception or Intellect — the second will be particular images or embodiments thereof.

To the intelligible world there are applicable two distinct modes of procedure — the Geometrical — the Dialectic. Geometrical procedure assumes diagrams.

Now in regard to these two portions of the conceivable or intelligible region, two different procedures of the mind are employed: the pure Dialectic, and the Geometrical, procedure. The Geometer or the Arithmetician begins with certain visible images, lines, figures, or numbered objects, of sense: he takes his departure from certain hypotheses or assumptions, such as given numbers, odd and even — given figures and angles, of three different sorts. He assumes these as data without rendering account of them, or allowing them to be called in question, as if they were self-evident to every one. From these premisses he deduces his conclusions, carrying them down by uncontradicted steps to the solution of the problem which he is examining. But though he has before his eyes the visible parallelogram inscribed on the sand, with its visible diagonal, and though all his propositions are affirmed respecting these — yet what he has really in his mind is something quite different — the Parallelogram per se, or the Form of a Parallelogram — the Form of a Diagonal, &c. The visible figure before him is used only as an image or representative of this self-existent form; which last he can contemplate only in conception, though all his propositions are intended to apply to it. He is unable to take his departure directly from this Form, as from a first principle: he is forced to assume the visible figure as his point of departure, and cannot ascend above it: he treats it as something privileged and self-evident.

Dialectic procedure assumes nothing. It departs from the highest Form, and steps gradually down to the lowest, without meddling with any thing except Forms.

From the geometrical procedure thus described, we must now distinguish the other section — the pure Dialectic. Here the Intellect ascends to the absolute Form, and grasps it directly. Particular assumptions or hypotheses are indeed employed, but only as intervening stepping-stones, by which the Intellect is to ascend to the Form: they are afterwards to be discarded: they are not used here for first principles of reasoning, as they are by the Geometer. The Dialectician uses for his first principle the highest absolute Form; he descends from this to the next highest, and so lower and lower through the orderly gradation of Forms, until he comes to the end or lowest: never employing throughout the whole descent any hypothesis or assumption, nor any illustrative aid from sense. He contemplates and reasons upon the pure intelligible essence, directly and immediately: whereas the Geometer can only contemplate it indirectly and mediately, through the intervening aid of particular assumptions.

Two distinct grades of Cognition — Direct or Superior — Noûs — Indirect or Inferior — Dianoia.

The distinction here indicated between the two different sections of the Intelligible Region, and the two different sections of the Region of Sense — we shall mark (continues Socrates) by appropriate terms. The Dialectician alone has Noûs or Intellect, direct or the highest cognition: he alone grasps and comprehends directly the pure intelligible essence or absolute Form. The Geometer does not ascend to this direct contemplation or intuition of the Form: he knows it only through the medium of particular assumptions, by indirect Cognition or Dianoia; which is a lower faculty than Noûs or Intellect, yet nevertheless higher than Opinion.

Two distinct grades of Opinion also in the Sensible World — Faith or Belief — Conjecture.

As we assign two distinct grades of Cognition to the Intelligible Region, so we also assign two distinct grades of Opinion to the Region of Sense, and its two sections. To the first of these two sections, or to real objects of sense, we assign the highest grade of Opinion, viz.: Faith or Belief. To the second of the two, or to the images of real objects of sense, we assign the lower grade, viz.: Conjecture.

Here then are the four grades. Two grades of Cognition — 1. Noûs, or Direct Cognition. 2. Dianoia, or Indirect Cognition: both of them belonging to the Intelligible Region, and both of them higher than Opinion. Next follow the two grades of Opinion. 3. The higher grade, Faith or Belief. 4. The lower grade, Conjecture. Both the two last belong to the sensible world; the first to real objects, the last to images of those objects.

Distinction between the philosopher and the unphilosophical public, illustrated by the simile of the Cave, and the captives imprisoned therein.

Socrates now proceeds to illustrate the contrast between the philosopher and the unphilosophical or ordinary man, by the memorable simile of the cave and its shadows. Mankind live in a cave, with its aperture directed towards the light of the sun; but they are so chained, that their backs are constantly turned towards this aperture, so that they cannot see the sun and sunlight. What they do see is by means of a fire which is always burning behind them. Between them and this fire there is a wall; along the wall are posted men who carry backwards and forwards representations or images of all sorts of objects; so that the shadows of these objects by the firelight are projected from behind these chained men upon the ground in front of them, and pass to and fro before their vision. All the experience which such chained men acquire, consists in what they observe of the appearance and disappearance, the transition, sequences, and co-existences, of these shadows, which they mistake for truth and realities, having no no acquaintance with any other phenomena.

If now we suppose any one of them to be liberated from his chains, turned round, and brought up to the light of the sun and to real objects — his eyesight would be at first altogether dazzled, confounded, and distressed. Distinguishing as yet nothing clearly, he would believe that the shadows which he had seen in his former state were true and distinct objects, and that the new mode of vision to which he had been suddenly introduced was illusory and unprofitable. He would require a long time to accustom him to daylight: at first his eyes would bear nothing but shadows — next images in the water — then the stars at night — lastly, the full brightness of the Sun. He would learn that it was the Sun which not only gave light, but was the cause of varying seasons, growth, and all the productions of the visible world. And when his mind had been thus opened, he would consider himself much to be envied for the change, looking back with pity on his companions still in the cave. He would think them all miserably ignorant, as being conversant not with realities, but only with the shadows which passed before their eyes. He would have no esteem even for the chosen few in the cave, who were honoured by their fellows as having best observed the co-existences and sequences among these shadows, so as to predict most exactly how the shadows would appear in future.

Moreover if, after having become fully accustomed to daylight and the contemplation of realities, he were to descend again into the cave, his eyesight would be dim and confused in that comparative darkness; so that he would not well recognise the shadows, and would get into disputes about them with his companions. They on their side would deride him as having spoilt his sight as well as his judgment, and would point him out as an example to deter others from emerging out of the cave into daylight. Far from wishing to emerge themselves, they would kill, if they could, any one who tried to unchain them and assist them in escaping.

By this simile (continues Socrates) I intend to illustrate, as far as I can, yet without speaking confidently, the relations of the sensible world to the intelligible world: the world of transitory shadows, dimly seen and admitting only opinion, contrasted with that of unchangeable realities steadily contemplated and known, illuminated by the Idea of Good, which is itself visible in the background, being the cause both of truth in speculation and of rectitude in action. No wonder that the few who can ascend into the intelligible region, amidst the clear contemplations of Truth and Justice per se, are averse to meddle again with the miseries of human affairs and to contend with the opinions formed by ordinary men respecting the shadows of Justice, the reality of which these ordinary men have never seen. There are two causes of temporary confused vision: one, when a man moves out of darkness into light — the other when he moves from light into darkness. It is from the latter cause that the philosopher suffers when he redescends into the obscure cave.

The great purpose of education is to turn a man round from his natural position at the bottom of this dark cave, where he sees nothing but shadows: to fix his eyes in the other direction, and to induce him to ascend into clear daylight. Education does not, as some suppose, either pour knowledge into an empty mind, or impart visual power to blind persons. Men have good eyes, but these eyes are turned in the wrong direction. The clever among them see sharply enough what is before them: but they have nothing before them except shadows, and the sharper their vision the more mischief they do.

What is required is to turn them round and draw them up so as to face the real objects of daylight. Their natural eyesight would then suffice to enable them to see these objects well. The task of our education must be, to turn round the men of superior natural aptitude, and to draw them up into the daylight of realities. Next, when they shall have become sufficiently initiated in truth and philosophy, we must not allow them to bury themselves permanently in such studies — as they will themselves be but too eager to do. We must compel them to come down again into the cave and exercise ascendancy among their companions, for whose benefit their superior mental condition will thus become available.

Coming as they do from the better light, they will, after a little temporary perplexity, be able to see the dim shadows better than those who have never looked at anything else. Having contemplated the true and real Forms of the Just, Beautiful, Good — they will better appreciate the images of these Forms which come and go, pass by and repass in the cave. They will indeed be very reluctant to undertake the duties or exercise the powers of government: their genuine delight is in philosophy; and if left to themselves, they would cultivate nothing else. But such reluctance is in itself one proof that they are the fittest persons to govern. If government be placed in the hands of men eager to possess it, there will be others eager to dispossess them, so that competition and factions will arise. Those who come forward to govern, having no good of their own, and seeking to extract their own good from the exercise of power, are both unworthy of trust and sure to be resisted by opponents of the like disposition. The philosopher alone has his own good in himself. He enjoys a life better than that of a ruler; which life he is compelled to forego when he accepts power and becomes a ruler.

Studies serving as introduction to philosophy — Arithmetic, its awakening power — shock to the mind by felt contradiction.

The main purpose of education, I have said (continues Socrates) is, to turn round the faces of the superior men, and to invite them upwards from darkness to light — from the region of perishable shadows to that of imperishable realities. Now what cognitions, calculated to aid such a purpose, can we find to teach? Gymnastic, music, the vulgar arts, are all useful to be taught: but they do not tend to that which we are here seeking. Arithmetic does so to a certain extent, if properly taught which at present it is not.

It furnishes a stimulus to awaken the dormant intellectual and reflective capacity. Among the variety of sensible phenomena, there are some in which the senses yield a clear and satisfactory judgment, leaving no demand in the mind for anything beyond: there are others in which the senses land us in apparent equivocation, puzzle, and contradiction — so that the mind is stung by this apparent perplexity, and instigated to find a solution by some intellectual effort.

Thus, if we see or feel the fingers of our hand, they always appear to the sense, fingers: in whatever order or manner they may be looked at, there is no contradiction or discrepancy in the judgment of sense. But if we see or feel them as great or small, thick or thin, hard or soft, &c., they then appear differently according as they are seen or felt in different order or under different circumstances. The same object which now appears great, will at another time appear small: it will seem to the sense hard or soft, light or heavy, according as it is seen under different comparisons and relations.

Here then, sense is involved in an apparent contradiction, declaring the same object to be both hard and soft, great and small, light and heavy, &c. The mind, painfully confounded by such a contradiction, is obliged to invoke intellectual reflection to clear it up. Great and small are presented by the sense as inhering in the same object. Are they one thing, or two separate things? Intellectual reflection informs us that they are two: enabling us to conceive separately two things, which to our sense appeared confounded together. Intellectual (or abstract) conception is thus developed in our mind, as distinguished from sense, and as a refuge from the confusion and difficulties of sense, which furnish the stimulus whereby it is awakened.

Now arithmetic, besides its practical usefulness for arrangements of war, includes difficulties and furnishes a stimulus of this nature. We see the same thing both as One and as infinite in multitude: as definite and indefinite in number. We can emerge from these difficulties only by intellectual and abstract reflection. It is for this purpose, and not for purposes of traffic, that our intended philosophers must learn Arithmetic. Their minds must be raised from the confusion of the sensible world to the clear daylight of the intelligible.

In teaching Arithmetic, the master sets before his pupils numbers in the concrete, that is, embodied in visible and tangible objects — so many balls or pebbles. Each of these balls he enumerates as One, though they be unequal in magnitude, and whatever be the magnitude of each. If you remark that the balls are unequal — and that each of them is Many as well as One, being divisible into as many parts as you please — he will laugh at the objection as irrelevant. He will tell you that the units to which his numeration refers are each Unum per se, indivisible and without parts; and all equal among themselves without the least shade of difference. He will add that such units cannot be exhibited to the senses, but can only be conceived by the intellect: that the balls before you are not such units in reality, but serve to suggest and facilitate the effort of abstract conception.In this manner arithmetical teaching conducts us to numbers in the abstract — to the real, intelligible, indivisible unit — the Unum per se.

Geometry conducts the mind towards Universal Ens.

Geometrical teaching conducts the mind to the same order of contemplations; leading it away from variable particulars to unchangeable universal Essence. Some persons extol Geometry chiefly on the ground of its usefulness in applications to practice. But this is a mistake: its real value is in conducing to knowledge, and to elevated contemplations of the mind. It does, however, like Arithmetic, yield useful results in practice: and both of them are farther valuable as auxiliaries to other studies.

Astronomy — how useful — not useful as now taught — must be studied by ideal figures, not by observation.

After Geometry — the measurement of lines and superficial areas — the proper immediate sequel is Stereometry, the measurement of solids. But this latter is nowhere properly honoured and cultivated: though from its intrinsic excellence, it forces its way partially even against public neglect and discouragement. Most persons omit it, and treat Astronomy as if it were the immediate sequel to Geometry: which is a mistake, for Astronomy relates to solid bodies in a state of rotatory movement, and ought to be preceded by the treatment of solid bodies generally. Assuming Stereometry, therefore, as if it existed, we proceed to Astronomy.

Certainly (remarks Glaukon) Astronomy, besides its usefulness in regard to the calendar, and the seasons, must be admitted by every one to carry the mind upwards, to the contemplation of things not below but on high. I do not admit this at all (replies Socrates), as Astronomy is now cultivated: at least in my sense of the words, looking upwards and looking downwards. If a man lies on his back, contemplating the ornaments of the ceiling, he may carry his eyes upward, but not his mind. To look upwards, as I understand it, is to carry the mind away from the contemplation of sensible things, whereof no science is attainable — to the contemplation of intelligible things, entities invisible and unchangeable, which alone are the objects of science. Observation of the stars, such as astronomers now teach, does not fulfil any such condition. The heavenly bodies are the most beautiful of all visible bodies and the most regular of all visible movements, approximating most nearly, though still with a long interval of inferiority, to the ideal figures and movements of genuine and self-existent Forms — quickness, slowness, number, figure, &c., as they are in themselves, not visible to the eye, but conceivable only by reason and intellect.

The movements of the heavenly bodies are exemplifications, approaching nearest to the perfection of these ideal movements, but still falling greatly short of them. They are like visible circles or triangles drawn by some very exact artist; which, however beautiful as works of art, are far from answering to the conditions of the idea and its definition, and from exhibiting exact equality and proportion. So about the movements of the sun and stars: they are comparatively regular, but they are yet bodily and visible, never attaining the perfect sameness and unchangeableness of the intelligible world and its forms. We cannot learn truth by observation of phenomena constantly fluctuating and varying. We must study astronomy, as we do geometry, not by observation, but by mathematical theorems and hypotheses: which is a far more arduous task than astronomy as taught at present. Only in this way can it be made available to improve and strengthen the intellectual organ of the mind.

In like manner (continues Socrates), Acoustics or Harmonics must be studied, not by the ear, listening to and comparing various sounds, but by the contemplative intellect, applying arithmetical relations and theories.

After going through all these different studies, the student will have his mind elevated so as to perceive the affinity of method and principle which pervades them all. In this state he will be prepared for entering on Dialectic, which is the final consummation of his intellectual career. He will then have ascended from the cave into daylight. He will have learnt to see real objects, and ultimately the Sun itself, instead of the dim and transitory shadows below. He will become qualified to grasp the pure Intelligible Form with his pure Intellect alone, without either aid or disturbance from sense. He will acquire that dialectical discursive power which deals exclusively with these Intelligible Forms, carrying on ratiocination by means of them only, with no reference to sensible objects. He will attain at length the last goal of the Dialectician — the contemplation of Bonum per se (the highest perfection and elevation of the Intelligible) with Intellect per se in its full purity: the best part of his mind will have been raised to the contemplation and knowledge of the best and purest entity.

I know not whether I ought to admit your doctrine, Socrates (observes Glaukon). There are difficulties both in admitting and denying it. However, let us assume it for the present. Your next step must be to tell us what is the characteristic function of this Dialectic power — what are its different varieties and ways of proceeding? I would willingly do so (replies Socrates), but you would not be able to follow me. I would lay before you not merely an image of the truth but the very truth itself; as it appears to me at least, whether I am correct or not — for I ought not to be sure of my own correctness.

He answers partially — It is the consummation of all the sciences, raising the student to the contemplation of pure Forms, and especially to that of the highest Form — Good.

But I am sure that the dialectic power is something of the nature which I have described. It is the only force which can make plain the full truth to students who have gone through the preliminary studies that we have described. It is the only study which investigates rationally real forms and essences — what each thing is, truly in itself. Other branches of study are directed either towards the opinions and preferences of men — or towards generation and combination of particular results — or towards upholding of combinations already produced or naturally springing up: while even as to geometry and the other kindred studies, we have seen that as to real essence, they have nothing better than dreams — and that they cannot see it as it is, so long as they take for their principle or point of departure certain assumptions or hypotheses of which they can render no account. The principle being thus unknown, and the conclusion as well as the intermediate items being spun together out of that unknown, how can such a convention deserve the name of Science?

Pursuant to custom, indeed, we call these by the name of Sciences. But they deserve no higher title than that of Intellectual Cognitions, lower than Science, yet higher than mere Opinion. It is the Dialectician alone who discards all assumptions, ascending at once to real essence as his principle and point of departure: defining, and discriminating by appropriate words, each variety of real essence — rendering account of it to others — and carrying it safely through the cross-examining process of question and answer. Whoever cannot discriminate in this way the Idea or Form of Good from every thing else, will have no proper cognition of Good itself, but only, at best, opinions respecting the various shadows of Good. Dialectic — the capacity of discriminating real Forms and maintaining them in cross-examining dialogue is thus the coping-stone, completion, or consummation, of all the other sciences.

The Synoptic view peculiar to the Dialectician.

Scale and duration of various studies for the Guardians, from youth upwards.

The preliminary sciences must be imparted to our Guardians during the earlier years of life, together with such bodily and mental training as may test their energy and perseverance of character.

After the age of twenty, those who have distinguished themselves in the juvenile studies and gymnastics, must be placed in a select class of honour above the rest, and must be initiated in a synoptic view of the affinity pervading all the separate cognitions which have been imparted to them. They must also be introduced to the view of Real Essence and its nature. This is the test of aptitude for Dialectics: it is the synoptic view only, which constitutes the Dialectician.

In these new studies they will continue until thirty years of age: after which a farther selection must be made, of those who have most distinguished themselves. The men selected will be enrolled in a class of yet higher honour, and will be tested by dialectic cross-examination: so that we may discover who among them are competent to apprehend true, pure, and real Essence, renouncing all visual and sensible perceptions. It is important that such Dialectic exercises should be deferred until this advanced age — and not imparted, as they are among us at present, to immature youths: who abuse the license of interrogation, find all their homegrown opinions uncertain, and end by losing all positive convictions.

Our students will remain under such dialectic tuition for five years, until they are thirty-five years of age: after which they must be brought again down into the cave, and constrained to acquire practical experience by undertaking military and administrative functions. In such employments they will spend fifteen years: during which they will undergo still farther scrutiny, to ascertain whether they can act up to their previous training, in spite of all provocations and temptations.

Those who well sustain all these trials will become, at fifty years of age, the finished Elders or Chiefs of the Republic. They will pass their remaining years partly in philosophical contemplations, partly in application of philosophy to the regulation of the city. It is these Elders whose mental eye will have been so trained as to contemplate the Real Essence of Good, and to copy it as an archetype in all their ordinances and administration. They will be the Moderators of the city: but they will perform this function as a matter of duty and necessity — not being at all ambitious of it as a matter of honour.

All these studies, and this education, are common to females as well as males.

What has here been said about the male guardians and philosophers must be understood to apply equally to the female. We recognise no difference in this respect between the two sexes. Those females who have gone through the same education and have shown themselves capable of enduring the same trials as males, will participate, after fifty years of age, in the like philosophical contemplations, and in superintendence of the city.

First formation of the Platonic city — how brought about: difficult, but not impossible.

I have thus shown (Socrates pursues) how the fundamental postulate for our city may be brought about. — That philosophers, a single man or a few, shall become possessed of supreme rule: being sufficiently exalted in character to despise the vulgar gratifications of ambition, and to carry out systematically the dictates of rectitude and justice. The postulate is indeed hard to be realised — yet not impossible. Such philosophical rulers, as a means for first introducing their system into a new city, will send all the inhabitants above ten years old away into the country, reserving only the children, whom they will train up in their own peculiar manners and principles. In this way the city, according to our scheme, will be first formed: when formed, it will itself be happy, and will confer inestimable benefit on the nation to which it belongs.

Plato thus assumes his city, and the individual man forming a parallel to his city, to be perfectly well constituted. Reason, the higher element, exercises steady controul: the lower elements, Energy and Appetite, both acquiesce contentedly in her right to controul, and obey her orders — the former constantly and forwardly — the latter sometimes requiring constraint by the strength of the former.

The city thus formed will last long, but not for ever. After a certain time, it will begin to degenerate. Stages of its degeneracy.

But even under the best possible administration, the city, though it will last long, will not last for ever. Eternal continuance belongs only to Ens; every thing generated must one day or other be destroyed. The fatal period will at length arrive, when the breed of Guardians will degenerate. A series of changes for the worse will then commence, whereby the Platonic city will pass successively into timocracy, oligarchy, democracy, despotism. The first change will be, that the love of individual wealth and landed property will get possession of the Guardians: who, having in themselves the force of the city, will divide the territory among themselves, and reduce the other citizens to dependence and slavery.

They will at the same time retain a part of their former mental training. They will continue their warlike habits and drill: they will be ashamed of their wealth, and will enjoy it only in secret: they will repudiate money-getting occupations as disgraceful. They will devote themselves to the contests of war and political ambition — the rational soul becoming subordinate to the energetic and courageous. The system which thus obtains footing will be analogous to the Spartan and Kretan, which have many admirers. The change in individual character will correspond to this change in the city. Reason partially losing its ascendancy, while energy and appetite both gain ground — an intermediate character is formed in which energy or courage predominates. We have the haughty, domineering, contentious, man.

1. Timocracy and the timocratical individual.
2. Oligarchy, and the oligarchical individual.

Out of this timocracy, or timarchy, the city will next pass into an oligarchy, or government of wealth. The rich will here govern, to the exclusion of the poor. Reason, in the timocracy, was under the dominion of energy or courage: in the oligarchy, it will be under the dominion of appetite. The love of wealth will become predominant, instead of the love of force and aggrandisement. Now the love of wealth is distinctly opposed to the love of virtue: virtue and wealth are like weights in opposite scales. The oligarchical city will lose all its unity, and will consist of a few rich with a multitude of discontented poor ready to rise against them. The character of the individual citizen will undergo a modification similar to that of the collective city. He will be under the rule of appetite: his reason will be only invoked as the servant of appetite, to teach him how he may best enrich himself. He will be frugal, — will abstain from all unnecessary expenditure, even for generous and liberal purposes — and will keep up a fair show of honesty, from the fear of losing what he has already got.

3. Democracy, and the democratical individual.

The oligarchical city will presently be transformed into a democracy, mainly through the abuse and exaggeration of its own ruling impulse — the love of wealth. The rulers, anxious to enrich themselves, rather encourage than check the extravagance of young spendthrifts, to whom they lend money at high interest, or whose property they buy on advantageous terms. In this manner there arises a class of energetic men, with ruined fortunes and habits of indulgence. Such are the adventurers who put themselves at the head of the discontented poor, and overthrow the oligarchy. The ruling few being expelled or put down, a democracy is established with equal franchise, and generally with officers chosen by lot.

The characteristic of the democracy is equal freedom and open speech to all, with liberty to each man to shape his own life as he chooses. Hence there arises a great diversity of individual taste and character. Uniformity of pursuit or conduct is scarcely enforced: there is little restraint upon any one. A man offers himself for office whenever he chooses and not unless he chooses. He is at war or at peace, not by obedience to any public authority, but according to his own individual preference. If he be even condemned by a court of justice, he remains in the city careless of the sentence, which is never enforced against him. This democracy is an equal, agreeable, diversified, society, with little or no government: equal in regard to all — to the good, bad, and indifferent.

So too the democratical individual. The son of one among these frugal and money-getting oligarchs, departing from the habits and disregarding the advice of his father, contracts a taste for expensive and varied indulgences. He loses sight of the distinction between what is necessary, and what is not necessary, in respect to desires and pleasures. If he be of a quiet temperament, not quite out of the reach of advice, he keeps clear of ruinous excess in any one direction; but he gives himself up to a great diversity of successive occupations and amusements, passing from one to the other without discrimination of good from bad, necessary from unnecessary. His life and character thus becomes an agreeable, unconstrained, changeful, comprehensive, miscellany, like the society to which he belongs.

4. Passage from democracy to despotism. Character of the despotic city.

Democracy, like oligarchy, becomes ultimately subverted by an abuse of its own characteristic principle. Freedom is gradually pushed into extravagance and excess, while all other considerations are neglected. No obedience is practised: no authority is recognised. The son feels himself equal to his father, the disciple to his teacher, the metic to the citizen, the wife to her husband, the slave to his master. Nay, even horses, asses, and dogs, go free about, so that they run against you in the road, if you do not make way for them. The laws are not obeyed: every man is his own master.

The subversion of such a democracy arises from the men who rise to be popular leaders in it: violent, ambitious, extravagant, men, who gain the favour of the people by distributing among them confiscations from the propproperty of the rich. The rich, resisting these injustices, become enemies to the constitution: the people, in order to put them down, range themselves under the banners of the most energetic popular leader, who takes advantage of such a position to render himself a despot.

He begins his rule by some acceptable measures, such as abolition of debts, and assignment of lands to the poorer citizens, until he has expelled or destroyed the parties opposed to him. He seeks pretences for foreign war, in order that the people may stand in need of a leader, and may be kept poor by the contributions necessary to sustain war. But presently he finds, or suspects, dissatisfaction among the more liberal spirits. He kills or banishes them as enemies: and to ensure the continuance of his rule, he is under the necessity of dispatching in like manner every citizen prominent either for magnanimity, intelligence, or wealth. Becoming thus odious to all the better citizens, he is obliged to seek support by enlisting a guard of mercenary foreigners and manumitted slaves. He cannot pay his guards, without plundering the temples, extorting perpetual contributions from the people, and grinding them down by severe oppression and suffering. Such is the government of the despot, which Euripides and other poets employ their genius in extolling.

Despotic individual corresponding to that city.

We have now to describe the despotic individual, the parallel of the despotised city. As the democratic individual arises from the son of an oligarchical citizen departing from the frugality of his father and contracting habits of costly indulgence: so the son of this democrat will contract desires still more immoderate and extravagant than his father, and will thus be put into training for the despotic character. He becomes intoxicated by insane appetites, which serve as seconds and auxiliaries to one despotic passion or mania, swaying his whole soul.

To gratify such desires, he spends all his possessions, and then begins to borrow money wherever he can. That resource being exhausted, he procures additional funds by fraud or extortion; he cheats and ruins his father and mother; he resorts to plunder and violence. If such men are only a small minority, amidst citizens of better character, they live by committing crimes on the smaller scale. But if they are more numerous, they set up as a despot the most unprincipled and energetic of their number, and become his agents for the enslavement of their fellow-citizens. The despotic man passes his life always in the company of masters, or instruments, or flatterers: he knows neither freedom nor true friendship — nothing but the relation of master and slave. The despot is the worst and most unjust of mankind: the longer he continues despot, the worse he becomes.

We have thus gone through the four successive depravations which our perfect city will undergo — timocracy, oligarchy, democracy, despotism. Step by step we have passed from the best to the worst — from one extreme to the other. As is the city, so is the individual citizen — good or bad: the despotic city is like the despotic individual, — and so about the rest. Now it remains to decide whether in each case happiness and misery is proportioned to good and evil: whether the best is the happiest, the worst the most miserable, — and so proportionally about the intermediate. On this point there is much difference of opinion.

Misery of the despotised city.

If we look at the condition of the despotised city, it plainly exhibits the extreme of misery; while our model city presents the extreme of happiness. Every one in the despotised city is miserable, according to universal admission, except the despot himself with his immediate favourites and guards. To be sure, in the eyes of superficial observers, the despots with these few favourites will appear perfectly happy and enviable. But if we penetrate beyond this false exterior show, and follow him into his interior, we shall find him too not less miserable than those over whom he tyrannises.

What is true of the despotised city, is true also of the despotising individual. The best parts of his mind are under subjection to the worst: the rational mind is trampled down by the appetitive mind, with its insane and unsatisfied cravings. He is full of perpetual perturbation, anxiety, and fear; grief when he fails, repentance even after he has succeeded. Speaking of his mind as a whole, he never does what he really wishes for the rational element, which alone can ensure satisfaction to the whole mind, and guide to the attainment of his real wishes, is enslaved by furious momentary impulses.

The man of despotical mind is thus miserable; and most of all miserable, the more completely he succeeds in subjugating his fellow-citizens and becoming a despot in reality. Knowing himself to be hated by everyone, he lives in constant fear of enemies within as well as enemies without, against whom he can obtain support only by courting the vilest of men as partisans. Though greedy of all sorts of enjoyment, he cannot venture to leave his city, or visit any of the frequented public festivals. He lives indoors like a woman, envying those who can go abroad and enjoy these spectacles.

He is in reality the poorest and most destitute of men, having the most vehement desires, which he can never satisfy. Such is the despot who, not being master even of himself, becomes master of others: in reality, the most wretched of men, though he may appear happy to superficial judges who look only at external show.

Conclusion

Thus then (concludes Socrates) we may affirm with confidence, having reference to the five distinct cities above described — (1. The Model-City, regal or aristocratical. 2. Timocracy. 3. Oligarchy. 4. Democracy. 5. Despotism) — that the first of these is happy, and the last miserable: the three intermediate cities being more or less happy in the order which they occupy from the first to the last.

The Just Man is happy in and through his Justice, however he may be treated by others. The Unjust Man, miserable.

Each of these cities has its parallel in an individual citizen. The individual citizen corresponding to the first is happy — he who corresponds to the last is miserable: and so proportionally for the individual corresponding to the three intermediate cities. He is happy or miserable, in and through himself, or essentially; whether he be known to Gods and men or not — whatever may be the sentiment entertained of him by others.

There are two other lines of argument (continues Socrates) establishing the same conclusion.

Other arguments proving the same conclusion — Pleasures of Intelligence are the best of all pleasures.

1. We have seen that both the collective city and the individual mind are distributed into three portions: Reason, Energy, Appetite. Each of these portions has its own peculiar pleasures and pains, desires and aversions, beginnings or principles of action: Love of Knowledge: Love of Honour: Love of Gain. If you question men in whom these three varieties of temper respectively preponderate, each of them will extol the pleasures of his own department above those belonging to the other two. The lover of wealth will declare the pleasures of acquisition and appetite to be far greater than those of honour or of knowledge: each of the other two will say the same for himself, and for the pleasures of his own department. Here then the question is opened, Which of the three is in the right? Which of the three varieties of pleasure and modes of life is the more honourable or base, the better or worse, the more pleasurable or painful? By what criterion, or by whose

judgment, is this question to be decided? It must be decided by experience, intelligence and rational discourse. Now it is certain that the lover of knowledge, or the philosopher, has greater experience of all the three varieties of pleasure than is possessed by either of the other two men. He must in his younger days have tasted and tried the pleasures of both; but the other two have never tasted his.

Moreover, each of the three acquires more or less of honour, if he succeeds in his own pursuits: accordingly the pleasures belonging to the love of honour are shared, and may be appreciated, by the philosopher; while the lover of honour as such, has no sense for the pleasures of philosophy. In the range of personal experience, therefore, the philosopher surpasses the other two: he surpasses them no less in exercised intelligence, and in rational discourse, which is his own principal instrument. If wealth and profit furnished the proper means of judgment, the money-lover would have been the best judge of the three: if honour and victory furnished the proper means, we should consult the lover of honour: but experience, intelligence, and rational discourse, have been shown to be the means — and therefore it is plain that the philosopher is a better authority than either of the other two. His verdict must be considered as final. He will assuredly tell us, that the pleasures belonging to the love of knowledge are the greatest: those belonging to the love of honour and power, the next: those belonging to the love of money and to appetite, the least.

They are the only pleasures completely true and pure. Comparison of pleasure and pain with neutrality. Prevalent illusions.

2. The second argument, establishing the same conclusion, is as follows:— No pleasures, except those belonging to philosophy or the love of wisdom, are completely true and pure. All the other pleasures are mere shadowy outlines, looking like pleasure at a distance, but not really pleasures when you contemplate them closely. Pleasure and pain are two conditions opposite to each other. Between them both is another state, neither one nor the other, called neutrality or indifference. Now a man who has been sick and is convalescent, will tell you that nothing is more pleasurable than being in health, but that he did not know what the pleasure of it was, until he became sick. So too men in pain affirm that nothing is more pleasurable than relief from pain. When a man is grieving, it is exemption or indifference, not enjoyment, which he extols as the greatest pleasure. Again, when a man has been in a state of enjoyment, and the enjoyment ceases, this cessation is painful. We thus see that the intermediate state — cessation, neutrality, indifference — will be some times pain, sometimes pleasure, according to circumstances. Now that which is neither pleasure nor pain cannot possibly be both. Pleasure is a positive movement or mutation of the

mind: so also is pain. Neutrality or indifference is a negative condition, intermediate between the two: no movement, but absence of movement: non-pain, non-pleasure. But non-pain is not really pleasure: non-pleasure is not really pain. When therefore neutrality or non-pain, succeeding immediately after pain, appears to be a pleasure — this is a mere appearance or illusion, not a reality. When neutrality or non-pleasure, succeeding immediately after pleasure, appears to be pain — this also is a mere appearance or illusion, not a reality. There is nothing sound or trustworthy in such appearances. Pleasure is not cessation of pain, but something essentially different: pain is not cessation of pleasure, but something essentially different.

Take, for example, the pleasures of smell, which are true and genuine pleasures, of great intensity: they spring up instantaneously without presupposing any anterior pain — they depart without leaving any subsequent pain. These are true and pure pleasures, radically different from cessation of pain: so also true and pure pains are different from cessation of pleasure. Most of the so-called pleasures, especially the more intense, which reach the mind through the body, are in reality not pleasures at all, but only cessations or reliefs from pain. The same may be said about the pleasures and pains of anticipation belonging to these so-called bodily pleasures. They may be represented by the following simile:— There is in nature a real Absolute Up and uppermost point — a real Absolute Down and lowest point — and a centre between them. A man borne from the lowest point to the centre will think himself moving upwards, and will be moving upwards relatively.

If his course be stopped in the centre, he will think himself at the absolute summit — on looking to the point from which he came, and ignorant as he is of any thing higher. If he be forced to return from the centre to the point from whence he came, he will think himself moving downwards, and will be really moving downwards, absolutely as well as relatively. Such misapprehension arises from his not knowing the portion of the Kosmos above the centre — the true and absolute Up or summit. Now the case of pleasure and pain is analogous to this. Pain is the absolute lowest — Pleasure the absolute highest — non-pleasure, non-pain, the centre intermediate between them.

But most men know nothing of the region above the centre, or the absolute highest — the region of true and pure pleasure: they know only the centre and what is below it, or the region of pain. When they fall from the centre to the point of pain, they conceive the situation truly, and they really are pained: but when they rise from the lowest point to the centre, they misconceive the change, and imagine themselves to be in a process of replenishment and acquisition of pleasure. They mistake the painless condition for pleasure, not knowing what true pleasure is: just as a man who has seen only black and not white, will fancy, if dun be shown to him, that he is looking on white.

Nourishment of the mind partakes more of real essence than nourishment of the body — Replenishment of the mind imparts fuller pleasure than replenishment of the body.

Hunger and thirst are states of emptiness in the body: ignorance and folly are states of emptiness in the mind. A hungry man in eating or drinking obtains replenishment: an ignorant man becoming instructed obtains replenishment also. Now replenishment derived from that which exists more fully and perfectly is truer and more real than replenishment from that which exists less fully and perfectly.

Let us then compare the food which serves for replenishment of the body, with that which serves for replenishment of the mind. Which of the two is most existent? Which of the two partakes most of pure essence? Meat and drink — or true opinions, knowledge, intelligence, and virtue? Which of the two exists most perfectly? That which embraces the true, eternal, and unchangeable — and which is itself of similar nature? Or that which embraces the mortal, the transient, and the ever variable — being itself of kindred nature? Assuredly the former. It is clear that what is necessary for the sustenance of the body partakes less of truth and real essence, than what is necessary for the sustenance of the mind. The mind is replenished with nourishment more real and essential: the body with nourishment less so: the mind itself is also more real and essential than the body. The mind therefore is more, and more thoroughly, replenished than the body. Accordingly, if pleasure consists in being replenished with what suits its peculiar nature, the mind will enjoy more pleasure and truer pleasure than the body.

Those who are destitute of intelligence and virtue, passing their lives in sensual pursuits, have never tasted any pure or lasting pleasure, nor ever carried their looks upwards to the higher region in which alone it resides. Their pleasures, though seeming intense, and raising vehement desires in their uninstructed minds, are yet only phantoms deriving a semblance of pleasure from contrast with pains: they are like the phantom of Helen, for which (as Stesichorus says) the Greeks and Trojans fought so many battles, knowing nothing about the true Helen, who was never in Troy.

The pleasures belonging to the Love of Honour (Energy or Passion) are no better than those belonging to the Love of Money (Appetite). In so far as the desires belonging to both these departments of mind are under the controul of the third or best department (Love of Wisdom, or Reason), the nearest approach to true pleasure, which it is in the nature of either of them to bestow, will be realised. But in so far as either of them throws off the controul of Reason, it will neither obtain its own truest pleasures, nor allow the other departments of mind to obtain theirs. The desires connected with love, and with despotic power, stand out more than the others, as recusant to Reason, Law, and Regulation. The kingly and moderate desires are most obedient to this authority. The lover and the despot, therefore, will enjoy the least pleasure: the kindly-minded man will enjoy the most. Of the three sorts of pleasure, one true and legitimate, two bastard, the despot goes most away from the legitimate, and to the farthest limit of the bastard. His condition is the most miserable, that of the kingly-minded man is the happiest: between the two come the oligarchical and the democratical man. The difference between the two extremes is as 1: 729.

The Just Man will be happy from his justice — He will look only to the good order of his own mind — He will stand aloof from public affairs, in cities as now constituted.

I have thus refuted (continues Socrates) the case of those who contend — That the unjust man is a gainer by his injustice, provided he could carry it on successfully, and with the reputation of being just. I have shown that injustice is the greatest possible mischief, intrinsically and in itself, apart from consequences and apart from public reputation: inasmuch as it enslaves the better part of the mind to the worse. Justice, on the other hand, is the greatest possible good, intrinsically and in itself, apart from consequences and reputation, because it keeps the worse parts of the mind under due controul and subordination to the better. Vice and infirmity of every kind is pernicious, because it puts the best parts of the mind under subjection to the worst.

No success in the acquisition of wealth, aggrandisement, or any other undue object, can compensate a man for the internal disorder which he introduces into his own mind by becoming unjust. A well-ordered mind, just and temperate, with the better part governing the worse, is the first of all objects: greater even than a healthy, strong, and beautiful body. To put his mind into this condition, and to acquire all the knowledge thereunto conducing, will be the purpose of a wise man's life. Even in the management of his body, he will look not so much to the health and strength of his body, as to the harmony and fit regulation of his mind. In the acquisition of money, he will keep the same end in view: he will not be tempted by the admiration and envy of people around him to seek great wealth, which will disturb the mental polity within him: he will, on the other hand, avoid depressing poverty, which might produce the same effect. He will take as little part as possible in public life, and will aspire to no political honours, in cities as at present constituted — nor in any other than the model-city which we have described.

Tenth Book — Censure of the poets is renewed — Mischiefs of imitation generally, as deceptive — Imitation from imitation.

The tenth and last book of the Republic commences with an argument of considerable length, repeating and confirming by farther reasons the sentence of expulsion which Plato had already pronounced against the poets in his second and third books. The Platonic Socrates here not only animadverts upon poetry, but extends his disapprobation to other imitative arts, such as painting. He attacks the process of imitation generally, as false and deceptive; pleasing to ignorant people, but perverting their minds by phantasms which they mistake for realities. The work of the imitator is not merely not reality, but is removed from it by two degrees. What is real is the Form or Idea: the one conceived object denoted by each appellative name common to many particulars. There is one Form or Idea, and only one, known by the name of Bed; another by the name of Table.

When the carpenter constructs a bed or a table, he fixes his contemplation on this Form or Idea, and tries to copy it. What he constructs, however, is not the true, real, existent, table, which alone exists in nature, and may be presumed to be made by the Gods — but a something like the real existent table: not true Ens, but only quasi-Ens: dim and indistinct, as compared with the truth, and standing far off from the truth. Next to the carpenter comes the painter, who copies not the real existent table, but the copy of that table made by the carpenter. The painter fixes his contemplation upon it, not as it really exists, but simply as it appears: he copies an appearance or phantasm, not a reality. Thus the table will have a different appearance, according as you look at it from near or far — from one side or the other: yet in reality it never differs from itself. It is one of these appearances that the painter copies, not the reality itself. He can in like manner paint any thing and every thing, since he hardly touches any thing at all — and nothing whatever except in appearance. He can paint all sorts of craftsmen and their works — carpenters, shoemakers, &c. without knowledge of any one of their arts.

The like is true also of the poets. Homer and the tragedians give us talk and affirmations about everything: government, legislation, war, medicine, husbandry, the character and proceedings of the Gods, the habits and training of men, &c. Some persons even extol Homer as the great educator of the Hellenic world, whose poems we ought to learn by heart as guides for education and administration. But Homer, Hesiod, and the other poets, had no real knowledge of the multifarious matters which they profess to describe. These poets know nothing except about appearances, and will describe only appearances, to the satisfaction of the ignorant multitude. The representations of the painter, reproducing only the appearances to sense, will be constantly fallacious and deceptive, requiring to be corrected by measuring, weighing, counting — which are processes belonging to Reason. The lower and the higher parts of the mind are here at variance; and the painter addresses himself to the lower, supplying falsehood as if it were truth. The painter does this through the eye, the poet through the ear.

The poet chiefly appeals to emotions — Mischiefs of such eloquent appeals, as disturbing the rational government of the mind.

In the various acts and situations of life a man is full of contradictions. He is swayed by manifold impulses, often directly contradicting each other. Hence we have affirmed that there are in his mind two distinct principles, one contradicting the other: the emotional and the rational. When a man suffers misfortune, emotion prompts him to indulge in extreme grief, and to abandon himself like a child to the momentary tide. Reason, on the contrary, exhorts him to resist, and to exert himself immediately in counsel to rectify or alleviate what has happened, adapting his conduct as well as he can to the actual throw of the dice which has befallen him. Now it is these vehement bursts of emotion which lend themselves most effectively to the genius of the poet, and which he must work up to please the multitude in the theatre: the state of rational self-command can hardly be described so as to touch their feelings. We see thus that the poet, like the painter, addresses himself to the lower department of the mind, exalting the emotional into preponderance over the rational — the foolish over the wise — the false over the true. He introduces bad government into the mind, giving to pleasure and pain the sceptre over reason. Hence we cannot tolerate the poet, in spite of all his sweets and captivations. We can only permit him to compose hymns for the Gods and encomiums for good men.

This quarrel between philosophy and poetry (continues the Platonic Socrates) is of ancient date. I myself am very sensible to the charms of poetry, especially that of Homer. I should be delighted if a case could be made out to justify me in admitting it into our city. But I cannot betray the cause of what seems to me truth. We must resist our sympathies and preferences, when they are incompatible with the right government of the mind.

Immortality of the soul affirmed and sustained by argument — Total number of souls always the same.

To maintain the right government and good condition of the soul or mind, is the first of all considerations: and will be seen yet farther to be such, when we consider that it is immortal and imperishable. Of this Plato proceeds to give a proof, concluding with a mythical sketch of the destiny of the soul after death. The soul being immortal (he says), the total number of souls is and always has been the same — neither increasing nor diminishing.

I have proved (the Platonic Socrates concludes) in the preceding discourse, that Justice is better, in itself and intrinsically, than Injustice, quite apart from consequences in the way of reward and honour; that a man for the sake of his own happiness, ought to be just, whatever may be thought of him by Gods or men — even though he possessed the magic ring of Gyges. Having proved this, and having made out the intrinsic superiority of justice to injustice, we may now take in the natural consequences and collateral bearings of both. We have hitherto reasoned upon the hypothesis that the just man was mistaken for unjust, and treated accordingly — that the unjust man found means to pass himself off for just, and to attract to himself the esteem and the rewards of justice. But this hypothesis concedes too much, and we must now take back the concession. The just man will be happier than the unjust, not simply from the intrinsic working of justice on his own mind, but also from the exterior consequences of justice. He will be favoured and rewarded both by Gods and men. Though he may be in poverty, sickness, or any other apparent state of evil, he may be assured that the Gods will compensate him for it by happiness either in life or after death. And men too, though they may for a time be mistaken about the just and the unjust character, will at last come to a right estimation of both. The just man will finally receive honour, reward, and power, from his fellow-citizens: the unjust man will be finally degraded and punished by them. And after death, the reward of the just man, as well as the punishment of the unjust, will be far greater than even during life.

This latter position is illustrated at some length by the mythe with which the Republic concludes, describing the realm of Hades, with the posthumous condition and treatment of the departed souls.

The Logic of the Pre-Socratic Philosophy

By William Arthur Heidel

It is not the purpose of this study to show that the Pre-Socratics possessed a system of logic which is now for the first time brought to the notice of the modern world. Indeed, there is nothing to indicate that they had reflected on mental processes in such a way as to call for an organized body of canons regulating the forms of concepts and conclusions. Aristotle attributed the discovery of the art of dialectic to Zeno the Eleatic, and we shall see in the sequel that there was much to justify the opinion. But logic, in the technical sense, is inconceivable without concepts, and from the days of Aristotle it has been universally believed that proper definitions owe their origin to Socrates. A few crude attempts at definition, if such they may be rightly called, are referred to Empedocles and Democritus. But in so far as they were conceived in the spirit of science, they essayed to define things materially by giving, so to speak, the chemical formula for their production. Significant as this very fact is, it shows that even the rudiments of the canons of thought were not the subjects of reflection.

In his Organon Aristotle makes it evident that the demand for a regulative art of scientific discourse was created by the eristic logic-chopping of those who were most deeply influenced by the Eleatic philosophy. Indeed, the case is quite parallel to the rise of the art of rhetoric. Aristotle regarded Empedocles as the originator of that art, as he referred the beginnings of dialectic to Zeno. But the formulation of both arts in well-rounded systems came much later. As men conducted lawsuits before the days of Tisias and Corax, so also were the essential principles of logic operative and effective in practice before Aristotle gave them their abstract formulation.

While it is true, therefore, that the Pre-Socratics had no formal logic, it is equally true, and far more significant, that they either received from their predecessors or themselves developed the conceptions and the presuppositions on which the Aristotelian logic is founded. One of the objects of this study is to institute a search for some of these basic conceptions of Greek thought, almost all of which existed before the days of Socrates, and to consider their origin as well as their logical significance. The other aim here kept in view is to trace the course of thought in which the logical principles, latent in all attempts to construct and verify theories, came into play.

It is impossible, no doubt, to discover a body of thought which does not ground itself upon presuppositions. They are the warp into which the woof of the system, itself too often consisting of frayed ends of other fabrics, is woven with the delight of a supposed creator. Rarely is the thinker so conscious of his own mental processes that he is aware of what he takes for granted. Ordinarily this retirement to an interior line takes place only when one has been driven back from the advanced position which could no longer be maintained. Emerson has somewhere said: "The foregoing generations beheld God and Nature face to face; we through their eyes. Why should not we also enjoy an original relation to the universe? Why should not we have a poetry and philosophy of insight and not of tradition, and a religion by revelation to us and not the history of theirs?" The difficulty lies precisely in our faith in immediate insight and revelation, which are themselves only short-cuts of induction, psychological short circuits, conducted by media we have disregarded. Only a fundamentally critical philosophy pushes its doubt to the limit of demanding the credentials of those conceptions which have come to be regarded as axiomatic.

The need of going back of Aristotle in our quest for the truth is well shown by his attitude toward the first principles of the several sciences. To him they are immediately given—ἄμεσοι προτάσεις—and hence are ultimate a priori. The historical significance of this fact is already apparent. It means that in his day these first principles, which sum up the outcome of previous inductive movements of thought, were regarded as so conclusively established that the steps by which they had been inferred were allowed to lapse from memory.

No account of the history of thought can hope to satisfy the demands of reason that does not explain the origin of the convictions thus embodied in principles. The only acceptable explanation would be in terms of will and interest. To give such an account would, however, require the knowledge of secular pursuits and ambitions no longer obtainable. It might be fruitful of results if we could discover even the theoretical interests of the age before Thales; but we know that in modern times the direction of interest characteristic of the purely practical pursuits manifests its reformative influences in speculation a century or more after it has begun to shape the course of common life. Hence we might misinterpret the historical data if they were obtainable. But general considerations, which we need not now rehearse, as well as indications contained in the later history of thought, hereinafter sketched, point to the primacy of the practical as yielding the direction of interest that determines the course it shall take.

It was said above that the principles of science are the result of an inductive movement, and that the inductive movement is directed by an interest. Hence the principles are contained in, or rather are the express definition of, the interest that gave them birth. In other words, there is implied in all induction a process of deduction. Every stream of thought embraces not only the main current, but also an eddy, which here and there re-enters it. And this is one way of explaining the phenomenon which has long engaged the thought of philosophers, namely, the fact of successful anticipations of the discoveries of science or, more generally still, the possibility of synthetic judgments a priori. The solution of the problem is ultimately contained in its statement.

To arrive at a stage of mentality not based on assumptions one would have, no doubt, to go back to its beginnings. Greek thought, even in the time of Thales, was well furnished with them. We cannot pause to catalogue them, but it may further our project if we consider a few of the more important. The precondition of thought as of life is that nature be uniform, or ultimately that the world be rational. This is not even, as it becomes later, a conscious demand; it is the primary ethical postulate which expresses itself in the confidence that it is so. Viewed from a certain angle it may be called the principle of sufficient reason. Closely associated with it is the universal belief of the early philosophers of Greece that everything that comes into being is bound up inseparably with that which has been before; more precisely, that there is no absolute, but only relative, Becoming. Corollaries of this axiom soon appeared in the postulates of the conservation of matter or mass, and the conservation of energy, or more properly for the ancients, of motion. Logically these principles appear to signify that the subject, while under definition, shall remain just what it is; and that, in the system constituted of subject, predicate, and copula, the terms shall "stay put" while the adjustment of verification is in progress. It is a matter of course that the constants in the great problem should become permanent landmarks.

Other corollaries derive from this same principle of uniformity. Seeing that all that comes to be in some sense already is, there appears the postulate of the unity of the world; and this unity manifests itself not only in the integrity and homogeneity of the world-ground, but also in the more ideal conception of a universal law to which all special modes of procedure in nature are ancillary. In these we recognize the insistent demand for the organization of predicate and copula. Side by side with these formulæ stands the other, which requires an ordered process of becoming and a graduated scale of existences, such as can mediate between the extremes of polarity. Such series meet us on every hand in early Greek thought. The process of rarefaction and condensation in Anaximenes, the ὁδὸς ἄνω κάτω of Heraclitus, the regular succession of the four Empedoclean elements in almost all later systems—these and other examples spontaneously occur to the mind. The significance of this conception, as the representative of an effective copula, will presently be seen. More subtle, perhaps, than any of these principles, though not allowed to go so long unchallenged, is the assumption of a φύσις, that is, the assumption that all nature is instinct with life. The logical interpretation of this postulate would seem to be that the concrete system of things—subject, predicate, copula—constitutes a totality complete in itself and needing no jog from without.

In this survey of the preconceptions of the early Greek philosophers I have employed the terms of the judgment without apology. The justification for this course must come ultimately, as for any assumption, from the success of its application to the facts. But if "logic" merely formulates in a schematic way that which in life is the manipulation of concrete experience, with a view to attaining practical ends, then its forms must apply here as well as anywhere. Logical terminology may therefore be assumed to be welcome to this field where judgments are formed, induction is made from certain facts to defined conceptions, and deductions are derived from principles or premises assumed. Speaking then in these terms we may say that the Pre-Socratics had three logical problems set for them: First, there was a demand for a predicate, or, in other words, for a theory of the world. Secondly, there was the need of ascertaining just what should be regarded as the subject, or, otherwise stated, just what it was that required explanation. Thirdly, there arose the necessity of discovering ways and means by which the theory could be predicated of the world and by which, in turn, the hypothesis erected could be made to account for the concrete experience of life: in terms of logic this problem is that of maintaining an efficient copula. It is not assumed that the sequence thus stated was historically observed without crossing and overlapping; but a survey of the history of the period will show that, in a general way, the logical requirements asserted themselves in this order.

1. Greek philosophy began its career with induction. We have already stated that the preconceptions with which it approached its task were the result of previous inductions, and indeed the epic and theogonic poetry of the Greeks abounds in thoughts indicative of the consciousness of all of these problems. Thus Homer is familiar with the notion that all things proceed from water, and that, when the human body decays, it resolves itself into earth and water. Other opinions might be enumerated, but they would add nothing to the purpose. When men began, in the spirit of philosophy, to theorize about the world, they assumed that it—the subject—was sufficiently known. Its existence was taken for granted, and that which engaged their attention was the problem of its meaning. What predicate—so we may formulate their question—should be given to the subject? It is noticeable that their induction was quite perfunctory. But such is always the case until there are rival theories competing for acceptance, and even then the impulse to gather up evidence derived from a wide field and assured by resort to experiment comes rather with the desire to test a hypothesis than to form it. It is the effort to verify that brings out details and also the negative instances. Hence we are not to blame Thales for rashness in making his generalization that all is Water. We do not know what indications led to this conclusion.

Aristotle ventured a guess, but the motives assumed for Thales agree too well with those which weighed with Hippo to admit of ready acceptance.

Anaximander, feeling the need of deduction as a sequel to induction, found his predicate in the Infinite. We cannot now delay to inquire just what he meant by the term; but it is not unlikely that its very vagueness recommended it to a man of genius who caught enthusiastically at the skirts of knowledge. Anaximenes, having pushed verification somewhat farther and eliciting some negative instances, rejected water and the Infinite and inferred that all was air. His ἀρχή must have the quality of infinity, but, a copula having been found in the process of rarefaction and condensation, it must occupy a determinate place in the series of typical forms of existence. The logical significance of this thought will engage our attention later.

Meanwhile it may be well to note that thus far only one predicate has been offered by each philosopher. This is doubtless due to the preconception of the unity and homogeneity of the world, of which we have already made mention. Although at the beginning its significance was little realized, the conception was destined to play a prominent part in Greek thought. It may be regarded from different points of view not necessarily antagonistic. One may say, as indeed has oftentimes been said, that it was due to ignorance. Men did not know the complexity of the world, and hence declared its substance to be simple. Again, it may be affirmed that the assumption was merely the naïve reflex of the ethical postulate that we shall unify our experience and organize it for the realization of our ideals. While increased knowledge has multiplied the so-called chemical elements, physics knows nothing of their differences, and chemistry itself demands their reduction.

The extension and enlarged scope of homogeneity came in two ways: First, it presented itself by way of abstraction from the particular predicates that may be given to things. This was due to the operation of the fundamental assumption that the world must be intelligible. Thus, even in Anaximander, the world-ground takes no account of the diversity of things except in the negative way of providing that the contrariety of experience shall arise from it. We are therefore referred for our predicate to a somewhat behind concrete experience. The Pythagoreans fix upon a single aspect of things as the essential, and find the meaning of the world in mathematical relations. The Eleatics press the conception of homogeneity until it is reduced to identity. Identity means the absence of difference; hence, spatially considered, it requires the negation of a void and the indivisibility of the world; viewed temporally, it precludes the succession of different states and hence the possibility of change.

We thus reach the acute stage of the problem of the One and the Many. The One is here the predicate, the subject is the Many. The solution of the difficulty is the task of the copula, and we shall recur to the theme in due time. It may be well, however, at this point to draw attention to the fact that the One is not always identical with the predicate, nor the Many with the subject. In the rhythmic movement of erecting and verifying hypotheses the interest shifts and what was but now the predicate, by taking the place of the premises, comes to be regarded as the given from which the particular is to be derived or deduced. There is thus likewise a shift in the positions of existence and meaning. The subject, or the world, was first assumed as the given means with which to construct the predicate, its meaning; once the hypothesis has been erected, the direction of interest shifts back to the beginning, and in the process of verification or deduction the quondam predicate, now the premises, becomes the given, and the task set for thought is the derivation of fact. For the moment, or until the return to the world is accomplished, the One is the only real, the Manifold remains mere appearance.

The second form in which the sense of the homogeneity of the world embodies itself is not, like the first, static, but is altogether dynamic. That which makes the whole world kin is neither the presence nor the absence of a quality, but a principle. The law thus revealed is, therefore, not a matter of the predicate, but is the copula itself. Hence we must defer a fuller consideration of it for the present.

2. As has already been said, the inductive movement implies the deductive, and not only as something preceding or accompanying it, but as its inner meaning and ultimate purpose. So too it was with the earliest Greek thinkers. Their object in setting up a predicate was the derivation of the subject from it. In other words their ambition was to discover the ἀρχή from which the genesis of the world proceeds. But deduction is really a much more serious task than would at first appear to one who is familiar with the Aristotelian machinery of premises and middle terms. The business of deduction is to reveal the subject, and ordinarily the subject quite vanishes from view. Induction is rapid, but deduction lags far behind. It may require but a momentary flash of "insight" on the part of the physical philosopher to discover a principle; if it is really significant, inventors will be engaged for centuries in deducing from it applications to the needs of life by means of contrivances. Thus after ages we come to know more of the subject, which is thereby enriched. The contrivances are the representatives of the copula in practical affairs; in quasi-theoretical spheres they are the apparatus for experimentation. It has just been remarked that by the application of the principles to life it is enriched; in other words, it receives new meaning, and new meaning signifies a new predicate. Theory is at times painfully aware of the multitude of new predicates proposed; rarely does it realize that there

has been created a new heaven and a new earth. Without the latter, the former would be absurd.

Men take very much for granted and regard almost every achievement as a matter of course. Hence they do not become aware of their changed position except as it reflects itself in new schemes and in a larger outlook. The subject receives only a summary glance to discover what new predicate shall be evolved. Hence, while there is in Greek philosophy a strongly marked deductive movement, the theoretical results to the subject are insignificant. Thales seems, indeed, to have had no means to offer for the derivation of the world, but he evidently had no doubt that it was possible. With him and with others the assumption, however vaguely understood, seems to have been that the subject, like the predicate, was simple. Thus the essential unity of the world, considered as existence no less than as meaning, is a foregone conclusion. The sense of a division in the subject seems to arise with Empedocles when, reaping the harvest of the Eleatic definition of substance, he parted the world, as subject and as predicate, into four elements.

We may, perhaps, pause a moment to consider the significance of the assumption of four elements which plays so large a part in subsequent philosophies. There is no need of enlarging on the importance of the association of multiple elements with the postulate that nothing is absolutely created and nothing absolutely passes away. These are indeed the pillars that support chemical science, and they further imply the existence of qualities of different rank; but that implication, as we shall see, lay even in the process of rarefaction and condensation introduced by Anaximenes. The four elements concern us here chiefly as testifying to the fact that certain practical interests had summed up the essential characteristics of nature in forms sufficiently significant to have maintained themselves even to our day. In regard to fire, air, and water this is not greatly to be wondered at; it is a somewhat different case with earth. If metallurgy and other pursuits which deal with that which is roughly classed as earth had been highly enough developed to have reacted upon the popular mind, this element could not possibly have been assumed to be so homogeneous. The conception clearly reflects the predominantly agricultural interest of the Greeks in their relation to the earth. This further illustrates the slow progress which deduction makes in the reconstitution of the subject.

It is different, however, with Anaxagoras and the Atomists. Apparently the movement begun by Empedocles soon ran its extreme course. Instead of four elements there is now an infinite number of substances, each differentiated from the other. The meaning of this wide swing of the pendulum is not altogether clear; but it is evident from the system of Anaxagoras that the metals, for example, possessed a significance which they can not have had for Empedocles.

The opposite swing of the pendulum is seen in the later course of the Eleatics. Given a predicate as fixed and unified as they assumed, the subject cannot possibly be conceived in terms of it and hence it is denied outright. In the dialectic of Zeno and Melissus, dealing with the problems of the One and the Many, there is much that suggests the solution offered by the Atomists; but it is probably impossible now to ascertain whether these passages criticise a doctrine already propounded or pointed the way for successors. While the Eleatics asserted the sole reality of the One, Anaxagoras and the Atomists postulated a multiplicity without essential unity. But the human mind seems to be incapable of resting in that decision; it demands that the world shall have not meanings, but a meaning. This demand calls not only for a unified predicate, but also for an effective copula.

3. We have already remarked that the steps by which the predicate was inferred are for the most part unknown. Certain suggestions are contained in the reports of Aristotle, but it is safe to say that they are generally guesses well or ill founded. The summary inductive mediation has left few traces; and the process of verification, in the course of which hypotheses were rejected and modified, can be followed only here and there in the records. Almost our only source of information is the dialectic of systems. Fortunately for our present purpose we do not need to know the precise form which a question assumed to the minds of the several philosophers; the efforts which they made to meet the imperious demands of logic here speak for themselves.

At first there was no scheme for the mediation of the predicate back to the subject. Indeed there seems not to have existed in the mind of Thales a sense of its need. Anaximander raised the question, but the process of segregation or separation (ἐκκρίνεσθαι) which he propounded was so vaguely conceived that it has created more problems than it solved. Anaximenes first proposed a scheme that has borne fruits. He said that things are produced from air by rarefaction and condensation. This process offers not only a principle of difference, but also a regulative conception, the evaluation of which engaged the thought of almost all the later Pre-Socratics. It implies that extension and mass constitute the essential characters of substance, and, fully apprehended, contains in germ the whole materialistic philosophy from Parmenides at one extreme to Democritus and Anaxagoras at the other. The difficulties inherent in the view were unknown to Anaximenes; for, having a unitary predicate, he assumed also a homogeneous subject.

The logical position of Heraclitus is similar to that of Anaximenes. He likewise posits a simple predicate and further signalizes its functional character by naming it Fire. Without venturing upon debatable ground we may say that it was the restless activity of the element that caused him to single it out as best expressing the meaning of things. Its rhythmic libration typified to him the principle of change in existence and of existence in change. It is the "ever-living" copula, devouring subject and predicate alike and re-creating them functionally as co-ordinate expressions of itself. That which alone is, the abiding, is not the physical composition of a thing, but the law of reciprocity by which it maintains a balance. This he calls variously by the names of Harmony, Logos, Necessity, Justice. In this system of functional co-ordinates nothing escapes the accounting on 'Change; all things are in continuous flux, only the nodes of the rhythm remaining constant. It is not surprising therefore that Heraclitus has been the subject of so much speculation and comment in modern times; for the functional character of all distinctions in his system marks the affinity of his doctrines for those of modern psychology and logic.

The Pythagoreans, having by abstraction obtained a predicate, acknowledged the existence of the subject, but did not feel the need of a copula in the theoretical sphere, except as it concerned the inner relation of the predicate. To them the world was number, but number itself was pluralistic, or let us rather say dualistic. The odd and the even, the generic constituents of number, had somehow to be brought together. The bond was found in Unity, or, again, in Harmony. When they inquired how numbers constituted the world, their answer was in general only a nugatory exercise of an unbridled fancy. Such and such a number was Justice, such another, Man. It was only in the wholly practical sphere of experiment that they reached a conclusion worth recording. Its significance they themselves did not perceive. Here, by the application of mathematical measurements to sounds, they discovered how to produce tones of a given pitch, and thus successfully demonstrated the efficiency of their copula.

The Eleatics followed the same general course of abstraction; but with them the sense of the unity of the world effaced its rich diversity. Xenophanes does not appear to have pressed the conception so far as to deny all change within the world. Parmenides, however, bated no jot of the legitimate consequences of his logical position, interpreting, as he did, the predicate, originally conceived as meaning, in terms of existence. That which is simply is. Thus there is left only a one-time predicate, now converted into a subject of which only itself, as a brute fact, can be predicated. Stated logically, Parmenides is capable only of uttering identical propositions: $A=A$. The fallacious character of the report of the senses and the impossibility of Becoming followed as a matter of course. Where the logical copula is a mere sign of equation there can be neither induction nor deduction. We are caught in a theoretical cul-de-sac.

We are not now concerned to know in what light the demand for a treatise on the world of Opinion may have appeared to Parmenides himself. The avenues by which men reach conclusions which are capable of simplification and syllogistic statement are too various to admit of plausible conjecture in the absence of specific evidence. But it is clear that his resort to the expedient reflected a consciousness of the state of deadlock. In that part of his philosophical poem he dealt with many questions of detail in a rather more practical spirit. Following the lead of Heraclitus and the Pythagoreans he was more successful here than in the field of metaphysics. Thus we see once more that the wounds of theory are healed by practice. But, as usual, even though the metaphysician does receive the answer to his doubts by falling into a severely practical pit and extricating himself by steps which he fashions with his hands, his mental habit is not thereby reconstructed. The fixed predicate of the Eleatics was bequeathed to the Platonic-Aristotelian formal logic, and induction and deduction remained for centuries in theory a race between the hedgehog and the hare. The true significance of the destructive criticism brought to bear by Zeno and Melissus on the concepts of unity, plurality, continuity, extension, time, and motion is simply this: that when by a shift of the attention a predicate becomes subject or meaning fossilizes as existence, the terms of the logical process lose their functional reference and grow to be unmeaning and self-contradictory.

We have already remarked that Empedocles, Anaxagoras, and the Atomists sought to solve the problem of the One and the Many, of the subject and the predicate, by shattering the unitary predicate and thus leaving the field to plurality in both spheres. But obviously they were merely postponing the real question. Thought, as well as action, demands a unity somewhere. Hence the absorbing task of these philosophers is to disclose or contrive such a bond of unity. The form which their quest assumed was the search for a basis for physical interaction.

Empedocles clearly believed that he was solving the difficulty in one form when he instituted the rhythmic libration between unity under the sway of Love and multiplicity under the domination of Hate. But even he was not satisfied with that. While Love brought all the elements together into a sphere and thus produced a unity, it was a unity constituted of a mixture of elements possessing inalienable characters not only different but actually antagonistic. On the other hand, Hate did indeed separate the confused particles, but it effected a sort of unity in that, by segregating the particles of the several elements from the others, it brought like and like together. In so far Aristotle was clearly right in attributing to Love the power to separate as well as to unite. Moreover, it would seem that there never was a moment in which both agencies were not conceived to be operative, to however small an extent.

Empedocles asserted, however, that a world could arise only in the intervals between the extremes of victory in the contest between Love and Hate, when, so to speak, the battle was drawn and there was a general mêlée of the combatants. It may be questioned, perhaps, whether he distinctly stated that in our world everything possessed its portion of each of the elements; but so indispensable did he consider this mixture that its function of providing a physical unity is unmistakable. A further evidence of his insistent demand for unity—the copula—is found in his doctrine that only like can act on like; and the scheme of pores and effluvia which he contrived bears eloquent testimony to the earnest consideration he gave to this matter. For he conceived that all interaction took place by means of them.

Empedocles, then, may be said to have annulled the decree of divorce he had issued for the elements at the beginning. But the solution here too is found, not in the theoretical, but in the practical, sphere; for he never retracts his assertion that the elements are distinct and antagonistic. But even so his problem is defined rather than solved; for after the elements have been brought within microscopic distance of each other in the mixture, since like can act only on like, the narrow space that separates them is still an impassable gulf.

Anaxagoras endowed his infinitely numerous substances with the same characters of fixity and contrariety that mark the four elements of Empedocles. For him, therefore, the difficulty of securing unity and co-operation in an effective copula is, if that be possible, further aggravated. His grasp of the problem, if we may judge from the relatively small body of documentary evidence, was not so sure as that of Empedocles, though he employed in general the same means for its solution. He too postulates a mixture of all substances, more consciously and definitely indeed than his predecessor. Believing that only like can act on like, he is led to assume not only an infinite multiplicity of substances, but also their complete mixture, so that everything, however small, contains a portion of every other. Food, for example, however seeming-simple, nourishes the most diverse tissues of the body. Thus we discover in the universal mixture of substances the basis for co-operation and interaction.

Anaxagoras, therefore, like Empedocles, feels the need of bridging the chasm which he has assumed to exist between his distinct substances. Their failure is alike great, and is due to the presuppositions they inherited from the Eleatic conception of a severe homogeneity which implies an absolute difference from everything else. The embarrassment of Anaxagoras increases with the introduction of the *Νοῦς*. This agency was conceived with a view to explaining the formation of the world; that is, with a view to mediating between the myriad substances in their essential aloofness and effecting the harmonious concord of concrete things. While, even on the basis of a universal mixture, the function of the Νοῦς was foredoomed to failure, its task was made more difficult still by the definition given to its nature. According to Anaxagoras it was the sole exception to the composite character of things; it is absolutely pure and simple in nature. By its definition, then, it is prevented from accomplishing the work it was contrived to do; and hence we cannot be surprised at the lamentations raised by Plato and Aristotle about the failure of Anaxagoras to employ the agency he had introduced. To be sure, the Νοῦς is no more a deus ex machina than were the ideas of Plato or the God of Aristotle. They all labored under the same restrictions.

The Atomists followed with the same recognition of the Many, in the infinitely various kinds of atoms; but it was tempered by the assumption of an essential homogeneity. One atom is distinguished from another by characteristics due to its spatial relations. Mass and weight are proportional to size. Aristotle reports that, though things and atoms have differences, it is not in virtue of their differences, but in virtue of their essential identity, that they interact. There is thus introduced a distinction which runs nearly, but not quite, parallel to that between primary and secondary qualities. Primary qualities are those of size, shape, and perhaps position; all others are secondary. On the other hand, that which is common to all atoms is their corporeity, which does indeed define itself with reference to the primary (spatial) qualities, but not alike in all. The atoms of which the world is constituted are alike in essential nature, but they differ most widely in position.

It is the void that breaks up the unity of the world—atomizes it, if we may use the expression. It is the basis of all discontinuity. Atoms and void are thus polar extremes reciprocally exclusive. The atoms in their utter isolation in space are incapable of producing a world. In order to bridge the chasm between atom and atom, recourse is had to motion eternal, omnipresent, and necessary. This it is that annihilates distances. In the course of their motion atoms collide, and in their impact one upon the other the Atomists find the precise mode of co-operation by which the world is formed. To this agency are due what Lucretius happily called "generating motions."

The problem, however, so insistently pursued the philosophers of this time that the Atomists did not content themselves with this solution, satisfactory as modern science has pretended to consider it. They followed the lead of Empedocles and Anaxagoras in postulating a widespread, if not absolutely universal, mixture. Having on principle excluded "essential" differences among the atoms, the impossibility of finally distinguishing essential and non-essential had its revenge. Important as the device of mixture was to Empedocles and Anaxagoras, just so unmeaning ought it to have been in the Atomic philosophy, provided that the hypothesis could accomplish what was claimed for it. It is not necessary to reassert that the assump-assumption of "individua," utterly alienated one from the other by a void, rendered the problem of the copula insoluble for the Atomists.

Diogenes of Apollonia is commonly treated contemptuously as a mere reactionary who harked back to Anaximenes and had no significance of his own. The best that can be said of such an attitude is that it regards philosophical theories as accidental utterances of individuals, naturally well or ill endowed, who happen to express conclusions with which men in after times agree or disagree. A philosophical tenet is an atom, set somewhere in a vacuum, utterly out of relation to everything else. But it is impossible to see how, on this theory, any system of thought should possess any significance for anybody, or how there should be any progress even, or retardation.

Viewed entirely from without, the doctrine of Diogenes would seem to be substantially a recrudescence of that of Anaximenes. Air is once more the element or ἀρχή out of which all proceeds and into which all returns. Again the process of transformation is seen in rarefaction and condensation; and the attributes of substance are those which were common to the early hylozoists. But there is present a keen sense of a problem unknown to Anaximenes. What the early philosopher asserted in the innocence of the youth of thought, the later physiologist reiterates with emphasis because he believes that the words are words of life.

The motive for recurring to the earlier system is supplied by the imperious demand for a copula which had so much distressed Empedocles, Anaxagoras, and the Atomists. And here we are not left to conjecture, but are able to refer to the ipsissima verba of our philosopher. After a brief prologue, in which he stated that one's starting-point must be beyond dispute, he immediately turned to his theme in these words: "In my opinion, to put the whole matter in a nutshell, all things are derived by alteration from the same substance, and indeed all are one and the same. And this is altogether evident. For if the things that now exist in the world—earth and water and air and fire and whatsoever else appears to exist in this world—if, I say, any one of these were different from the other, different that is to say in its proper peculiar nature, and did not rather, being one and the same, change and alter in many ways, then in no-wise would things be able to mix with one another, nor would help or harm come to one from the other, nor would any plant spring from the earth, nor any other living thing come into being, if things were not so constituted as to be one and the same."

These words contain a singularly interesting expression of the need of restoring the integrity of the process which had been lost in the effort to solve the problem of the One and the Many without abandoning the point of view won by the Eleatics. Aristotle and Theophrastus paraphrase and sum up the passage above quoted by saying that interaction is impossible except on the assumption that all the world is one and the same. Hence it is manifest, as was said above, that the return of Diogenes to the monistic system of Anaximenes had for its conscious motive the avoidance of the dualism that had sprung up in the interval and had rendered futile the multiplied efforts to secure an effective copula.

We should note, however, that in the attempt thus made to undo the work of several generations Diogenes retained the principle which had wrought the mischief. We have before remarked that the germ of the Atomic philosophy was contained in the process of rarefaction and condensation. Hence, in accepting it along with the remainder of Anaximenes's theory, the fatal assumption was reinstated. It is the story of human systems in epitome. The superstructure is overthrown, and with the débris a new edifice is built upon the old foundations.

In the entire course of philosophical thought from Thales onward the suggestion of an opposition between the subject and the predicate had appeared. It has often been said that it was expressed by the search for a φύσις, or a true nature, in contrast with the world as practically accepted. There is a certain truth in this view; for the effort to attain a predicate which does not merely repeat the subject does imply that there is an opposition. But the efforts made to return from the predicate to the subject, in a deductive movement, shows that the difference was not believed to be absolute. This is true, however, only of those fields of speculation that lie next to the highways of practical life, which lead equally in both directions, or, let us rather say, which unite while they mark separation. In the sphere of abstract ideas the sense of embarrassment was deep and constantly growing deeper. The reconstruction, accomplished on lower levels, did not attain unto those heights. Men doubted conclusions, but did not think to demand the credentials of their common presuppositions.

Side by side with the later philosophers whom we have mentioned there walked men whom we are wont to call the Sophists. They were the journalists and pamphleteers of those days, men who, without dealing profoundly with any special problem, familiarized themselves with the generalizations of workers in special fields and combined these ideas for the entertainment of the public. They were neither philosophers nor physicists, but, like some men whom we might cite from our own times, endeavored to popularize the teachings of both. Naturally they seized upon the most sweeping generalizations and the preconceptions which disclosed themselves in manifold forms. Just as naturally they had no eyes with which to detect the significance of the besetting problems at which, in matters more concrete, the masters were toiling. Hence the contradictions, revealed in the analysis we have just given of the philosophy of the age, stood out in utter nakedness.

The result was inevitable. The inability to discover a unitary predicate, more still, the failure to attain a working copula, led directly to the denial of the possibility of predication. There was no truth. Granted that it existed, it could not be known. Even if known, it could not be communicated. In these incisive words of Gorgias the conclusion of the ineffectual effort to establish a logic of science is clearly stated. But the statement is happily only the half-truth, which is almost a complete falsehood. It takes no account of the indications, everywhere present, of a needed reconstruction. Least of all does it catch the meaning of such a demand.

The Sophists did not, however, merely repeat in abstract from the teachings of the philosophers. It matters not whether they originated the movement or not; at all events they were pioneers in the field of moral philosophy. Here it was that they chiefly drew the inferences from the distinction between φύσει and νόμῳ. Nothing could have been more effective in disengaging the firmly rooted moral pre-possessions and rendering them amenable to philosophy. Just here, at last, we catch a hint of the significance of the logical process. In a striking passage in Plato's *Protagoras*, which one is fain to regard as an essentially true reproduction of a discourse by that great man, Justice and Reverence are accorded true validity. On inquiring to what characteristic this honorable distinction is due, we find that it does not reside in themselves; it is due to the assumption that a state must exist.

Here, then, in a word, is the upshot of the logical movement. Logical predicates are essentially hypothetical, deriving their validity from the interest that moves men to affirm them. When they lose this hypothetical character, as terms within a volitional system, and set up as entities at large, they cease to function and forfeit their right to exist.

The Pre-Socratics

By Benjamin Cocker

Of all the monuments of the greatness of Athens which have survived the changes and the wastes of time, the most perfect and the most enduring is her philosophy. The Propylaea, the Parthenon, and the Erechtheum, those peerless gems of Grecian architecture, are now in ruins. The magnificent sculpture of Phidias, which adorned the pediment, and outer cornice, and inner frieze of these temples, and the unrivalled statuary of gods and heroes which crowded the platform of the Acropolis, making it an earthly Olympus, are now no more, save a few broken fragments which have been carried to other lands, and, in their exile, tell the mournful story of the departed grandeur of their ancient home. The brazen statue of Minerva, cast from the spoils of Marathon, which rose in giant grandeur above the buildings of the Acropolis, and the flashing of whose helmet plumes was seen by the mariner as soon as he had rounded the Sunian promontory; and that other brazen Pallas, called, by pre-eminence, "the Beautiful;" and the enormous Colossus of ivory and of gold, "the Immortal Maid"--the protecting goddess of the Parthenon--these have perished. But whilst the fingers of time have crumbled the Pentelic marble, and the glorious statuary has been broken to pieces by vandal hands, and the gold and brass have been melted in the crucibles of needy monarchs and converted into vulgar money, the philosophic thought of Athens, which culminated in the dialectic of Plato, still survives. Not one of all the vessels, freighted with immortal thought, which Plato launched upon the stream of time, has foundered. And after the vast critical movement of European thought during the past two centuries, in which all philosophic systems have been subjected to the severest scrutiny, the method of Plato still preserves, if not its exclusive authority unquestioned, at least its intellectual pre-eminence unshaken. "Platonism is immortal, because its principles are immortal in the human intellect and heart."

Philosophy is, then, the world-enduring monument of the greatness and the glory of Athens. Whilst Greece will be forever memorable as "the country of wisdom and of wise men," Athens will always be pre-eminently memorable as the University of Greece. This was the home of Socrates, and Plato, and Aristotle--the three imperial names which, for twenty centuries, reigned supreme in the world of philosophic thought. Here schools of philosophy were founded to which students were attracted from every part of the civilized world, and by which an impulse and a direction was given to human thought in every land and in every age. Standing on the Acropolis at Athens, and looking over the city and the open country, the Apostle would see these places which are inseparably associated with the names of the men who have always been recognized as the great teachers of the pagan world, and who have also exerted a powerful influence upon Christian minds of every age. "In opposite directions he would see the suburbs where Plato and Aristotle, the two pupils of Socrates, held their illustrious schools. The streamless bed of the Ilissus passes between the Acropolis and Hymettus in a south-westerly direction, until it vanishes in the low ground which separates the city from the Piraeus." Looking towards the upper part of this channel, Paul would see gardens of plane-trees and thickets of angus-castus, "with other torrent-loving shrubs of Greece." Near the base of Lycabettus was a sacred inclosure which Pericles had ornamented with fountains. Here stood a statue of Apollo Lycius, which gave the name to the Lyceum. Here, among the plane-trees, Aristotle walked, and, as he walked, taught his disciples. Hence the name Peripatetics (the Walkers), which has always designated the disciples of the Stagirite philosopher.

On the opposite side of the city, the most beautiful of the Athenian suburbs, we have the scene of Plato's teaching. Beyond the outer Ceramicus, which was crowded with the sepulchres of those Athenians who had fallen in battle, and were buried at the public expense, the eye of Paul would rest on the favored stream of the Cephisus, flowing towards the west. On the banks of this stream the Academy was situated. A wall, built at great expense by Hipparchus, surrounded it, and Cimon planted long avenues of trees and erected fountains. Beneath the plane-trees which shaded the numerous walks there assembled the master-spirits of the age. This was the favorite resort of poets and philosophers. Here the divine spirit of Plato poured forth its sublimest speculations in streams of matchless eloquence; and here he founded a school which was destined to exert a powerful and perennial influence on human minds and hearts in all coming time.

Looking down from the Acropolis upon the Agora, Paul would distinguish a cloister or colonnade. This is the Stoa Poecile, or "Painted Porch," so called because its walls were decorated with fresco paintings of the legendary wars of Greece, and the more glorious struggle at Marathon. It was here that Zeno first opened that celebrated school which thence received the name of Stoic. The site of the garden where Epicurus taught is now unknown. It was no doubt within the city walls, and not far distant from the Agora. It was well known in the time of Cicero, who visited Athens as a student little more than a century before the Apostle. It could not have been forgotten in the time of Paul. In this "tranquil garden," in the society of his friends, Epicurus passed a life of speculation and of pleasure. His disciples were called, after him, the Epicureans.

Here, then, in Athens the Apostle was brought into immediate contact with all the phases of philosophic thought which had appeared in the ancient world. "Amongst those who sauntered beneath the cool shadows of the plane-trees in the Agora, and gathered in knots under the porticoes, eagerly discussing the questions of the day, were the philosophers, in the garb of their several sects, ready for any new question on which they might exercise their subtlety or display their rhetoric." If there were any in that motley group who cherished the principles and retained the spirit of the true Platonic school, we may presume they felt an inward intellectual sympathy with the doctrine enounced by Paul. With Plato, "philosophy was only another name for religion: philosophy is the love of perfect Wisdom; perfect Wisdom and perfect Goodness are identical: the perfect Good is God himself; philosophy is the love of God." He confessed the need of divine assistance to attain "the good," and of divine interposition to deliver men from moral ruin. Like Socrates, he longed for a supernatural--a divine light to guide him, and he acknowledged his need thereof continually. He was one of those who, in heathen lands, waited for "the desire of nations;" and, had he lived in Christian times, no doubt his "spirit of faith" would have joyfully "embraced the Saviour in all the completeness of his revelation and advent." And in so far as the spirit of Plato survived among his disciples, we may be sure they were not among the number who "mocked," and ridiculed, and opposed the "new doctrine" proclaimed by Paul. It was "the philosophers of the Epicureans and of the Stoics who encountered Paul." The leading tenets of both these sects were diametrically opposed to the doctrines of Christianity. The ruling spirit of each was alien from the spirit of Christ. The haughty pride of the Stoic, the Epicurean abandonment to pleasure, placed them in direct antagonism to him who proclaimed the crucified and risen Christ to be "the wisdom of God."

If, however, we would justly appreciate the relation of pagan philosophy to Christian truth, we must note that, when Paul arrived in Athens, the age of Athenian glory had passed away. Not only had her national greatness waned, and her national spirit degenerated, but her intellectual power exhibited unmistakable signs of exhaustion, and weakness, and decay. If philosophy had borne any fruit, of course that fruit remained. If, in the palmy days of Athenian greatness, any field of human inquiry had been successfully explored; if human reason had achieved any conquests; if any thing true and good had been obtained, that must endure as an heir-loom for all coming time; and if those centuries of agonizing wrestlings with nature, and of ceaseless questioning of the human heart, had yielded no results, then, at least, the lesson of their failure and defeat remained for the instruction of future generations. Either the problems they sought to solve were proved to be insoluble, or their methods of solution were found to be inadequate; for here the mightiest minds had grappled with the great problems of being and of destiny. Here vigorous intellects had struggled to pierce the darkness which hangs alike over the beginning and the end of human existence. Here profoundly earnest men had questioned nature, reason, antiquity, oracles, in the hope they might learn something of that invisible world of real being which they instinctively felt must lie beneath the world of fleeting forms and ever-changing appearances. Here philosophy had directed her course towards every point in the compass of thought, and touched every accessible point. The sun of human reason had reached its zenith, and illuminated every field that lay within the reach of human ken. And this sublime era of Greek philosophy is of inestimable value to us who live in Christian times, because it is an exhaustive effort of human reason to solve the problem of being, and in its history we have a record of the power and weakness of the human mind, at once on the grandest scale and in the fairest characters.

It will at once be obvious, even to those who are least conversant with our theme, that it would be fruitless to attempt the answer to these important questions before we have made a careful survey of the entire history of philosophic thought in Greece. We must have a clear and definite conception of the problems they sought to solve, and we must comprehend their methods of inquiry, before we can hope to appreciate the results they reached, or determine whether they did arrive at any definite and valuable conclusions. It will, therefore, devolve upon us to present a brief and yet comprehensive epitome of the history of Grecian speculative thought.

"Philosophy," says Cousin, "is reflection, and nothing else than reflection, in a vast form"--"Reflection elevated to the rank and authority of a method." It is the mind looking back upon its own sensations, perceptions, cognitions, ideas, and from thence to the causes of these sensations, cognitions, and ideas. It is thought passing beyond the simple perceptions of things, beyond the mere spontaneous operations of the mind in the cognition of things to seek the ground, and reason, and law of things. It is the effort of reason to solve the great problem of "Being and Becoming," of appearance and reality, of the changeful and the permanent. Beneath the endless diversity of the universe, of existence and action, there must be a principle of unity; below all fleeting appearances there must be a permanent substance; beyond this everlasting flow and change, this beginning and ending of finite existence, there must be an eternal being, the source and cause of all we see and know, What is that principle of unity, that permanent substance, or principle, or being?

This fundamental question has assumed three separate forms or aspects in the history of philosophy. These forms have been determined by the objective phenomena which most immediately arrested and engaged the atten-attention of men. If external nature has been the chief object of attention, then the problem of philosophy has been, What is the ἀρχή--the beginning; what are the first principles--the elements from which, the ideas or laws according to which, the efficient cause or energy by which, and the reason or end for which the universe exists? During this period reflective thought was a *Philosophy Of Nature*. If the phenomena of mind--the opinions, beliefs, judgments of men--are the chief object of attention, then the problem of philosophy has been, What are the fundamental Ideas which are unchangeable and permanent amid all the diversities of human opinions, connecting appearance with reality, and constituting a ground of certain knowledge or absolute truth? Reflective thought is now a *Philosophy Of Ideas*.

Then, lastly, if the practical activities of life and the means of well-being be the grand object of attention, then the problem of philosophy has been, What is the ultimate standard by which, amid all the diversities of human conduct, we may determine what is right and good in individual, social, and political life? And now reflective thought is a *Philosophy Of Life*. These are the grand problems with which philosophy has grappled ever since the dawn of reflection. They all appear in Greek philosophy, and have a marked chronology. As systems they succeed each other, just as rigorously as the phenomena of Greek civilization. The Greek schools of philosophy have been classified from various points of view. In view of their geographical relations, they have been divided into the Ionian, the Italian, the Eleatic, the Athenian, and the Alexandrian. In view of their prevailing spirit and tendency, they have been classified by Cousin as the Sensational, the Idealistic, the Skeptical, and the Mystical. The most natural and obvious method is that which (regarding Socrates as the father of Greek philosophy in the truest sense) arranges all schools from the Socratic stand point, and therefore in the chronological order of development:

I. THE PRE-SOCRATIC SCHOOLS.
II. THE SOCRATIC SCHOOLS.
III. THE POST-SOCRATIC SCHOOLS.

The history of philosophy is thus divided into three grand epochs. The first reaching from Thales to the time of Socrates (B.C. 639-469): the second from the birth of Socrates to the death of Aristotle (B.C. 469-322); the third from the death of Aristotle to the Christian era (B.C. 322, A.D. 1). Greek philosophy during the first period was almost exclusively a philosophy of nature; during the second period, a philosophy of mind; during the last period, a philosophy of life.

Nature, man, and society complete the circle of thought. Successive systems, of course, overlap each other, both in the order of time and as subjects of human speculation; and the results of one epoch of thought are transmitted to and appropriated by another; but, in a general sense, the order of succession has been very much as here indicated. Setting aside minor schools and merely incidental discussions, and fixing our attention on the general aspects of each historic period, we shall discover that the first period was eminently Physical, the second Psychological, the last Ethical. Every stage of progress which reason, on à priori grounds, would suggest as the natural order of thought, or of which the development of an individual mind would furnish an analogy, had a corresponding realization in the development of Grecian thought from the time of Thales to the Christian era.

"Thought," says Cousin, "in the first trial of its strength is drawn without."

The first object which engages the attention of the child is the outer world. He asks the "how" and "why" of all he sees. His reason urges him to seek an explanation of the universe. So it was in the childhood of philosophy. The first essays of human thought were, almost without exception, discourses περὶ φύσεως (*De rerum natura*), of the nature of things. Then the rebound of baffled reason from the impenetrable bulwarks of the universe drove the mind back upon itself. If the youth can not interpret nature, he can at least "know himself," and find within himself the ground and reason of all existence. There are "ideas" in the human mind which are copies of those "archetypal ideas" which dwell in the Creative Mind, and after which the universe was built. If by "analysis" and "definition" these universal notions can be distinguished from that which is particular and contingent in the aggregate of human knowledge, then so much of eternal truth has been attained. The achievements of philosophic thought in this direction, during the Socratic age, have marked it as the most brilliant period in the history of philosophy--the period of its youthful vigor. Deeply immersed in the practical concerns and conflicts of public life, manhood is mainly occupied with questions of personal duty, and individual and social well-being. And so, during the hopeless turmoil of civil disturbance which marked the decline of national greatness in Grecian history, philosophy was chiefly occupied with questions of personal interest and personal happiness. The poetic enthusiasm with which a nobler age had longed for truth, and sought it as the highest good, has all disappeared, and now one sect seeks refuge from the storms and agitations of the age in Stoical indifference, the other in Epicurean effeminacy.

If now we have succeeded in presenting the real problem of philosophy, it will at once be obvious that the inquiry was not, in any proper sense, theological. Speculative thought, during the period we have marked as the era of Greek philosophy, was not an inquiry concerning the existence or nature of God, or concerning the relations of man to God, or the duties which man owes to God. These questions were all remitted to the theologian. There was a clear line of demarkation separating the domains of religion and philosophy. Religion rested solely on authority, and appealed to the instinctive faith of the human heart. She permitted no encroachment upon her settled usages, and no questioning of her ancient beliefs. Philosophy rested on reason alone. It was an independent effort of thought to interpret nature, and attain the fundamental grounds of human knowledge--to find an ἀρχή--a first principle, which, being assumed, should furnish a rational explanation of all existence. If philosophy reach the conclusion that the *ἀρχή* was water, or air, or fire, or a chaotic mixture of all the elements or atoms, extended and self-moved, or monads, or τὸ πᾶν, or uncreated mind, and that conclusion harmonized with the ancient standards of religious faith--well; if not, philosophy must present some method of conciliation. The conflicts of faith and reason; the stragglings of traditional authority to maintain supremacy; the accommodations and conciliations attempted in those primitive times, would furnish a chapter of peculiar interest, could it now be written.

The poets who appeared in the dim twilight of Grecian civilization--Orpheus, Musæus, Homer, Hesiod--seem to have occupied the same relation to the popular mind in Greece which the Bible now sustains to Christian communities. Not that we regard them as standing on equal ground of authority, or in any sense a revelation. But, in the eye of the wondering Greek, they were invested with the highest sacredness and the supremest authority. The high poetic inspiration which pervaded them was a supernatural gift. Their sublime utterances were accepted as proceeding from a divine afflatus. They were the product of an age in which it was believed by all that the gods assumed a human form, and held a real intercourse with gifted men. This universal faith is regarded by some as being a relic of still more distant times, a faint remembrance of the glory of patriarchal days. The more natural opinion is, that it was begotten of that universal longing of the human heart for some knowledge of that unseen world of real being, which man instinctively felt must lie beyond the world of fleeting change and delusive appearances. It was a prolepsis of the soul, reaching upward towards its source and goal. The poet felt within him some native affinities therewith, and longed for some stirring breath of heaven to sweep the harp-strings of the soul. He invoked the inspiration of the Goddess of Song, and waited for, no doubt believed in, some "deific impulse" descending on him. And the people eagerly accepted his utterance as the teaching of the gods. They were too eager for some knowledge from that unseen world to question their credentials. Orpheus, Hesiod, Homer, were the θεολόγοι -- the theologians of that age.

These ancient poems, then, were the public documents of the religion of Greece--the repositories of the national faith. And it is deserving of especial note that the philosopher was just as anxious to sustain his speculations by quoting the high traditional authority of the ancient theologian, as the propounder of modern novelties is to sustain his notions by the authority of the Sacred Scriptures. Numerous examples of this solicitude will recur at once to the remembrance of the student of Plato. All encroachments of philosophy upon the domains of religion were watched as jealously in Athens in the sixth century before Christ, as the encroachments of science upon the fields of theology were watched in Rome in the seventeenth century after Christ. The court of the Areopagus was as earnest, though not as fanatical and cruel, in the defense of the ancient faith, as the court of the Inquisition was in the defense of the dogmas of the Romish Church. The people, also, as "the sacred wars" of Greece attest, were ready quickly to repel every assault upon the majesty of their religion. And so philosophy even had its martyrs. The tears of Pericles were needed to save Aspasia, because she was suspected of philosophy. But neither his eloquence nor his tears could save his friend Anaxagoras, and he was ostracized. Aristotle had the greatest difficulty to save his life. And Plato was twice imprisoned, and once sold into slavery.

It is unnecessary that we should, in this place, again attempt the delineation of the theological opinions of the earlier periods of Grecian civilization. That the ancient Greeks believed in one Supreme God has been conclusively proved by Cudworth. The argument of his fourth chapter is incontrovertible. However great the number of "generated gods" who crowded the Olympus, and composed the ghostly array of Greek mythology, they were all subordinate agents, "demiurges," employed in the framing of the world and all material things, or else the ministers of the moral and providential government of the εἷς Θεὸς ἀγέντος -- the one uncreated God. Beneath, or beyond the whole system of pagan polytheism, we recognize a faith in an Uncreated Mind, the Source of all the intelligence, and order, and harmony which pervades the universe the Fountain of law and justice; the Ruler of the world; the Avenger of injured innocence; and the final Judge of men. The immortality of the soul and a state of future retribution were necessary corollaries of this sublime faith. This primitive theology was unquestionably the people's faith; the faith, also, of the philosopher, in his inmost heart, however far he might wander in speculative thought. The instinctive feeling of the human heart, the spontaneous intuitions of the human reason, have led man, in every age, to recognize a God. It is within the fields of speculative thought that skepticism has had its birth. Any thing like atheism has only made its appearance amid the efforts of human reason to explain the universe. The native sentiments of the heart and the spontaneous movements of the reason have always been towards faith, that is, towards "a religious movement of the soul."

Unbridled speculative thought, which turns towards the outer world alone, and disregards "the voices of the soul," tends towards doubt and irreligion. But, as Cousin has said, "a complete extravagance, a total delusion (except in case of real derangement), is impossible." "Beneath reflection there is still spontaneity, when the scholar has denied the existence of a God; listen to the man, interrogate him unawares, and you will see that all his words betray the idea of a God, and that faith in a God is, without his recognition, at the bottom of his heart."

Let us not, therefore, be too hasty in representing the early philosophers as destitute of the idea of a God, because in the imperfect and fragmentary representations which are given us of the philosophical opinions of Thales, and Anaximenes, and Heraclitus, and Diogenes of Apollonia, we find no explicit allusions to the Uncreated Mind as the first principle and cause of all. A few sentences will comprehend the whole of what remains of the opinions of the earliest philosophers, and these were transmitted for ages by oral tradition. To Plato and Aristotle we are chiefly indebted for a stereotype of those scattered, fragmentary sentences which came to their hands through the dim and distorting medium of more than two centuries. Surely no one imagines these few sentences contain and sum up the results of a lifetime of earnest thought, or represent all the opinions and beliefs of the earliest philosophers! And should we find therein no recognition of a personal God, would it not be most unfair and illogical to assert that they were utterly ignorant of a God, or wickedly denied his being? If they say "there is no God," then they are foolish Atheists; if they are silent on that subject, we have a right to assume they were Theists, for it is most natural to believe in God. And yet it has been quite customary for Christian teachers, after the manner of some Patristic writers, to deny to those early sages the smallest glimpse of underived and independent knowledge of a Divine Being, in their zeal to assert for the Sacred Scriptures the exclusive prerogative of revealing Him.

Now in regard to the theological opinions of the Greek philosophers, we shall venture this general lemma -- the majority of them recognized an "incorporeal substance" an uncreated Intelligence, an ordering, governing Mind. Leucippus, Democritus, and Epicurus, who were Materialists, are perhaps the only exceptions. Many of them were Pantheists, in the higher form of Pantheism, which, though it associates the universe with its framer and mover, still makes "the moving principle" superior to that which is moved. The world was a living organism,

"Whose body nature is, and God the soul."

Unquestionably most on them recognized the existence of two first principles, substances essentially distinct, which had co-existed from eternity-- an incorporeal Deity and matter. We grant that the free production of a universe by a creative fiat--the calling of matter into being by a simple act of omnipotence -- is not elementary to human reason. The famous physical axiom of antiquity, "De nihilo nihil, in nihilum posse reverti" under one aspect, may be regarded as the expression of the universal consciousness of a mental inability to conceive a creation out of nothing, or an annihilation.

"We can not conceive, either, on the one hand, nothing becoming something, or something becoming nothing, on the other hand. When God is said to create the universe out of nothing, we think this by supposing that he evolves the universe out of himself; and in like manner, we conceive annihilation only by conceiving the Creator to withdraw his creation from actuality into power."

"It is by faith we understand the worlds were framed by the word of God, so that things which are were not made from things which do appear"--that is, from pre-existent matter.

Those writers are, therefore, clearly in error who assert that the earliest question of Greek philosophy was, What is God? and that various and discordant answers were given, Thales saying, water is God, Anaximenes, air; Heraclitus, fire; Pythagoras, numbers; and so on. The idea of God is a native intuition of the mind. It springs up spontaneously from the depths of the human soul. The human mind naturally recognizes God as an uncreated Mind, and recognizes itself as "the offspring of God." And, therefore, it is simply impossible for it to acknowledge water, or air, or fire, or any material thing to be its God. Now they who reject this fundamental principle evidently misapprehend the real problem of early Grecian philosophic thought.

The external world, the material universe, was the first object of their inquiry, and the method of their inquiry was, at the first stage, purely physical. Every object of sense had a beginning and an end; it rose out of something, and it fell back into something. Beneath this ceaseless flow and change there must be some permanent principle. What is that στοιχεῖον -- that first element? The changes in the universe seem to obey some principle of law--they have an orderly succession.

What is that μορφή--that form, or ideal, or archetype, proper to each thing, and according to which all things are produced? These changes must be produced by some efficient cause, some power or being which is itself immobile, and permanent, and eternal, and adequate to their production. What is that ἀρχὴ τῆς κινήσεως -- that first principle of movement Then, lastly, there must be an end for which all things exist--a good reason why things are as they are, and not otherwise. What is that τὸ οὗ ἕνεκεν καὶ τὸ ἀγαθόν -- that reason and good of all things? Now these are all ἀρχαί or first principles of the universe.

"Common to all first principles," says Aristotle, "is the being, the original, from which a thing is, or is produced, or is known." First principles, therefore, include both elements and causes, and, under certain aspects, elements are also causes, in so far as they are that without which a thing can not be produced. Hence that highest generalization by Aristotle of all first principles; as -- 1. The Material Cause; 2. The Formal Cause; 3. The Efficient Cause; 4. The Final Cause. The grand subject of inquiry in ancient philosophy was not alone what is the final element from which all things have been produced? nor yet what is the efficient cause of the movement and the order of the universe? but what are those First Principles which, being assumed, shall furnish a rational explanation of all phenomena, of all becoming?

THE PRE-SOCRATIC SCHOOLS

"The first act in the drama of Grecian speculation was performed on the varied theatre of the Grecian colonies--Asiatic, insular, and Italian, verging at length (in Anaxagoras) towards Athens." During the progress of this drama two distinct schools of philosophy were developed, having distinct geographical provinces, one on the east, the other on the west, of the peninsula of Greece, and deriving their names from the localities in which they flourished. The earliest was the Ionian; the latter was the Italian school.

It would be extremely difficult, at this remote period, to estimate the influence which geographical conditions and ethnical relations exerted in determining the course of philosophic thought in these schools. Unquestionably those conditions contributed somewhat towards fixing their individuality. At the same time, it must be granted that the distinction in these two schools of philosophy is of a deeper character than can be represented or explained by geographical surroundings; it is a distinction reaching to the very foundation of their habits of thought. These schools represent two distinct aspects of philosophic thought, two distinct methods in which the human mind has essayed to solve the problem of the universe.

The ante-Socratic schools were chiefly occupied with the study of external nature. "Greek philosophy was, at its first appearance, a philosophy of nature." It was an effort of the reason to reach a "first principle" which should explain the universe. This early attempt was purely speculative. It sought to interpret all phenomena by hypotheses, that is, by suppositions, more or less plausible, suggested by physical analogies or by à priori rational conceptions.

Now there are two distinct aspects under which nature presents itself to the observant mind. The first and most obvious is the simple phenomena as perceived by the senses. The second is the relations of phenomena, cognized by the reason alone. Let phenomena, which are indeed the first objects of perception, continue to be the chief and almost exclusive object of thought, and philosophy is on the highway of pure physics. On the other hand, instead of stopping at phenomena, let their relations become the sole object of thought, and philosophy is now on the road of purely mathematical or metaphysical abstraction. Thus two schools of philosophy are developed, the one *sensational*, the other *idealist*. Now these, it will be found, are the leading and characteristic tendencies of the two grand divisions of the pre-Socratic schools; the Ionian is sensational, the Italian is idealist.

These two schools have again been the subject of a further subdivision based upon diverse habits of thought. The Ionian school sought to explain the universe by physical analogies. Of these there are two clear and obvious divisions--analogies suggested by living organisms, and analogies suggested by mechanical arrangements. One class of philosophers in the Ionian school laid hold on the first analogy. They regarded the world as a living being, spontaneously evolving itself -- a vital organism whose successive developments and transformations constitute all visible phenomena. A second class laid hold on the analogy suggested by mechanical arrangements. For them the universe was a grand superstructure, built up from elemental particles, arranged and united by some ab-extra power or force, or else aggregated by some inherent mutual affinity. Thus we have two sects of the Ionian school; the first, Dynamical or vital; the second, Mechanical.

The Italian school sought to explain the universe by rational conceptions and à priori ideas. Now to those who seek, by simple reflection, to investigate the relations of the external world this marked distinction will present itself: some are relations between sensible phenomena--relations of time, of place, of number, of proportion, and of harmony; others are relations of phenomena to essential being--relations of qualities to substance, of becoming to being, of the finite to the infinite. The former constituted the field of

Pythagorean the latter of Eleatic contemplation. The Pythagoreans sought to explain the universe by numbers, forms, and harmonies; the Eleatics by the a priori ideas of unity, substance, Being in se, the Infinite. Thus were constituted a Mathematical and a Metaphysical sect in the Italian school.

I. The Ionian or Physical School. -- We have premised that the philosophers of this school attempted the explanation of the universe by physical analogies.

One class of these early speculators, the Dynamical, or vital theorists, proceeded on the supposition of a living energy infolded in nature, which in its spontaneous development continuously undergoes alteration both of quality and form. This imperfect analogy is the first hypothesis of childhood. The child personifies the stone that hurts him, and his first impulse is to resent the injury as though he imagined it to be endowed with consciousness, and to be acting with design. The childhood of superstition (whose genius is multiplicity) personifies each individual existence -- a rude fetishism, which imagines a supernatural power and presence enshrined in every object of nature, in every plant, and stock, and stone. The childhood of philosophy (whose genius is unity) personifies the universe. It regards the earth as one vast organism, animated by one soul, and this soul of the world as a "created god." The first efforts of philosophy were, therefore, simply an attempt to explain the universe in harmony with the popular theological beliefs. The cosmogonies of the early speculators in the Ionian school were an elaboration of the ancient theogonies, but still an elaboration conducted under the guidance of that law of thought which constrains man to seek for unity, and reduce the many to the one.

Therefore, in attempting to construct a theory of the universe they commenced by postulating an ἀρχή -- a first principle or element out of which, by a vital process, all else should be produced. "Accordingly, whatever seemed the most subtle or pliable, as well as universal element in the mass of the visible world, was marked as the seminal principle whose successive developments and transformations produced all the rest." With this seminal principle the living, animating principle seems to have been associated -- in some instances perhaps confounded, and in most instances called by the same name. And having pursued this analogy so far, we shall find the most decided and conclusive evidence of a tendency to regard the soul of man as similar, in its nature, to the soul which animates the world.

Thales of Miletus (B.C. 636-542) was the first to lead the way in the perilous inquiry after an ἀρχή, or first principle, which should furnish a rational explanation of the universe. Following, as it would seem, the genealogy of Hesiod, he supposed water to be the primal element out of which all material things were produced. Aristotle supposes he was impressed with this idea from observing that all things are nourished by moisture; warmth itself, he declared, proceeded from moisture; the seeds of all things are moist; water, when condensed, becomes earth. Thus convinced of the universal presence of water, he declared it to be the first principle of things.

And now, from this brief statement of the Thalean physics, are we to conclude that he recognized only a material cause of the universe? Such is the impression we receive from the reading of the First Book of Aristotle's Metaphysics. His evident purpose is to prove that the first philosophers of the Ionian school did not recognize an efficient cause. In his opinion, they were decidedly materialistic. Now to question the authority of Aristotle may appear to many an act of presumption. But Aristotle was not infallible; and nothing is more certain than that in more than one instance he does great injustice to his predecessors. To him, unquestionably, belongs the honor of having made a complete and exhaustive classification of causes, but there certainly does appear something more than vanity in the assumption that he, of all the Greek philosophers, was the only one who recognized them all. His sagacious classification was simply a resumè of the labors of his predecessors. His "principles" or "causes" were incipient in the thought of the first speculators in philosophy. Their accurate definition and clearer presentation was the work of ages of analytic thought. The phrases "efficient," "formal," "final" cause, are, we grant, peculiar to Aristotle; the ideas were equally the possession of his predecessors.

The evidence, we think, is conclusive that, with this primal element (water), Thales associated a formative principle of motion; to the "material" he added the "efficient" cause. A strong presumption in favor of this opinion is grounded on the psychological views of Thales. The author of "De Placitis Philosophorum" associates him with Pythagoras and Plato, in teaching that the soul is incorporeal, making it naturally self-active, and an intelligent substance. And it is admitted by Aristotle (rather unwillingly, we grant, but his testimony is all the more valuable on that account) that, in his time, the opinion that the soul is a principle, $ἀεικίνητον$ -- ever moving, or essentially self-active, was currently ascribed to Thales. "If we may rely on the notices of Thales, he too would seem to have conceived the soul as a moving principle." Extending this idea, that the soul is a moving principle, he held that all motion in the universe was due to the presence of a living soul. "He is reported to have said that the loadstone possessed a soul because it could move iron."

And he taught that "the world itself is animated, and full of gods."

"Some think that soul and life is mingled with the whole universe; and thence, perhaps, was that [opinion] of Thales that all things are full of gods," portions, as Aristotle said, of the universal soul. These views are quite in harmony with the theology which makes the Deity the moving energy of the universe -- the energy which wrought the successive transformations of the primitive aqueous element. They also furnish a strong corroboration of the positive statement of Cicero -- "Aquam, dixit Thales, esse initium rerum, Deum autem eam mentem quae ex aqua cuncta fingeret."

Thales said that water is the first principle of things, but God was that mind which formed all things out of water; as also that still more remarkable saying of Thales, recorded by Diogenes Laertius; "God is the most ancient of all things, for he had no birth; the world is the most beautiful of all things, for it is the workmanship of God." We are aware that some historians of philosophy reject the statement of Cicero, because, say they, "it does violence to the chronology of speculation." Following Hegel, they assert that Thales could have no conception of God as Intelligence, since that is a conception of a more advanced philosophy. Such an opinion may be naturally expected from the philosopher who places God, not at the commencement, but at the end of things, God becoming conscious and intelligent in humanity. If, then, Hegel teaches that God himself has had a progressive development, it is no wonder he should assert that the idea of God has also had an historic development, the last term of which is an intelligent God. But he who believes that the idea of God as the infinite and the perfect is native to the human mind, and that God stands at the beginning of the entire system of things, will feel there is a strong a priori ground for the belief that Thales recognized the existence of an intelligent God who fashioned the universe.

Anaximenes of Miletus (B.C. 529 - 480) we place next to Thales in the consecutive history of thought. It has been usual to rank Anaximander next to the founder of the Ionian School. The entire complexion of his system is, however, unlike that of a pupil of Thales. And we think a careful consideration of his views will justify our placing him at the head of the Mechanical or Atomic division of the Ionian school. Anaximenes is the historical successor of Thales; he was unquestionably a vitalist. He took up the speculation where Thales had left it, and he carried it a step forward in its development.

Pursuing the same method as Thales, he was not, however, satisfied with the conclusion he had reached. Water was not to Anaximenes the most significant, neither was it the most universal element. But air seemed universally present. "The earth was a broad leaf resting upon it. All things were produced from it; all things were resolved into it. When he breathed he drew in a part of this universal life. All things are nourished by air." Was not, therefore, air the ἀρχή, or primal element of things?

This brief notice of the physical speculations of Anaximenes is all that has survived of his opinions. We search in vain for some intimations of his theological views. On this merely negative ground, some writers have unjustly charged him with Atheism. Were we to venture a conjecture, we would rather say that there are indications of a tendency to Pantheism in that form of it which associates God necessarily with the universe, but does not utterly confound them. His fixing upon "air" as the primal element, seems an effort to reconcile, in some apparently intermediate substance, the opposite qualities of corporeal and spiritual natures. Air is invisible, impalpable, all-penetrating, and yet in some manner appreciable to sense. May not the vital transformations of this element have produced all the rest? The writer of the Article on Anaximenes in the *Encyclopedia Britannica* tells us (on what ancient authorities he saith not) that "he asserted this air was God, since the divine power resides in it and agitates it."

Some indications of the views of Anaximenes may perhaps be gathered from the teachings of Diogenes of Apollonia (B.C. 520-490,) who was the disciple, and is generally regarded as the commentator and expounder of the views of Anaximenes. The air of Diogenes was a soul; therefore it was living, and not only living, but conscious and intelligent. "It knows much," says he; "for without reason it would be impossible for all to be arranged duly and proportionately; and whatever objects we consider will be found to be so arranged and ordered in the best and most beautiful manner." Here we have a distinct recognition of the fundamental axiom that mind is the only valid explanation of the order and harmony which pervades the universe. With Diogenes the first principle is a "divine air," which is vital, conscious, and intelligent, which spontaneously evolves itself, and which, by its ceaseless transformations, produces all phenomena. The soul of man is a detached portion of this divine element; his body is developed or evolved therefrom. The theology of Diogenes, and, as we believe, of his master, Anaximenes also, was a species of Materialistic Pantheism.

Heraclitus of Ephesus(B.C. 503-420) comes next in the order of speculative thought. In his philosophy, fire is the ἀρχή, or first principle; but not fire in the usual acceptation of that term. The Heraclitean "fire" is not flame, which is only an intensity of fire, but a warm, dry vapor--an ether, which may be illustrated, perhaps, by the "caloric" of modern chemistry. This "ether" was the primal element out of which the universe was formed; it was also a vital power or principle which animated the universe, and, in fact, the cause of all its successive phenomenal changes. "The world," he said, "was neither made by the gods nor men, and it was, and is, and ever shall be, an ever-living fire, in due proportion self-enkindled, and in due measure self-extinguished." The universe is thus reduced to "an eternal fire," whose ceaseless energy is manifested openly in the work of dissolution, and yet secretly, but universally, in the work of renovation. The phenomena of the universe are explained by Heraclitus as "the concurrence of opposite tendencies and efforts in the motions of this ever-living fire, out of which results the most beautiful harmony. This harmony of the world is one of conflicting impulses, like the lyre and the bow. The strife between opposite tendencies is the parent of all things. All life is change, and change is strife."

Heraclitus was the first to proclaim the doctrine of the perpetual fluxion of the universe (τὸ ῥέον, τὸ γιγνόμενον--Unrest and Development), the endless changes of matter, and the mutability and perishability of all individual things. This restless, changing flow of things, which never are, but always are becoming, he pronounced to be the One and the All.

From this statement of the physical theory of Heraclitus we might naturally infer that he was a Hylopathean Atheist. Such an hypothesis would not, however, be truthful or legitimate. On a more careful examination, his system will be found to stand half-way between the materialistic and the spiritual conception of the Author of the universe, and marks, indeed, a transition from the one to the other. Heraclitus unquestionably held that all substance is material, for a philosopher who proclaims, as he did, that the senses are the only source of knowledge, must necessarily attach himself to a material element as the primary one. And yet he seems to have spiritualized matter. "The moving unit of Heraclitus--the Becoming--is as immaterial as the resting unit of the Eleatics--the Being."

The Heraclitean "fire" is endowed with spiritual attributes. "Aristotle calls it ψυχή--soul, and says that it is ἀσωματώτατον, or absolutely incorporeal ("De Anima," i. 2. 16). It is, in effect, the common ground of the phenomena both of mind and matter it is not only the animating, but also the intelligent and regulating principle of the universe; the universal Word or Reason, which it behooves all men to follow." The psychology of Heraclitus throws additional light upon his theological opinions. With him human intelligence is a detached portion of the Universal Reason. "Inhaling," said he, "through the breath the Universal Ether, which is Divine Reason, we become conscious." The errors and imperfections of humanity are consequently to be ascribed to a deficiency of the Divine Reason in man. Whilst, therefore, the theory of Heraclitus seems to materialize mind, it may, with equal fairness, be said to spiritualize matter.

The general inference, therefore, from all that remains of the doctrine of Heraclitus is that he was a Materialistic Pantheist. His God was a living, rational, intelligent Ether -- a soul pervading the universe. The form of the universe, its ever-changing phenomena, were a necessary emanation from, or a perpetual transformation of, this universal soul.

With Heraclitus we close our survey of that sect of the physical school which regarded the world as a living organism.

The second subdivision of the physical school, the Mechanical or Atomist theorists, attempted the explanation of the universe by analogies derived from mechanical collocations, arrangements, and movements. The universe was regarded by them as a vast superstructure built up from elemental particles, aggregated by some inherent force or mutual affinity.

Anaximander of Miletus (born B.C. 610) we place at the head of the Mechanical sect of the Ionian school; first, on the authority of Aristotle, who intimates that the philosophic dogmata of Anaximander "resemble those of Democritus," who was certainly an Atomist; and, secondly, because we can clearly trace a genetic connection between the opinions of Democritus and Leucippus and those of Anaximander.

The ἀρχή, or first principle of Anaximander, was τὸ ἄπειρον, the boundless, the illimitable, the infinite. Some historians of philosophy have imagined that the infinite of Anaximander was the "unlimited all," and have therefore placed him at the head of the Italian or "idealistic school." These writers are manifestly in error. Anaximander was unquestionably a sensationalist. Whatever his "infinite" may be found to be, one thing is clear, it was not a "metaphysical infinite"--it did not include infinite power, much less infinite mind.

The testimony of Aristotle is conclusive that by "the infinite" Anaximander understood the multitude of primary, material particles. He calls it "a μῖγμα, or mixture of elements." It was, in fact, a chaos--an original state in which the primary elements existed in a chaotic combination without limitation or division. He assumed a certain "prima materia," which was neither air, nor water, nor fire, but a "mixture" of all, to be the first principle of the universe. The account of the opinions of Anaximander which is given by Plutarch ("De Placita," etc.) is a further confirmation of our interpretation of his infinite. "Anaximander, the Milesian, affirmed the infinite to be the first principle, and that all things are generated out of it, and corrupted again into it. His infinite is nothing else but matter."

"Whence," says Cudworth, "we conclude that Anaximander's infinite was nothing else but an infinite chaos of matter, in which were actually or potentially contained all manner of qualities, by the fortuitous secretion and segregation of which he supposed infinite worlds to be successively generated and corrupted. So that we may easily guess whence Leucippus and Democritus had their infinite worlds, and perceive how near akin these two Atheistic hypotheses were." The reader, whose curiosity may lead him to consult the authorities collected by Cudworth (pp. 185-188), will find in the doctrine of Anaximander a rude anticipation of the modern theories of "spontaneous generation" and "the transmutation of species." In the fragments of Anaximander that remain we find no recognition of an ordering Mind, and his philosophy is the dawn of a Materialistic school.

Leucippus of Miletus (B.C. 500-400) appears, in the order of speculation, as the successor of Anaximander. Atoms and space are, in his philosophy, the ἀρχαί, or first principles of all things. "Leucippus (and his companion, Democritus) assert that the plenum and the vacuum [i.e., body and space] are the first principles, whereof one is the Ens, the other Non-ens; the differences of the body, which are only figure, order, and position, are the causes of all others."

He also taught that the elements, and the worlds derived from them, are infinite. He describes the manner in which the worlds are produced as follows: "Many bodies of various kinds and shapes are borne by amputation from the infinite [i.e., the chaotic μῖγμα of Anaximander] into a vast vacuum, and then they, being collected together, produce a vortex; according to which, they, dashing against each other, and whirling about in every direction, are separated in such a way that like attaches itself to like; bodies are thus, without ceasing, united according to the impulse given by the vortex, and in this way the earth was produced." Thus, through a boundless void, atoms infinite in number and endlessly diversified in form are eternally wandering; and, by their aggregation, infinite worlds are successively produced. These atoms are governed in their movements by a dark negation of intelligence, designated "Fate," and all traces of a Supreme Mind disappear in his philosophy. It is a system of pure materialism, which, in fact, is Atheism.

Democritus of Abdera (B.C. 460-357), the companion of Leucippus, also taught "that atoms and the vacuum were the beginning of the universe." These atoms, he taught, were infinite in number, homogeneous, extended, and possessed of those primary qualities of matter which are necessarily involved in extension in space--as size, figure, situation, divisibility, and mobility. From the combination of these atoms all other existences are produced; fire, air, earth, and water; sun, moon, and stars; plants, animals, and men; the soul itself is an aggregation of round, moving atoms. And "motion, which is the cause of the production of every thing, he calls necessity." Atoms are thus the only real existences; these, without any pre-existent mind, or intelligence, were the original of all things.

The psychological opinions of Democritus were as decidedly materialistic as his physical theories. All knowledge is derived from sensation. It is only by material impact that we can know the external world, and every sense is, in reality, a kind of touch. Material images are being continually thrown off from the surface of external objects which come into actual contact with the organs of sense. The primary qualities of matter, that is, those which are involved in extension in space, are the only objects of real knowledge; the secondary qualities of matter, as softness, hardness, sweetness, bitterness, and the like, are but modifications of the human sensibilities.

"The sweet exists only in form -- the bitter in form, hot in form, color in form; but in causal reality only atoms and space exist. The sensible things which are supposed by opinion to exist have no real existence, but atoms and space alone exist."

Thus by Democritus was laid the basis of a system of absolute materialism, which was elaborated and completed by Epicurus, and has been transmitted to our times. It has undergone some slight modifications, adapting it to the progress of physical science; but it is to-day substantially the theory of Democritus. In Democritus we have the culmination of the mechanical theory of the Ionian or Physical school. In physics and psychology it terminated in pure materialism. In theology it ends in positive Atheism.

The fundamental error of all the philosophers of the physical school was the assumption, tacitly or avowedly, that sense-perception is the only source of knowledge. This was the fruitful source of all their erroneous conclusions, the parent of all their materialistic tendencies. This led them continually to seek an $ἀρχή$, or first principle of the universe, which should, under some form, be appreciable to sense; and consequently the course of thought tended naturally towards materialism.

Thales was unquestionably a dualist. Instructed by traditional intimations, or more probably guided by the spontaneous apperceptions of reason, he recognized, with more or less distinctness, an incorporeal Deity as the moving, animating, and organizing cause of the universe. The idea of God is a truth so self-evident as to need no demonstration. The human mind does not attain to the idea of a God as the last consequence of a series of antecedent principles. It comes at once, by an inherent and necessary movement of thought, to the recognition of God as the First Principle of all principles. But when, instead of hearkening to the simple and spontaneous intuitions of the mind, man turns to the world of sense, and loses himself in discursive thought, the conviction of a personal God becomes obscured. Then, amid the endlessly diversified phenomena of the universe, he seeks for a cause or origin which in some form shall be appreciable to sense. The mere study of material phenomena, scientifically or unscientifically conducted, will never yield the sense of the living God. Nature must be interpreted, can only be interpreted in the light of certain a priori principles of reason, or we can never "ascend from nature up to nature's God."

Within the circle of mere sense-perception, the dim and undeveloped consciousness of God will be confounded with the universe. Thus, in Anaximenes, God is partially confounded with "air," which becomes a symbol; then a vehicle of the informing mind; and the result is a semi-pantheism. In Heraclitus, the "ether" is, at first, a semi-symbol of the Deity; at length, God is utterly confounded with this ether, or "rational fire," and the result is a definite materialistic pantheism. And, finally, when this feeling or dim consciousness of God, which dwells in all human souls, is not only disregarded, but pronounced to be an illusion -- a phantasy; when all the analogies which intelligence suggests are disregarded, and a purely mechanical theory of the universe is adopted, the result is the utter negation of an Intelligent Cause, that is, absolute Atheism, as in Leucippus and Democritus.

Printed in Great Britain
by Amazon